SUGAR-FREE RELIGION

Trimming the Fluff from a Fragmented Faith

Denny C. Wise

Order this book online at www.trafford.com
or email orders@trafford.com

Most Trafford titles are also available at major online book retailers.

Printed in the United States of America.

ISBN: 978-1-4907-3887-1 (sc)
ISBN: 978-1-4907-3889-5 (hc)
ISBN: 978-1-4907-3888-8 (e)

Library of Congress Control Number: 2014910293

Trafford rev. 06/24/2014

Trafford
PUBLISHING®   www.trafford.com
North America & international
toll-free: 1 888 232 4444 (USA & Canada)
fax: 812 355 4082

Bible Citations

Most scripture quotations in this book are from the New Oxford Annotated Bible (the Revised Standard Version containing the Old and New Testaments) as follows: translated from the original languages, being the version set forth AD 1611, revised AD 1881–1885, and AD 1901, © 1962, 1973 by Oxford University Press Inc.; Revised Standard Version of the Bible, Old Testament Section, © 1952; New Testament Section, First Edition, © 1946, New Testament Section, Second Edition © 1971 by Division of Christian Education of the National Council of the Churches of Christ in the United States of America.

CONTENTS

ACKNOWLEDGMENTS

I WOULD LIKE TO thank my wonderful wife, Judy, who tirelessly donated her time, talent, energy, and patience typing and proofing to make this book possible. Regretfully, I will not have the time or space to list all the other countless church members, fellow pastors, teachers, and professors who offered me insight and inspiration along the way but to whom I am deeply indebted. You are legend, and I thank you. We do not arrive at who we are, independent of those with whom we bounce our thoughts and ideas on our unique journey.

However, this book is only an opinion piece. It is in no way a research paper. I can give neither credit nor blame to my research department because there was none. There was only me. Like most "preachers," I have attended lectures; read books; collected newspaper and magazine clippings; and watched plays, movies, TV shows, and the like while keeping notes and scribbles on little scraps of paper. There was no computer, Internet, or Google during most of my ministry, and I have this awful dread that some of my quotes and credits may be imperfect. But I have done my very best to be faithful. Thank you for your patience and tolerance.

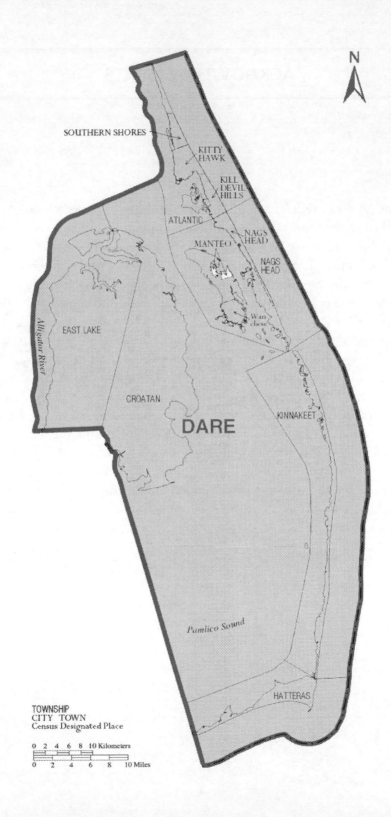

N

SOUTHERN SHORES

KITTY
HAWK

KILL
DEVIL
HILLS

ATLANTIC

NAGS
HEAD

MANTEO

NAGS
HEAD

Wan
chese

EAST LAKE

Alligator River

CROATAN

DARE

KINNAKEET

Pamlico Sound

HATTERAS

TOWNSHIP
CITY TOWN
Census Designated Place

0 2 4 6 8 10 Kilometers

0 2 4 6 8 10 Miles

WHAT THE HECK IS SUGAR-FREE RELIGION?

My thoughts are not your thoughts, nor are my ways your ways," says the Lord.

—Isaiah 55:8

THIS BOOK ATTEMPTS to do for religion what Teflon did for cooking. I want to teach you how to keep the sanctimonious "ick" from attaching itself to the Christian faith. And I believe the non-stick agent to accomplish this is relationships. With the word "religion," I am making reference only to the Christian religion, not to any other world religions. By "sugar-free," I mean a faith void of what Bonhoeffer called "cheap grace." Cheap grace is a feel-good kind of faith without sacrifice, commitment, or intellectual toughness. Cheap grace offers a brand of painless Christianity that refuses to stand up to social injustice. I want to refute that "cotton-candy" type of piety that tries to bring the sovereign *God* of creation down to our level. I am upset with those who would turn the holy "Lion of Judah" into Mary's little lamb or the exalted judge of creation into a divine butler—ever eager to please and do our bidding.

Consider the egocentric attitude revealed in the following prayer:

> My precious Lord, it's me again, just seeking another blessing from above! You will be pleased to know that I find you worthy of my praise. Please wrap me safely in your everlasting arms, as we hang together in all of my trivial pursuits. I want you to touch my heart and make me feel all fuzzy and warm inside, tingling with spiritual goose bumps. And could you please, as Jabez prayed of old, "increase my territory," expand my successes, and make me more healthy, wealthy, and wise? Thank you, sweet Jesus. Amen.

In such a shallow prayer as that, one can hardly recognize the Jesus of scripture, who calls us to make sacrifices for others, deny ourselves, humbly take up our cross, and follow him. The Jesus I worship calls us to reach outwardly to defend the less fortunate, not inwardly to feel good about ourselves! Yes, feelings are indeed fundamental to our faith, but feelings should never trump good deeds. Something within us almost compels us to praise God. The book of Psalms attests to that. Emotions should set us in motion and lead us to do good works. But feelings should never become idolatrous ends in themselves!

Being from a United Methodist background, I will mention John Wesley quite a bit in this book. Get used to it! For example, when John Wesley said, "There is no holiness but social holiness," he was not talking about church socials and covered dish dinners. He was talking about being "doers" of the Word together, through actions that can make a difference in society. He believed that, with God's help, we could change the world for the better (something he actually accomplished in eighteenth-century England). I believe that is still our mandate today.

Also, I regard as false all divisive attitudes that choose up sides, deciding that certain people are offensive or "undesirable." These groups can often make us feel uncomfortable because of race, religious viewpoint, or sexual orientation. When Jesus reached out to the lepers or hung with hookers, I believe he was teaching us a lesson about tolerance, compassion, and inclusiveness. Exclusiveness, on the other hand, tends to be rooted in negative narrow-minded attitudes, like arrogance, hypocrisy, legalism, literalism, and prejudice.

So amid the world's beautiful diversity, Jesus calls us to be nonjudgmental healers, seeking peace and unity with all God's children. How? This can be accomplished through expressions of love, respect, kindness, forgiveness, mutual understanding, and genuine dialogue. We are called to be "ambassadors for Christ." God makes his appeal for reconciliation to a broken world through us (2 Corinthians 5:21). This is why "sugar-free religion" takes seriously our Christian responsibility to care for the less fortunate and the unlovely. We should never hide behind piety or politics as a way of ignoring the plight of the poor. Indeed, we should reach out, in love, to all God's children. I regard such a call (for oneness in spite of differences) to be pure Gospel! (John 17:20–21)

Also, I wonder why we would think that scientific knowledge is a threat to God. God does not need to be protected from new discoveries or enlightenment. Indeed, we are commanded to love God with "all" our *minds* as well as "all" our *hearts*! I also question the ongoing speculation about the "end times." Instead, we need to deal with our own responsibilities of service, to life in the now. God takes care of the Eschaton, not us. All God asks us to do is to stay alert, keep busy, remain faithful servants, and keep our heads on straight.

With these perspectives in mind, I invite you to join me on a spiritual quest for a vital genuine faith. As pilgrims together, we will seek new enlightenment with open hearts and open minds. We will explore fresh insights into the very nature of truth itself. But please don't forget, as you pack your proverbial bags for the journey, to bring along your brain as well as your heart. Our assigned task is to seek a firm and honest theological foundation without having the frying pan of our faith all gummed up with too much sticky pompous goo!

> **By contrast, the fruit of the spirit is love, joy, peace, patience, kindness, generosity, faithfulness, gentleness, and self-control.**
> **—Galatians 5:22–23**

THE TRAGEDY OF A HUMPTY-DUMPTY CHURCH

If a house is divided against itself, that house cannot stand.
—Mark 3:25

MY FIRST APPOINTMENT was to Trinity United Methodist Church in Marshallberg, a quaint fishing village on the coast of North Carolina. My wife, Judy, came from the central part of the state and the thought of living on a tiny peninsula did unnerve her a bit. "What about hurricanes?" she sobbed.

At the time, Marshallberg was fifteen miles from the nearest supermarket. But don't feel too sorry for my young bride and me, as we were constantly getting oysters, shrimp, and fresh fish delivered to the parsonage door. Once, a neighbor brought a bushel of live crabs. I was away visiting at the time, so when he asked Judy, "Where would you like this basket, Ma'am?" she hesitated, but said with feigned assurance, "Oh, just put them on the washing machine."

By the time I got home, Judy was frantic. She had a life-long fear of spiders, and now there were slimy spider-like things scampering sideways all over the house with threatening claws held high. I would love to have that scene on a video. It was quite a show, as I scrambled on hands and knees, trying to corner those slithering blue-green crustaceans—without getting pinched. One was even under the couch. I knew if I failed to corral even one of those critters, it would die and ruin our lovely new parsonage. Fortunately, I was able to capture, clean, cook and devour every one. Yummm! Thanks be to God!

In those days, I was young and brash. I thought I could change the world. "I know your problem," I would say, "and I can help!" The people would reply, "What problem?" A concern we immediately observed in our tiny village, was the absence of anything for the teenagers. So with our teens on board, we decided to turn an old community building there into a youth center.

Unbelievably, in only one month at our new appointment, we managed to organize a little carnival as a fund-raiser. We had balloons, games, a bake sale, bag races, a bike-decorating contest, a watermelon-eating contest, and a talent show. We started the day off with a parade. Since almost everyone had boats and trailers, we challenged the village people to turn their boats into floats. It worked—even better than expected. Judy dressed up as a clown and went down the parade route, bouncing a four-foot beach ball while a dog nipped at her legs. People thought it was all part of the act, and so they cheered and clapped with delight. What a trooper she was, with teeth marks to prove it!

Now the reason I tell you this story is that Marshallberg just happened to be roughly divided, both numerically and geographically, between Methodists and Baptists. In order to get to the community building, our parade had to cross into Baptist territory. You could see Baptist mothers restraining their eager children behind screen doors as the parade went by. Those desperate housewives did not want the Methodists corrupting their little ones with dart throwing and other forms of "gambling" and "sin!" Even after successfully opening the Community Youth Center, there were still Baptist parents who wouldn't let their teens participate. Over the years, I have encountered many other examples of senseless division, as God's children scatter like crabs, slithering off sideways in a thousand different directions.

One day a man pulled to a stop at a traffic light and read the sticker on the car in front of him. It said, "Honk if you love Jesus." So he honked. A matronly lady leaped from the car in anger, pointing up to the light. "Look, you fool, the %$#$ light is still red!" So how do we heal this broken world when we can't even heal the rifts between ourselves?

WHAT IS WRONG WITH THIS PICTURE?

Has Christ been divided?
—1 Corinthians 1:13

At a time when we desperately need to stand together, Christendom finds itself fragmented, almost beyond repair. Devout believers turn on one another in hate, to ridicule and even kill in the name of God. I am saddened when the pope proclaims that only Roman Catholics are true Christians or the KKK invokes Jesus to justify hating Jews, Hispanics, and blacks—all of whom were created in his own image. I am appalled when Christians kill doctors who perform abortions or align themselves against all gun restrictions, along with the NRA.

There are even hidden divisive messages in books like the *Left Behind* series. I suspect you have seen those bold bumper stickers that so arrogantly proclaim, "In case of the rapture, this car will be unmanned." Did Jesus shed his blood on Calvary to encourage schisms and divisions or did he die to bring *unity*?

To me, that bumper sticker is saying, "Na, na, na, na, na! I will take flight, rising up like a weather balloon to meet Jesus in the air, while you slobs will be left behind. You and all other nonbelievers will suffer terrible torment in the tribulation. So too bad for you and too bad for all sinners, homosexuals, pagans, prostitutes, alcoholics, drug addicts, believers in pro-choice, and believers in evolution. Get off the bus; you're not one of us!"

WHY CAN'T WE LEARN TO GET ALONG?

I ask you, when some churches call themselves "full Gospel," does that mean the rest of us are (at best) only "half Gospel?" And when they call themselves "Bible believers," does this not imply the rest of us are "Bible nonbelievers?" Why can't we learn from each other and grow? Charismatic denominations certainly could use a little more reason in their worship, and mainline denominations could certainly use a lot more enthusiasm in theirs! Can't we tolerate our differences and celebrate the same Lord we all hold dear? God must weep to see us so divided! Jesus shed tears like drops of blood, praying we would all be perfectly one, but look at us. There are hundreds of different "Christian" sects in America—with millions of duplications of buildings, literature, and resources. What a waste, what a tragedy, what a sin!

Even King David understood that sometimes God prepares a table before us in the presence of our enemies! Surely, there is room at God's table for more than one point of view. After all, we have four different Gospels. We do not have to think exactly alike to find a place at the Lord's Table. John Wesley said, "Let my soul lie with these Christians, whosoever they are, and whatsoever opinion they are of." Surely God is not so narrow-minded that he would condemn a person to everlasting torment because they belong to a certain denomination or are brought up in a certain religion.

Once upon a time, an Indian medicine man was sitting by the river on a huge flat rock near the entrance to a large cavern, eating a sweet potato. Suddenly, the heavens were opened, and he saw wondrous visions of God! Immediately, he returned home to share his sacred experience with the people of his village. They, in turn, responded by hurrying down to the river bank. There they all huddled together to meditate on the huge flat rock in front of the cavern, eating sweet potatoes.

Don't you get it? The villagers missed the point! Neither the big flat rock nor the cave, nor the river, nor the sweet potato had anything to do with the holy man's religious experience. This has been the story of the church for two thousand years. Christians have squabbled over the trivial stuff such as immersion versus sprinkling. At the same time, they have missed the spiritual message of unity and tolerance and the *wonder* that Jesus came to bring.

You have probably heard the story of the man and his wife who were riding together on a bicycle built for two. "Phew! Thank God we finally made it!" the weary man moaned, as he crested an especially steep hill. "Honey, I know exactly what you mean," sighed his wife. "If I hadn't kept my foot on the brake the whole way up, we both would have slid right down that terrible hill!" Is this a parable of the church?

Remember when Jesus began his ministry? The ultra-traditionalist groups, the Sadducees, the Scribes, and the Pharisees were always there to block his path and challenge his every purpose. These were not bad people, they sincerely meant well. Their intentions were quite noble. In fact, they were the most moral and religious leaders of his day. But because Jesus was different, they saw him as a radical threat to their conservative way of life. They saw themselves as an elite moral people, set apart to come to God's defense! They were fighting against the invasion of strange new beliefs from Romans, Hellenist, pagans, and "false prophets." So they tried to put the brakes on Jesus, simply in God's defense! How little times have changed! There are many devout conservative Christians today with the same mindset. They believe God needs them to run interference for him, and protect him from evil people, like "socialists!" (See Acts 2:44–45)

Occasionally, I will receive a list of "Christian" candidates they say deserve my vote. Certain groups proudly claim that Jesus is on their side, when in truth, if he were to run for president, he would be unelectable. Can you imagine, for example, what the image handlers would do with one who tells this affluent, self-indulgent society to deny themselves and make sacrifices for the needy, instead of creating tax breaks for themselves? Ouch! And how would Wall Street bankers react to his embarrassing request to lend only to those who could *not* pay them back? (Luke 6:34–36)

My point is, just when you think you have Jesus safely tucked away, he comes out with some outlandish word to remind us that he is God, and God's ways are not our ways.

> **And blessed is he who takes no offense at me.**
> **—Matthew 11:6**

WHAT'S THE THING YOU DON'T LIKE ABOUT JESUS?

In the late 1960s, I helped organize a coffeehouse beach ministry at Atlantic Beach, known as the Koinonia House. One of the theme songs we used was a song entitled, "That's the Thing I Don't Like about Jesus." It made the point that sooner or later, the vertical will of God will confront the horizontal will of man, forming a cross, and on that conflicting cross, Jesus had to die! For example, perhaps you don't like our Lord's stand on "turning the other cheek." Perhaps, he sounds far too much like a bleeding-heart, liberal pacifist to you! Then again, if you consider yourself to be a liberal, Jesus may not satisfy you either or sound nearly liberal enough to suit you. After all, he could have said a lot more about social justice and corruption in high places, for your tastes. And he could have said a lot less about personal sacrifice and absolute devotion to duty. You see, whatever the issue, Jesus was always an *equal opportunity offender*.

AH, HOLY JESUS, HOW HAST THOU OFFENDED?

> *Who has believed what we have heard? And to whom has the arm of the lord been revealed? For he grew up before him like a young plant, and like a root out of dry ground, he had no form*

or majesty that we should look at him, nothing in his appearance that we should desire him. He was despised and rejected by others; a man of suffering "and acquainted with infirmity; and as one from whom others hide their faces" he was despised and we held him of no account. Surely he has borne our infirmities and carried our diseases; yet we accounted him stricken struck down by God and afflicted. But he was wounded for our transgressions, crushed for our iniquities; upon him was the punishment that made us whole, and by his bruises we are healed.

—Isaiah 53:1–6

In my early years of Sunday school, the walls of our classroom always had a picture of Jesus. This picture was always of a handsome, slightly effeminate, gentle-looking man who wouldn't hurt a fly. No wonder almost every group, no matter how off-the-wall (including the KKK), liked to claim Jesus was on their side. He is so popular that car dealers have used him to boost sales. But the frustrating thing about Jesus is that he absolutely refuses to choose up sides. Instead, he offers both judgment and grace to all, even me and you! He calls us all to repent. The truth is that our sweet gentle Jesus could make people mad—mad enough to kill him.

If you abuse drugs and alcohol, surely Jesus will call you to account, yet he made 160 gallons of wine at a wedding party. He called the unrighteous to repent, but he was also called a friend of publicans and sinners. He offered free grace but said the way to salvation was narrow and hard and few would find it (Matthew 7:14). He was a man of peace, but some of his twelve disciples carried swords by his command (Luke 22:36). Still, he said only two swords were "enough" (sword control?) (Luke 22:38).

He often ate with rich men and talked a lot about investments, but he told the rich young ruler to redistribute his wealth to the less fortunate (Matthew 19:21, Mark 10:21, Luke 18:22) and proclaimed the year of Jubilee as "good news to the poor" (Luke 4:16–20). If you are rich, he said that it would be easier for a camel to go through the eye of a needle than for you to enter the kingdom of heaven. But if you are poor, he said "the poor you will always have with you" (as our responsibility perhaps?) (See Deuteronomy 15:7–11).

So to the advocates of free speech, he might say, "I tell you, on the day of judgment, you will have to give an account of every careless word you utter, for by your words you will be justified and by your words you will be condemned" (Matthew 12:36), and "woe to anyone who would place a stumbling block before one of these little ones" (Matthew 18:6). However, if you support censorship, he said, "Nothing is covered that will not be uncovered, and nothing secret that will not be made known. What I tell you in the dark, utter in the light, and what you hear whispered, proclaim to the housetops" (Matthew 10:26–27).

If you just love to gobble up the sweet aroma and syrupy fluff of cotton-candy praise worship, he would say, "Not everyone who says, 'Lord, Lord' will enter the kingdom of heaven, but he who *does* the will of my father who is in heaven . . ." (Matthew 7:21) But if your worship is "zombie"—cold, dry, and formal—he would say, "I know you have the reputation of being alive, but you are dead" (Revelation 3:1). If you seek a sweet and gentle Jesus, he would say, "I have come not to bring peace, but a sword" (Matthew 10:34), "I have come to set father against son and mother against daughter" (Luke 12:53). But if you are a hawk, he said, "Blessed are the peacemakers, they shall be called the Children of God" (Matthew 5:9).

If you interpret the Bible literally, he would say, "You have heard it said of old . . . but I say unto you." (He was correcting an Old Testament error!) But if you interpret the Bible loosely, he said, "Not one letter, not one stroke of a letter, will pass from the law *until all is accomplished*" (See Matthew 5:18 and John 19:30).

If you are pro-life, he is for "life" too. In fact, he invented it! But he just might ask you, "If you are pro-life, then why do you also support the death penalty and oppose any form of gun control? And why do you ignore the life of the baby after it is born?" Where is your concern for starving babies; AIDS babies; crack babies; alcohol syndrome babies; babies from rape and incest; deformed babies; diseased babies; and abused, unloved, and unwanted babies? And there are the innocent ones who are victimized and die at the hands of the very ones who are supposed to take care of them. If you are pro-choice, Jesus would surely condemn you for the callous way that you can snuff out the life of a potential human being as if it were merely a legitimate and convenient form of birth control. That too would be offensive to him! (Complicated, isn't it?)

I think you get the point. Life is complex, and every situation is unique; so just when you expect judgment, Jesus offers grace, and just when you expect grace, Jesus offers judgment. He afflicts the comfortable. He comforts the afflicted. So do you really think that the ad men, the message handlers, and the spin doctors could tie Jesus down or keep him from telling it like it is? No way! If there is one thing that convinces me he is God, it is this constant clash between human expectation and divine will. The awful truth is if Jesus ran for president today, he would surely be *crucified.* Why? Because he would refuse to choose up sides or take bribes from lobbyists or special interest groups. In addition, he would love and judge, both the blue states and the red states, liberals and conservatives, hawks and doves, traditionalists and modernists. So no matter what side you are on, Jesus is already on your side—without partiality! *But* he also calls both sides to account. Thus, the real the question is, *"Are we on his side?"*

He was in the world, and the world came into being through him, yet the world did not know him. He came to what was his own and *his own people did not accept him.* But to all who received him, who believed in his name, he gave power to become the children of God who were born not of blood, or the will of the flesh, but of *God.* (John 1:10–13).

So why do we treat other Christians as competitors instead of fellow pilgrims and team players? Why do we try to hold each other back, instead of lending support as a part of the family of God? Why do we limit the amazing variety of ways that God can enrich our lives? Once, the Disciples came to Jesus saying, "There is a man who is casting out demons in your name. What should we do?" Jesus replied, "Whoever is not against us is for us" (Mark 9:40). Can't we see how that opens up room for so much diversity within the body of Christ? Isn't it time to stop being so exclusive, closed off and narrow-minded? I say, "It is time to trust in the power of Pentecost"—where the spirit moved among everyone and spoke to a broad spectrum of different cultures at the same time, each in their own native tongue? I call that real Pentecostal power!

MOVING WITH THE SPIRIT

In 1874, the Methodist people in the marshy lowlands of Swan Quarter, North Carolina, decided they needed a new church. So they sought out a landowner named Sam Saddler and asked about a lot he owned on good high ground. But Sam was a shrewd businessman, and the price he quoted was prime market value. Since the Methodists were low on funds, they decided to settle instead for a less desirable piece of land they could better afford.

So on September 16, 1876, the tiny one-room church was dedicated. One week later, a terrible Nor'easter lashed the North Carolina coast and rain fell in torrents. The next morning, the people of Swan Quarter woke to an incredible sight. They rolled up their shades and saw their new Methodist Church floating up Oyster Creek Road—being pushed toward higher ground, by the rising tide.

Immediately, the men and women of the community waded out into the rushing waters, tying ropes and halyards to moor the tiny church to trees and posts. They pulled on the ropes, trying to hold the church back, but the stubborn little church moved on up the street. When it reached Main Street, it suddenly stopped, as though pondering where to go next, made a mysterious ninety-degree turn to the right and proceeded down Main Street. Still, the people tried to hold it back but to no avail. The little church moved on. Then suddenly, as if it knew exactly where it was going, it veered off Main Street and headed down what is now known as "Church Street." There, it turned again, backed onto a vacant lot and stopped dead in its tracks—settling down on higher ground. Indeed, it was that very same piece of prime property owned by Mr. Saddler. Today Providence United Methodist Church is a brick building, but behind it sits a little one-room wooden structure with documents and sworn statements about the "Church that God moved." It is said that Sam Saddler made a mad dash, wading to the courthouse saying, "If God wants my property that bad, then he can have it for free!"

I see this as a modern parable of the church. First, it describes a group of people who settled for less than the best, who took the low ground instead of the high ground, trading convenience for sacrifice. Second, it describes a group of people who reacted to seeing the church move by tying ropes around it to try holding it back. Third, it reminds us that it is God's church, not ours. Our God is not powerless, and if you are not willing to keep up with his movement, then you had better get out of the way because God will find someone to keep things moving.

I dedicate this book as a bridge of reconciliation between opposing Christian camps; and a healer of old festering wounds!

"WHAT DO *YOU* THINK ABOUT ME?"

I WISH I DID not have to get in the way of what I have to say in this book, because it is really more about you than it is about me. My dilemma is simply this—how can I get you to trust me enough to hear what I have to say, unless I give you some sense of who I am? So who am I? Alfred Lord Tennyson penned it nicely on the lips of Ulysses when he wrote, "I am a part of all that I have met." So are we all. Our personhood comes into being through our experiences and relationships with other persons across the space of our lifetime and beyond. It is our unique encounters with the world and other persons, including the person of God that makes us who we are and gives wings to our souls.

My story begins on the outer banks of North Carolina on the historic island of Roanoke, in the tiny coastal village of Manteo. It was there that the English first settled on the white sandy beaches of the "New World." Manteo is home to Paul Green's open air drama, the "Lost Colony," that tells the tale of that first settlement. That, plus the attraction of a long strip of gorgeous beach, caused an annual invasion to our small town by that strange breed of humanity known as, "the summer tourist."

"Hey, buddy," they would yell from their convertibles, "can you tell me how to find the Lost Colony?"

"Yes, sir, just turn right at the next light and drive to the north end of the island and look for the signs. You can't miss it!"

"You don't say," they would yell back, "and we heard that it was lost. Ha, ha!" I fell for that same joke more than once! But on the whole, Manteo was a wholesome place for a kid to grow up.

I walked or rode my bike all over town—to school, to meet up with friends or to go downtown to the movies. The owner of the theater even knew me by name. The area was rich with things to do. We went fishing, boating, swimming, crabbing, clamming, and hunting. And the huge sand dunes were great places to play. I suppose this is where I got my love of all things coastal—especially seafood and most especially, oysters. Sometimes, we would go out on the skiff for only an hour or two and come back with a "mess of fish" for supper. Life was very good!

My kid sister Wanda was four years younger than me, and in my father's eyes, she could do no wrong. My eyes were not so clouded. When we'd share a Coke from my grandfather's supermarket, I would try to pour an equal amount in our two glasses. But every time I poured, she would suck off the foam. I kept trying to tell her it wasn't fair because the foam would reform into liquid, but she was astute enough to ignore me.

Once, when Mom and Dad were out and I had to babysit the cute little dear, I accidentally stepped on some of the dishes from her plastic tea set. Plastic was very cheap and thin in those days, so they shattered into a multitude of pieces. I apologized, but Wanda went into hysterics. In desperation to stop the crying, I bribed her with candy and even let her play with my most cherished toys—the ones that were always off limits to her. Finally, she calmed down and seemed smugly content—that is until Mom and Dad opened the front door. Then all hell broke loose. She was wailing like a lost puppy. You would have thought her best friend had died.

"What's the matter, dear?"

"It's Denny, he broke my favorite dishes, and he did it on purpose." After I had received what I regarded as an unjust punishment, I felt angry at Wanda and very sorry for myself. Then I heard Wanda praying loudly in her bedroom down the hall, "Dear God, Denny was mean to me again today. He broke my dishes on purpose."

"Mother," I yelled, "that's not fair, don't let her tell God that!"

In those days, I pictured God as a divine despot—an all-powerful busybody, a spy in the sky who kept an eye on me all the time everywhere I went. He even knew my every thought. To make matters worse, like a cosmic elephant, God never forgot a single sin I committed. Just in case, he had a big black book to remind him.

To me, the purpose of religion was to keep us all tied up in "do-nots." Do not drink or smoke or chew, and stay away from those who do! One of the most traumatic moments of judgment occurred when my dad caught me and a girl down the street playing doctor. After we had both been severely punished, she and I secretly placed our hands on the Holy

Bible and swore to God that we would never, ever do anything like that again for the rest of our lives. Right!

While my beloved home church, Mount Olivet Methodist, was a big part of our family life, at times it made me very uncomfortable. After all, God was all too eager to dole out punishment on sinners such as me. As Dennis the Menace once put it, "Dear God, bless all the good people on earth, and have mercy on the rest of us." Nevertheless, the oysters were plentiful, the beach was close by, and as I said, life was good!

PARADISE LOST

Little did I know that my idyllic days of sea and sand were about to come to an abrupt end. As long as I could remember, my dad had been the butcher in my grandfather's store, but suddenly Dad got "the call." Almost overnight, he put down his meat cleaver, picked up his Bible, and went into the ministry.

The next thing I knew, Mom and Dad were pulling me out of school, away from my friends, and moving us to my dad's first appointment in beautiful, historic Bath, the oldest town in North Carolina. The old moss-covered cypress trees and the high vermilion cliffs overlooking Bath Creek, reminded me of a scene out of a Faulkner novel. Edward Teach or Blackbeard, the meanest pirate on the Atlantic coast, often visited Bath. In fact, the governor of North Carolina, at that time, Charles Eden, had conspired with Teach to share his pirate booty.

So we kids were convinced that pirate treasure was hidden somewhere in those eighteen-foot high cliffs along Bath Creek. We dug many a cave looking for gold, in vain, of course. It is said that when the famous preacher, George Whitfield, was poorly received at Bath centuries back, he angrily brushed the dust off his feet and swore the town would never grow—and it never did!

LEARNING TO PRACTICE
WHAT MY FATHER PREACHED

The quaint little white frame Methodist Church in Bath was right next to the parsonage on a dirt street. My best friend was Bradley, the principal's son. He and I both found ourselves in a similar glass fish bowl. I suspect the reason people say "preacher's kids" are bad is because they are on a quest to be accepted as normal. "Shh! don't tell that joke, here comes the preacher's kid." I call it hypocrisy in reverse. "I'll show you, I can be just as bad as you; maybe worse!" It is also a self-fulfilling prophecy that many adults have about the nature of "PKs." They almost expected us to behave badly.

One Sunday in worship, Bradley and I were sitting right behind a tiny old lady named Ms. Waters. Ms. Waters loved to sing, but was so deaf she was unable to stay in pitch. She was like the piccolo in a band. You could hear her distinctive voice, singing high above everyone else. Bradley and I thought this to be very funny. It was summer and my dad was proudly wearing his brand-new white polyester robe for Communion Sunday.

After the sermon, the ushers began to guide us to the altar. As luck would have it, Ms. Waters ended up kneeling right next to Bradley and me. Dad had passed the little squares of white bread and was now serving the juice in those tiny individual glasses. Bradley nudged me, just as I put the little glass to my lips, whispering in my ear, "I'll bet a shot of this Welch's grape juice will work wonders for Old Lady Water's screech." Have you ever tried not to laugh? All that accomplishes is to make everything funnier. The end result was that I exploded in laughter and splattered grape juice all over the altar area—including my father's new white robe.

That day at lunch, no one spoke. Every time a fork hit the plate it sounded like a Chinese gong. I could hear myself chewing the food in my mouth. Heck, I could hear everyone at the table chewing their food. After dessert, my dad said, "Denny, I need to see you upstairs." I knew exactly what that meant, but I did not think it was fair. I couldn't help that Bradley made me laugh. It wasn't my fault!

Upstairs, Dad took off his belt and asked me to lie face down on the bed. But I just looked up at him with all the defiance I could muster in my young body. Whereupon, Dad said what parents have been saying to their children for a million years, "I am only doing this for your own good." He then waxed into a little sermon about what a high privilege it was for him to be able to share the sacred elements of bread and wine in reverence for his Savior, the Lord Jesus Christ and how he could not allow it to become a sacrilege, especially by his own son! Then he added, reaching once again into that primordial archive of universal parental wisdom, "Son, I just want you to know this hurts me a whole lot more than it hurts you!"

"Oh yeah!" I smirked as I looked back at him with all the defiant courage I had in me.

"Oh yeah," Dad replied, "and if you don't believe me, then here, you take the belt and you punish me for what you have done because someone has to pay." With that, he handed me the belt and lay face down on the bed. "Go ahead, you can punish me in your place."

My first reaction, I am ashamed to say, was, "Oh boy, justice at last! This is great!" But as I raised my hand to strike the first blow, that belt became so heavy and my arm so weak that I hesitated.

"Hit me!" he said. So halfheartedly, I let the belt fall upon his back. "Is that the best you can do?" he yelled.

Tears filled my eyes as I dropped to the floor on my knees and pleaded, "No, Daddy, no! Please don't make me hit you again!"

Soon, we were embracing and crying together as I had inadvertently stumbled upon the central paradigm of the Gospel—namely, "Reconciliation." Please understand that, at the time I in no way grasped the universal significance of this sacred moment. But looking back, I am amazed at how eloquently it expresses the primary message of salvation in the Holy Scriptures:

"For while we were enemies, we were reconciled to God," Romans 5:10.
"All this is from God who through Christ reconciled us to himself and gave us the ministry of reconciliation," 2 Corinthians 5:18.
"And through him to reconcile to himself all things," Colossians 1:19.
"That they all might be perfectly one," John 17:23.
"And I, when I am lifted up from the earth, will draw all people to myself," John 12:32.

So here is the problem: if the core of the Gospel is reconciliation, then why do we remain so darn divided?

THE BRIDGE

*For we are not peddlers of God's word like so many, but
in Christ we speak as persons of sincerity, and persons sent from
God, and standing in his presence.*

—1 Corinthians 2:17

BEFORE I TRANSFERRED to Duke Divinity School, I attended
Emory University's, Candler School of Theology in Atlanta for one
year. During that time, I would drive seventy miles every weekend to
Macon, Georgia, where I served as youth director at Centenary UMC.
One weekend, my MG-A broke down, as those cars were so notoriously
prone to do, and I had to take the bus. In the Atlanta terminal I was
about to board when I was confronted by a rather pushy, matronly lady.
She rudely tried to stop me just to hand me a tract with a tombstone
pictured on the cover. I confess that she immediately turned me off, but
I reluctantly took her tiny blue paper pamphlet entitled, "Where are the
dead?"

I then tried to make my way around her, but she was determined to
block my path. "Son, have you been sanctified by the Holy Ghost? Have
you been saved?" she asked urgently. "Saved from what, YOU?" I barked
impatiently. "No silly, saved from eternal damnation in the fiery pits of
hell, that's what!" she responded. About that time the bus driver yelled at
me, "Hey, Bud, are you getting on this bus or not?"

"Excuse me lady," I said sarcastically. With that, I made a quick jig to
the right and dashed onto the bus. As we pulled out of the station, she
had already found a new startled victim to save.

I must say that I felt guilty about the way I blew "Tract Lady" off.
Here I was a seminary student studying to be a Christian minister, angry
with an obviously devout and dedicated Christian. After all, Tract Lady
was freely volunteering her time to serve the Lord. So why did she make
me feel so uncomfortable, not to mention angry?

All the way to Macon, I thought about that encounter, and I finally
decided it was the impersonal nature of the experience that upset me.
She made me feel used instead of loved. She wasn't interested in me as a
person. She didn't want to know my hopes or aspirations. She never even
asked my name, nor did she offer hers. To her, I was just another notch

in her salvation belt or a "star in her crown." At least, that is the way she made me feel. Jesus never went around passing out papers, yelling, "Read all about it!" What Jesus offered was himself, person to person, heart to heart, and soul to soul. "If you have known me, you have known the Father," he said. But we have made religion about dogmatic beliefs and stern regulations, instead of personal relationships.

As I pondered this strange absence of union in our Christian communion, it occurred to me that the root of our division lies partially in a crisis of perception. It is the old apples-and-oranges dilemma. What we need is a common framework for dialogue. We need a starting point we can all agree upon—in spite of our differences—on which we can hang our differing ideas. As simplistic as it sounds, I began to see that we could build a bridge that would transcend our varied opinions and points of view about religion, about God, and about faith. The secret is to insist that all discourse over differences be placed in the context of relationships. The more I studied this, the more I began to see many of the traditional tenants of the faith, not from the perspective of doctrines, dogmas, and regulations, but from a new and exciting prospective of *relationships*!

THE LITTLE PRINCE

Most everyone has heard of the French book for children, *The Little Prince*. But this wonderful, whimsical book is not really a book for children. It is a spiritual allegory for adults about relationships. In one scene, the little prince has an encounter with a fox, and the fox says, "I have no need of you. And you have no need of me. To you I am nothing more than a fox, like a hundred thousand other foxes. But if you tame me, then we will truly need each other. To me you will be unique in all the world . . . Men have forgotten this truth, but you must never forget it. You become responsible forever for whatever you have tamed."

Isn't that why God sent his Son into the world, in order to touch us deep inside? God gives himself only to those who are willing to be tamed. And all those protective layers, we so carefully construct throughout our lives, serve only to distance us from one another and insulate us from really deep personal contact.

Now that you have heard his philosophy, I will tell you the rest of the story. Antoine de Saint-Exupéry, author of *The Little Prince*, was a devout

Catholic. He was a French pilot who despised fascism and died, fighting the Nazis. His battle against fascism went back to the Spanish Civil War.

According to Hanoch McCarty, he hid part of his own autobiography in one of his short stories. As a young soldier, Antoine was captured by the enemy and thrown into a Spanish prison. He sensed from the rude treatment he received from the guards that he was going to be killed. Nervous and distraught, he fumbled in his pockets to see if there were any cigarettes and found one that had escaped their search. "Do you have a light?" he said to the Spanish jailer. As the guard came closer and lit a match, their eyes inadvertently locked, smiles were exchanged and a spark jumped across the gap between their two distant souls. The jailer didn't want to look his enemy in the eye, much less smile, but he did. Suddenly, his look took on a new dimension.

"Do you have kids?" he asked. Antoine fumbled for the pictures in his wallet. Then the guard shared pictures of his own family. Soon they were talking about hopes and dreams for the future, as Antoine's eyes began to fill with tears. "I knew and he knew that I would probably never see my family again." Suddenly, without a word, the guard unlocked the cell and let Antoine go free. "I can't explain it," he said, "but my life was changed by a smile." Yes, a natural intimate connection, unaffected and unplanned, leaped through prison bars to generate a genuine spiritual bond between two sworn "enemies."

This experience helped inspire Saint-Exupéry's beautiful philosophy of life. He believed that beneath all of those self-protective defenses that hide our souls from one another, is a common spiritual need for connection. He urged us to look beyond our false pride, our position, our status and our need to feel important. Surely, if our souls really touched, then we would not be enemies anymore. We would no longer have room for violence, envy or war. We would see our sacred connectedness. Jesus said for this to happen, first you must be willing to give yourself away. If you want to know who you really are, you must be bold enough to find your life by losing it. That takes risk. It is not an easy or natural thing to do. I have found it so very hard to do my whole life. In order to do it you need divine help to break down those dividing walls that keep us apart.

If you could save yourself, then you wouldn't need a savior. That is why John Calvin said centuries ago, "No man can turn to the contemplation of himself, without immediately turning to the contemplation of God." After all, the most perfect and complete self in history was the most selfless person in history. He was the man for others, who, though he was in the form of God, emptied himself and took the form of a servant washing his disciple's feet. He came, not to be ministered unto, but to minister! He gave his life away so that we might no longer live for ourselves, but for him who lived and died for us!

I once read about a child who was locked in a dark closet for seven years. That child could never be normal, because we only become authentic persons through contact with other persons. You are not born with a complete personality. You have to become a whole person through relationships. You have the potential and the possibility to become an authentic "self," but only through interacting with other "selves." Only as our souls bounce off of one another and make some kind of real contact, can we truly come alive.

Your so-called self is much more than some private independent spark of consciousness buried deep inside your being, waiting to be released—through self-reflection or self-discovery. Instead, you have to connect with other "selves," reaching out beyond yourself to discover who you really are. That is why; the more you give yourself away, the more you become your authentic self.

A mother was preparing pancakes for her two sons, Kevin, age five, and Ryan, age three. As they waited for the pancakes to come off the griddle, they began to fuss over who would get the first one. At this point, the mother saw a wonderful opportunity to teach a moral lesson about sharing. "Boys," she said, "if Jesus were sitting here at the table, he would say, 'Let my brother have the first pancake, I can wait.'" It was then that Kevin turned to his younger brother and said, "OK, Ryan, you get to be Jesus!"

But that's just the point! As Christians, we are all called to be like Jesus, as we no longer live for ourselves but for him who gave himself for us. He set us an example and then told us to go and do likewise. "If I have washed your feet, you ought to wash each other's feet." So if you really want to expand your consciousness and find your true authentic self, then why not try looking at every person you meet as a special gift from God? Every stranger is a wonderful opportunity for you to experience new joy, self-fulfillment and self-discovery. You can actually encounter God and find out who you are just by knowing this person! So reach out and touch someone! Comfort a friend who is hurting. Give hugs to someone who needs it. Be kind to a lonely child. Visit the aged in nursing homes. Take flowers to someone who is sick. Bring cheer to someone who is dying. Give comfort to someone in grief. Gladly give yourself away. That is how you find your life by losing it!

> **"Though we cannot think alike, may we not love alike? May we not be of one heart, though we are not of one opinion?"**
>
> **—John Wesley**

AN ONTOLOGY OF CONNECTEDNESS

By this we know that we abide in him and he in us, because he has given us his spirit.

—1 John 4:13

I T WAS PATTY Black's first day on the job as a loan officer. But the first client to walk into her office was a big blue frog. Just as she was about to scream, the frog said, "Lady, please remain calm. I am only here to take out a $5,000 loan. That's all!"

"But how can you talk?" she asked in amazement.

"Well, my father used to be a frog, but he persuaded a beautiful woman to kiss him, and poof, he turned into Mick Jagger, while she, my poor mom, turned into a frog. And that's where I came from. Haven't you ever wondered why Mick Jagger's mouth is so large? Well, now you know!"

"OK, but what about collateral?" she asked.

"Well," he said, "I own this tiny scale-model statue of my father, like nothing else on earth. It is probably worth a fortune."

So Patty took the art piece to her boss to see what he would make of it, and the bank manager replied, "It's a knickknack, Patty Black, give the frog a loan, his old man's a Rolling Stone!"

You might say frog-kissing is what Jesus's followers are called to do!

I believe we are called to be Christian change agents. As such, I believe we must be willing to relate not only to the beautiful people of this world, but to the not so beautiful as well. We are called to give hope to the hopeless, and love to the unlovely. That is what Jesus did, and that is what he calls us to do. In short, the whole Gospel is not about following the right rules. It is about following Jesus and loving your neighbor. It is not about believing the right stuff; it is about personal life-changing "relationships."

I do not claim this truth as original in any way. On the contrary, I decided to write this book precisely because so many decent people seem to ignore the obvious. Why else would so-called Christians, who like to flaunt their devotion to Jesus, insist on excluding countless others simply because they were different? On what grounds did Jesus ever tell us not to love someone? Was it because they were enemies? Was it because they came from another religion, another race, or another sexual orientation? I don't remember that rule! Do you?

When I was in seminary, I read a book by Emil Brunner entitled *Truth is Encounter* and a book by a Jew named Martin Buber entitled *I and Thou*. Both books taught me that ultimate knowledge is personal knowledge—not detached empirical knowledge. Truth comes through relationships. Mr. Buber argued that the Bible was really about "I/Thou" as opposed to "I/It!"

In other words, I can view you as an object, an "it." I can study things about you, like your size, your clothing, your favorite brand names, and the color of your skin; but that's not you! To really know you, I must meet you as a person, soul to soul or "I/Thou." Therefore, only you can reveal yourself to me.

Emil Brunner latched on to that same concept to explain how Jesus is the way, the truth and the life. Real knowing, he argued, comes "not" from the way we know facts or gather information, but rather from personal encounter, the way we know people heart to heart. We do not collect truth, and file it under "T." Instead, we encounter truth through relationships. So taking this to its logical conclusion, I believe that to totally reject other people for any reason is to reject God.

One of the greatest miracles in the universe is *you*! The fact that I can relate to you and you to me, and be able to go question the nature of the universe at all, is a real miracle! No wonder we are said to be made in the image of God. After all, where else does this consciousness, this personality, this self-awareness come from, if not from God? Just as your spirit is invisible, so is the Spirit of the universe! Your soul is hidden from me—unless you choose to reveal it and the same thing holds true for God.

"No one has ever seen God," said John, "but the only Son who is in the bosom of the father, he has made him known" (John 1:18). So

God chooses not to keep his soul to himself and remain hidden and aloof. Instead, God is light, and like the sun, God constantly reaches out to give himself away. He reaches out to us through Jesus, "the sun of righteousness with healing on his wings" (Malachi 4:2). That is to say, "in Jesus," God makes himself known, not in the way we know facts, things, computer programs, books or philosophical concepts, but the way we know persons—heart to heart, soul to soul, and mind to mind. You don't memorize or debate ultimate truth; you encounter Truth in the person of Jesus! Listen to the passion and excitement of John, in his first letter, as he contemplates this idea:

> That which was from the beginning, which we have heard, which we have seen with our eyes, which we have looked upon and touched with our hands, concerning the word of life—the life was made manifest, and we saw it, and testify to it, and proclaim to you the eternal life which was with the father and was made manifest to us—that which we have seen and heard we proclaim also to you, so that you may have fellowship with us; and our fellowship is with the Father and with his Son Jesus Christ. And we are writing this that our joy may be complete. (1 John 1:1–4)

Now that is powerful! Can you feel his excitement and enthusiasm—the genuine intimacy? This was not like a lecture presented in dull monotones at Duke Divinity School or a dreary Supreme Court deliberation, or the mindless half-hearted simpering sentimentality of a jazzed-up contemporary worship service, devoid of very little intelligent theological depth or meaning. No, rather this came from deep down in his heart and soul! This meant something intimate, personal, and life-changing to him.

I contend that either you meet God as a "thou" instead of an "it" or you will never meet God at all. You cannot know God the way you know a baseball score. God cannot be objectified, analyzed, scrutinized, or described in any book! Nor is he simply your best buddy! God is holy *other*, which is why he must initiate the dialogue. We cannot sneak up on God, to learn God's nature, or predict what God will do next. We can only know God the way he chooses to be known which is personally through Jesus Christ. (That is to say, on his terms, not ours.) We call that revelation.

Unfortunately, we sometimes treat both God and other people, impersonally. We judge people as objects, by their shape or outward appearance, the color of their skin, their wealth or position, the way they talk or dress; but that external stuff is not really knowing them at all. *Real* knowing requires direct interpersonal involvement in a committed caring relationship. That is why I believe a crisis of perception occurs anytime we discuss religious issues outside the context of relationships. Otherwise, dialogue can quickly breakdown as the conversation shifts from grace and honest sharing to be replaced by the traps of narrow-mindedness, literalism, rigid legalism, or even sentimental fluff.

For example, the church has argued for ages over the nature of the Eucharist. Is Jesus present "in" the bread or "with" the bread? Is Jesus there by transubstantiation or consubstantiation or what? I agree with Saint Augustine. We miss the point! It is not about the bread! "We neither consume God nor excrete God," he said. Rather, we commune with him and each other spiritually through relationships. I always liked the historic way the late great Anglican, Archbishop Thomas Cranmer (sixteenth century), put it: "Feed on him in thy heart, by faith, with thanksgiving." I believe that is what true "Holy Communion" is all about!

When Jesus was confronted by the deeply entrenched conservative and legalistic beliefs of the Pharisees, he had a simple response. If you love the Lord your God with all your heart, with all your mind, and with all your strength and love your neighbor as yourself, then on these two "relationships" hang all the law and the prophets—which is to say the entire Bible. Or as Saint Augustine put it: "Love God and do as you please." Why? Because if you love God, then you will be pleased to do what is pleasing to him—not because you have to, but because, in gratitude, you want to. Therefore, I challenge you to name one religious term that cannot be explained in the context of relationships. There are a host of examples:

> **SIN** is estrangement, rebellion, and self-alienation from God and one another.
> **SALVATION** is to be reconciled with God and made a whole person.
> **JUSTIFICATION** is to be *put right* with God, restored by grace.

ATONEMENT is to be put *at one* with God through reconciliation.

THE CHURCH (*koinonia*) is a faith community of "fellowship," as together, we become the *Body of Christ*.

HOLY SPIRIT (intimate agape) is the Holy Person, the Invisible Presence.

HOLY COMMUNION is "union with" Christ, God, and fellow Christians.

KNOWLEDGE is, literally in Hebrew, "to be at one with," as in Adam "knew" Eve. This is a personal relational kind of knowing, not an objective, impersonal, or informational kind of knowing.

HEAVEN is "knowing," being "at one with" Jesus and God (*John 17:3*).

GOD is love. (We learned that truth in kindergarten.)

LOVE (agape) is the ultimate relationship that defines all others.

TRINITY is as Jesus described it, "I and the Father are one." Three distinct personhoods made perfectly one by interconnecting relationships.

SANCTIFICATION is to be transformed through a personal relationship with Jesus Christ into a new creation, as we are changed by degrees into his likeness.

PRAYER is a personal or communal dialogue in relationship with God.

FAITH . . . to be continued . . .

THAT'S NOT WHAT MY MOTHER TOLD ME!

For by grace you have been saved through faith, and this is not your own doing, it is the gift of God—not the result of works, so that no one may boast.

—Ephesians 2:8–9

A CERTAIN SEMINARY PROFESSOR used to address the incoming freshmen class by saying something like this: Some people have probably warned you that this school will take away your religion. That is not true! Believe me, we can't do that! We can help you explore your religion. We can test your religious convictions. We can improve your understanding. We can teach you Hebrew, Greek, Latin, theology, church history, and logic, but you learned your religion on your mother's knee, long before you got to this seminary. And what she taught you there on her knee, no one can ever take away from you, except you. Hopefully, however, we can help you understand your faith and interpret it more intelligently.

One of the central tenants of the Protestant Reformation was the Doctrine of Justification by Faith. Faith is, however, a very complex concept. Therefore, I wish to challenge almost every definition of faith you have ever heard, even if it was on your mother's knee that you heard it! Like a diamond, faith has many facets, but what most of us think faith is, is not at all what the apostle Paul talked about in his letter to the Ephesians. Let me begin by saying that the very worst place to look for the true definition of almost any religious term is a secular dictionary. I have looked through at least half a dozen different versions and all of them come up with definitions that sound something like this: *Faith* is unquestioning belief, complete confidence, blind trust; belief that is not based on empirical evidence or proof. *Faith* is strong religious convictions beyond reason. *Faith* is a system of doctrines or creeds that are to be believed. *Faith* is a certain kind of religion, the obligation of loyalty and fidelity to God or to a religion.

The common problem with all of these definitions is that they start as a human enterprise and end there, as if faith goes from the ground up, instead of from God down. Faith then becomes a bold human effort—a blind leap into the dark void, a daring plunge into the unknown abyss, an assent of the intellect—beyond knowledge, experience or reason. All of these understandings define faith as an act of man instead of an act of God, as a human accomplishment rather than a divine gift, as something we do to God, rather than something God works in us. Often, the man on the street is even more confused. He gets the impression that faith is like shadow boxing in the dark. He may even regard faith as optimistic ignorance, naive gullibility.

One man said to me, "When I round the curve in my car at sixty miles per hour, I have faith that the bridge won't be out," as if faith were little more than the power of positive thinking, blind confidence or sheer will. You know how it works: if you can concentrate hard enough, grit your teeth tight enough, and strain until your make the veins on your neck pop out . . . if you can do all of this then, "Oops, there goes another rubber tree plant," or another illness, or another "mountain" of a problem—right? Wrong! A lady in an iron lung once had a charismatic group come to pray for her, and when she did not improve they said: "You just didn't have enough faith!" From then on, she felt like her illness was all her fault. How sad!

If our own belief efforts could accomplish that kind of stuff, who would need God? We could all become healthy, wealthy, and wise by sheer will power! But Jesus never told us to have faith in faith, he told us to have faith in God! It is God, not belief that makes the mountains move. Faith is not a do-it-yourself proposition. Faith is not a personal skill or human achievement. It is not a special talent or a feat of self-actualization that one can develop apart from God.

A woman enters a bookstore to buy a Bible. She looks through the religious section, but not one is to be found. She says to the clerk, "I know the secular press never puts it on the list, but isn't the Bible still the no. 1 best seller?"

"Yes, ma'am, it is," says the clerk.

"Well," says the woman, "why don't you have any for sale?"

"Oh, we do, but some people don't like to go into the religious section, so we now display them with the self-help books."

Self-help—we have turned faith from "God's help" into "self-help!" You may have belief all by yourself, by your own bold efforts and volition. You might have optimism, trust, "positive thinking" or "possibility thinking," all by yourself apart from God, but true faith requires the help of a savior, and only God makes that kind of faith work! Real faith is not so much something you have, as it is an experience that has you! It is not a feat of exceptional skill or a personal accomplishment; it is a humbling divine gift of grace. In short, faith is a personal communion with God.

So faith is the opposite of sin. Listen to what Paul told the Ephesians, "And you he made alive when you were dead…for by grace you have been saved, through faith." (Note: He did not say "by faith," but "through faith.") "And this is not your doing, it is the gift of God, not because of works but lest any man should boast." And listen to what Paul told the Corinthians: "Now concerning spiritual gifts, there are a variety of gifts, the same Lord inspires them all."

"To one is given through the spirit the utterance of wisdom, to another *faith,* by the same spirit." So *faith is a gift* inspired by *the Spirit.* When the apostle Paul clearly tells us over and over again that faith is a divine gift, why in heaven's name do we still insist on regarding it as a personal achievement?

I believe this problem actually began as early as the first century when the church became infested with a bunch of arrogant self-righteous charismatics, who became so proud of their piety they came to believe that they had the inside track on faith. They had exclusive access to the Holy Spirit. So if you did not believe their particular brand of religion or show their spectacular spiritual skills, like speaking in tongues, then you did not cut it as a true Christian. At best, you were little more than a second-class "Christian." Isn't that exactly why Jesus got angry with the Pharisees? When I become proud of my faith, as if it were some talent I possess, then humility and gratitude go out the window to be replaced by arrogant selfish pride in my own personal accomplishments.

In the second century, a theologian named Tertullian took this logic to its ultimate extreme. He said, "I believe because it is absurd." He found some of the stories in the Bible so outlandish that he concluded that there must be some special saving merit in believing the unbelievable! He reasoned that the more far out and unbelievable a story was the more brownie points you earned for yourself in heaven by believing it anyway. Faith, for him, simply became a new work, a new way to earn your own salvation. It was like pulling yourself up to heaven by your own suspenders, by sheer force of will, as you coerce yourself to believe. But faith is not a human skill-set, or enterprise. It is not a heroic act of true grit. "Lord, you made it tough, but I made myself believe anyway, and boy, am I proud." Listen to what the apostle Paul says, "This is not your doing! We are God's workmanship."

So our response to faith should be humility and gratitude, not gloating, personal smugness, and self-satisfaction! Martin Luther said, "Man gives his all, but God does it all." Jesus tried to explain this idea to his followers, only to make some of them mad. "No one," he said, "can come to me unless it is granted him by the Father." Some of his followers quit then and there and went home. He then turned to the twelve and said, "Will you also leave me?" They said, "No, Lord, for you have the words of eternal life" (John 6:66–69).

My point is when Jesus came into my heart, I did not feel a need to brag about it because he came, in spite of me, by his power, not mine. He washed over me like a mighty wave; I could not help myself. Indeed, I had sworn that I would never be a preacher! So how could I boast or try to take credit for that . . . no way! It was not my doing; it was God doing something wonderful in me! He pulled me kicking and screaming into the ministry in spite of myself. Thanks be to God!

Martin Luther put it this way over five hundred years ago in his commentary. "Faith is not what some people think it is. They think that when you hear the Gospel, you start working, creating, by your own strength, a thankful heart, which says, 'I believe.' Instead, faith is God's work in us that changes us, and gives new birth. It kills the old Adam and makes us completely different people. It changes our hearts, our spirits, and our thoughts. Such knowledge of God's grace makes you happy, joyful and bold in your relationship with God. The Holy Spirit makes this happen! So ask God to work faith in you, or else you will remain forever without faith. No matter what you wish or say or do."

The sad thing is that even before Martin Luther's dead body was cold in his grave, the people had already begun to turn faith into a new saving work. "Just believe the Bible and you will be saved." they would say. Or "Believe in Jesus, and believing will save you!"

"So you believe," wrote Saint James, "even the devils believe and tremble" (James 2:19). So what? They don't know God personally nor care about God nor worship God nor walk in God's paths, but they believe, all right? So much for mere belief. Belief is a human activity. Have you ever heard someone say "It really doesn't matter what you believe so long as you believe in something"? That is a lie! I can believe the moon is made of green cheese all I want to, but believing won't make it so! Having belief does not save us; we are saved by a right relationship with a savior!

So here is my "definition of faith." Faith is a relationship of personal communion with Christ in our hearts that comes to us as a gift through the Holy Spirit. Faith creates in us trust, hope, assurance, and new birth. Faith quickens us, transforms us, renews us, completes us, and makes us whole. Faith puts a new radiance on our face, a new wonder in our hearts and a new joy in our soul. We are changed into new creatures by God's grace. As Saint Augustine put it, "I would not have found Thee if Thou had not first found me."

Friends, you can believe whatever you want, all by yourself; but faith is a two-way event, a personal correspondence, a co-response between you and God. In other words, faith doesn't just bring grace or make grace happen. Faith *is* grace!

I am certainly not discounting the value of spiritual formation, prayer or personal self-discipline. And I appreciate the value of service, good works, Bible reading, and concern for others. These are all good things, wonderful things—but they will not save you. They are only outward manifestations of the in-dwelling spirit. Spiritual discipline is merely a response to the gift of faith; it is not the source of it. But only God and God alone is the source. To God be the Glory.

When I lived in Laurinburg, North Carolina, in the 1990s, I would drive over the state line to buy gas in McColl, South Carolina, where it was quite a bit cheaper. On top of that the stations there were "full-service." For those of you born after the 1970s, full-service meant that an attendant put your gas in your tank, checked your oil, washed your windshield, took your money, and you never had to leave the comfort of your vehicle. Hard to believe, I know!

The apostle Paul described faith as being "filled with the fullness of God" (Ephesians 3:19). And so I ask you, if faith is being filled with the fullness of God, can you get it from a self-service pump? Can you receive the fullness of God by yourself or does God have to do the filling?

What do you think? "Can a leopard change his spots?" asked the prophet Jeremiah. Of course, he can't, and neither can we transform ourselves, or fill our own empty tanks, or give ourselves new birth. "Fill my cup, Lord!"

That is why if God is to dwell in us, then God must be actively involved in the whole process, as he takes up residence in our hearts. That is why "faith is the assurance of things hoped for" (Hebrews 11:1). The experience of faith authenticates itself. "You ask me how I know he lives. He lives within my heart." (Alfred Ackley).

In the words of John Wesley, "Faith is a gift of God, no man is able to work it in himself, no merit in man precedes the forgiving love of God. There is no such thing as faith without God's being involved and active in every part of it."

Surely, you say, we must do something! The answer is "Yes! Yes, we do." We respond! Faith is like a handshake. First, God offers his hand, and then we receive it! Faith is not a crowbar to pry open the gates of heaven in order to sneak in. Rather, faith is a foretaste of heaven, *right now*! Paul called it a guarantee or earnest money, a down payment, so to speak, on eternal life.

An elementary school teacher asked a student, "Johnny, can you tell us the capital of Nebraska?"

Johnny replied, "What do you think, Teacher?"

"I don't think, I know," the teacher replied in a huff.

"I'm with you, Teacher," said Johnny, "because I don't think I know either."

But in faith you know! Faith is not blind ignorance; faith is passionate knowing, ultimate knowing. "Blessed assurance," said Fannie Crosby, "Jesus is mine, oh, what a foretaste of glory divine." So faith is not a blind leap, because in faith, "you already know." You have had a foretaste. Faith not only brings salvation; faith *is* salvation. "Anything that is not from faith is sin" (Romans 14:23). In faith, we link spirits, get connected, and become one with God. Try doing that by yourself!

I had a seminary professor who used to say, "Never move anybody out of their house of faith, until you find them a better place to live." Well, I invite you to move into a new house, where the new synonym for faith is not belief but love! Can you control love? No! Can you define love? No! Can you turn love off and on like a water faucet? No! Can you name the time you decided to love your parents? Of course not! They loved you first. You simply returned that love back to them. Like love, faith is a gift that first comes to you from above. Through it, we are born again—or literally—" born from above." We can't make that happen. The wind blows where it wills. We can only experience the wind. "In this is love," John said, "not that we love God, but that God first loved us!" (1 John 4:10)

The same thing is true for faith. Faith is not something I have; faith is encountering someone who has me! It is the indwelling of God's Holy Spirit. Faith is not a rational decision I make. It is a life-changing experience. Faith takes no special skill or talent on my part. Faith is relinquishing the reins to a higher power. It is letting go. It is surrender. It is not forcing myself to believe hard-to-believe stuff. It is handing over the controls and leaving the driving to God. After all, if we know God is trustworthy, steadfast, and faithful, we can trust God to steer us in the right direction! As Paul put it, "The life I now live . . . I live by faith in the Son of God who loved me and gave himself for me" (Galatians 2:20).

One day the late Dwight L. Moody was down in the dark basement trying to fix a light when his young daughter came looking for him. "Daddy," she said, "I know you are down there somewhere, but it's so dark I can't see you."

"But I can see you, baby, so just jump, and I'll catch you," said her father.

Then without a moment's hesitation, she leaped into the darkness! She was not at all afraid because she already knew her daddy. She already knew he was able to catch her, that he would catch her, and he did. That is faith.

On May 24, 1738, John Wesley did not give rebirth to himself. It was not a decision he made, but something that happened to him and in him that was beyond his control. He even admits that when he attended that little prayer meeting on Aldersgate Street, he went very "unwillingly." But as a layman began to read Martin Luther's preface to his commentary on Romans, something wonderful happened in Wesley's heart. These were his words: "While he (Luther) was describing the change, which God works in the heart through faith in Christ, I felt my heart strangely warmed. I felt that I did trust in Christ, Christ alone, for salvation, and an assurance was given to me that he had taken away my sins (even mine) and saved me from the law of sin and death." *That, my Christian friends, is the true nature of faith, no matter what your mother may have told you!*

WHAT WE HAVE HERE IS A FAILURE TO COMMUNICATE

For my thoughts are not your thoughts, neither are your ways my ways, says the Lord. For as the heavens are higher than the earth, so are my ways higher than your ways and my thoughts higher than your thoughts.

—Isaiah 55:8–9

WHEN I RETIRED, after forty years in the ministry, my first thought was, "I need to write a book and use all the wisdom I have gleaned from the school of hard knocks." In the church we chose to attend, when I was invited to become a substitute teacher for the senior high Sunday school class, I jumped at the opportunity. I thought, "What better a sounding board for my book than a group of open-minded, bright, young leaders of tomorrow—whose intellect and creativity had not yet been dulled by the pressures of convention." I began to envision exciting, no-holds-barred dialogue to stretch my horizons as well as theirs. Unfortunately, I was too late. They no longer thought for themselves. Their young minds had already been set.

The subject was Genesis. So I said, "You need to remember that the Bible often speaks of invisible and eternal things in figurative picture language. Even God is described in symbolic anthropomorphic terms. For example: God is an invisible spirit, but the Bible says that humanity was made in God's image and that God walked with Adam and Eve in the garden in the cool of the day.

"Does this mean that God has a nose, teeth, and toenails?" I asked. One bright, attractive young lady, in a fluffy black and white dress, sitting with her arms crossed in defiance, shot back, "He could if he wanted to!" In her defense, I suppose she could have been talking about the incarnation, but that was not even dreamed of when the book of

Genesis was written. Instead, God was usually pictured as all-powerful, transcendent and Holy Other. The God of the Old Testament was an awesome wrathful force to be feared. He was not your best pal or the sweet gentle Jesus. In any case, her remark pretty well ended any further discussion on that topic for the day. This is an excellent example of the defensive attitudes that so often divide us and stop real communication!

I am reminded of the student, who asked his Sunday school teacher, "Could God build a rock so big that God couldn't move it?" My question is, even if God could do such a thing, what would be the point? How would it change our lives one way or the other? How would it make the world a better place? How would it help me be kinder to my neighbor? Remember the devout young lady, I spoke of earlier? Well, let me assure you she was no dummy. She was a leader in her youth group, and I am quite sure near the top of her class. Yet her dead serious answer stopped all further conversation.

I had also asked the class how long it took God to create the earth. Some of them had problems with six twenty-four-hour days; others did not. I pointed out that we measure our days by the sun, while according to Genesis, God did not even create the sun until day four. So with no sun, how does one measure a day, certainly not in twenty-four-hour segments. As the psalmist said, "For a thousand years in thy sight are but as yesterday, when it is passed or as a watch in the night" (Psalm 90). So let us not nitpick the Bible to pieces or use it to hammer away at scientific knowledge!

The point I was trying to make to the class was that the Bible is not a book of science and astronomy "on how the heavens go," but rather it is a book of faith and relationships "on how to go to heaven." Even the Biblical writers did not agree on the "how." That is why they could place two distinctly different creation stories side by side, without apology. Why? Because what mattered to them was not *how*, but *who*! The class all agreed that *God* was the creator, no matter how God did it. So at one point, I divided the class into two groups and asked them to answer the same question. Group 1 was to glean their answer from Genesis 1, and group 2 was to glean their answer from Genesis 2. The question was, "According to your chapter, in what order was life on earth created?"

At first, they had a very hard time not sneaking into the other chapter, but in the end, their conclusion was this. Group 1 found that God created in an evolutionary kind of sequence that began with plants, then sea creatures, then land animals, and finally at the top of the pyramid, man and woman (created together at the same time). The second group found, in chapter two, that man alone was created first, then plants, then animals, and finally, at the pinnacle of creation, God created woman.

It is important to note that these differences did not bother the ancient writers in the least. Why? Because they were more interested in the meaning of the story. They were more interested in our relationship with God and neighbor than in cold hard facts. From our modern rational perspective, however, we sometimes wonder, who did Cain marry? But that kind of silly nitpicking question did not even occur to the original authors. They simply passed on, faithfully, two distinctively different traditions. But in both cases, their main concern was our human condition. They were more interested in the *who* and *why* of creation than the *how*. Consider this, most of the Bible was written in, or before the Bronze Age, so even if God gave precise detailed schematics of how he created the universe, how, in their primitive world view, would they even begin to comprehend it? Even in this scientific age of sophistication, I doubt someone, on the caliber of a Stephen Hawking, could fully understand it either.

Therefore, to turn the book of Genesis into a scientific explanation for the origins of the universe could only prove to be both frustrating and embarrassing. Yet sadly, some sincere fundamentalist groups want to force public schools into teaching Genesis as a part of the school science curriculum. The truth is that, the ancient Jewish exiles in Babylonia, actually borrowed, from that culture, the concept of a three-story universe with oceans above, an air pocket with oceans and land in the middle, and pillars underneath to support the whole structure. In this view, before creation, there supposedly were oceans of chaos even above the clouds.

Listen, for example to the words of 2 Peter 3:5–6, "The earth was formed, out of water and by means of water." Many other scriptures say the same thing: (Explanatory notes in parenthesis are mine!) "Darkness was before the face of the deep (ocean) and the wind (Spirit) of God swept over the face of the waters (ocean)" (Genesis 1:2, Genesis 1:6–8), "And God said, 'Let there be a dome (firmament) in the midst of the waters and let it separate the waters (ocean) from the waters (ocean).' So God made the dome and separated the waters (ocean) that were under the dome from the waters (ocean) that were above the dome."

"Can you like him, spread out the sky (heavens) hard as a molten mirror?" (Job 37:18) Imagine a large fish bowl shoved into a large vat of water, and sitting on four blocks, creating an air pocket inside the bowl, with water above and water beneath. Now slip a bumpy block of tree bark to float inside the bowl, and guess what?—You have dry land.

Compare this with Psalm 104:2–9, "You (God) stretch out the heavens (sky) like a tent, you set the beams of your chambers on the waters, you make the clouds your chariot, you ride on the wings of the wind, you make the winds your messengers, fire and flame your ministers. You set the earth on its foundation, so that it shall never be shaken. You cover it with the deep as with a garment; the waters stood above the mountains. At thy rebuke they flee; at the sound of your thunder they took to flight. They rose up to the mountains, ran down to the valleys to the place that you appointed for them. You set a boundary they may not pass, so that they might not again cover the earth."

Proverbs 8:28–29 on "Wisdom" [Sophia] as an agent in creation: "When he established the heavens I (Sophia) was there, when he drew a circle on the face of the deep, when he made firm the skies above, when he established the fountains of the deep, when he assigned to sea its limit, so that the waters might not transgress his command, when he marked out the foundations of the earth."

God gave us minds, and it is a sin not to use them. Just because three thousand years ago, people thought the world was flat—sitting on four pillars—and the sky was "hard as a molten mirror" to hold back the primordial oceans of chaos, does that mean we in the twenty-first century have to believe that too in order to be saved? Surely, the doors of the church can be raised high enough that intelligent, educated people can enter without having to leave their heads on the outside. But instead, at some point in time, a group of well-meaning clergy and laity decided that spiritual truth was far too fragile to be left in the hands of ordinary people. So they decided to run interference for God, as if God was in dire need of their protection.

Thus, anyone who dared offer fresh insight, or an unfamiliar truth, was branded as an infidel and silenced. Thus, the seeds of division were sown. At first, it was the Inquisition and powers within the Catholic Church that sought to suppress scientific truth, such as astronomy, and later, it was the Fundamentalist movement that railed against evolution and other things, like stem cell research. It was almost as if the same overprotective Pharisees, who had once tried so hard to suppress the teachings of Jesus, have somehow reappeared through the ages and even in our time in order to shelter God's people from truth. But I believe that Christians should never ever be afraid of any kind of *truth* (world or spiritual). Why else would God have given us minds, in the first place, if we were not supposed to use them? Think about it!

> **Then you will know the truth,**
> **and the truth will set you free.**
> **—John 8:32**

TRUTH AS RELATIONSHIP

> *Jesus answered, "My kingship is not of this world; if my kingship were of this world, my servants would fight, that I might not be handed over to the Jews; but my kingship is not from the world." Pilate said to him, "So you are a king?" Jesus answered, "You say that I am a king. For this I was born, and for this I have come into the world, to bear witness to the truth. Everyone who is of the truth hears my voice." Pilate said to him, "What is truth?"*
>
> —John 18:36–38

WHEN JESUS ANSWERED Pilate, "my kingdom is not of this world," he meant that his kingdom is not subject to or limited by the empirical evidence of this world. Indeed, by all outward physical appearances, Jesus was no threat to Pilate whatsoever, as Pilate quickly perceived and declared him innocent. Nevertheless, we believe that in another realm, in an unseen dimension, he was, and is, King of Kings and Lord of Lords. Did you notice how Jesus makes a clear distinction between eternal truth and world truth, between literal truth and spiritual truth, between the finite visible realm and the infinite invisible realm?

In order to communicate this idea to my senior high Sunday school class, I drew a picture of a brick wall on the blackboard. I marked one brick with an X. Then I asked them, "If I removed brick X from the wall, would it still be the same brick?"

We put it to a vote. Five voted "Yes, it would be the same," and three voted "No, it would not." Two abstained.

Then I asked them to defend their positions. The "Yes" team went first. It was still a brick because X = X. It had the same chemistry and properties, such as size, shape, etc. It had the same "brick-ness"; hence, it was the very same brick.

Team 2, however, said, "No, brick X was not the same brick." Why? Because it had changed location and function. It had lost its purpose as part of a wall and was no longer related to the other bricks in the wall. Consequently, it had lost its "wall-ness," that is to say its meaning or its reason for being. It had even lost the intention of the bricklayer and the architect of the wall. In short, brick X had lost both its connections and its relationships, not only with the other bricks but also with the wall builder.

Then I told them they both were right. There were two correct answers. "For example," I said, "pick the three most connected words out of these four—"add, subtract, increase, multiply." They all agreed there were two correct answers—add, subtract, multiply (three forms of math) or add, increase, multiply (three concepts that imply growth). My point is that we can choose to understand brick X either literally (physically) or relationally (spiritually).

We can regard truth as visible, material, measurable facts or we can see a higher truth and regard truth as spiritual and invisible. Love, for example, is invisible and cannot be quantified. If a mother has five children, she loves them all with her whole self. She does not give each child 20 percent of her love. Hence, science depends on one kind of truth; religion depends on another, non-materialistic truth. But both truths—world truth and spiritual truth—are still true; they are just different kinds of truth.

I am reminded of the words of the apostle Paul: "We look not to things that are seen, but to things that are unseen. For the things that are seen are transient, but the things that are unseen are eternal" (2 Corinthians 4:18). My next step was to ask the class to come up with some distinctions between these two different forms of truth. If you will forgive the oversimplification, I think the results may prove enlightening. Here are some examples:

WORLD TRUTH	GOD TRUTH
Material	Spiritual
Visible	Invisible
Physical	Nonphysical
Measurable	Immeasurable

How?	Why
Function	Purpose
Use	Meaning
Literalism	Symbolism
Body	Soul
Physical	Spiritual
Facts	Parables or symbols
Flesh	Spirit
Finite	Infinite
Concrete	Abstract
Quantification	Figurative Language
Prose	Poetry
Human animal	Human spirit
Coincidence	Providence
Life is an accident	Life is a gift
Survival of the fittest	Meek will inherit earth
Book words	The Living Word
Power rules	Compassion rules
Skepticism, doubt	Faith, assurance
Treasures on earth	Treasures in heaven
Detachment	Involvement
The whole is equal to the sum of its parts	The whole is greater than the sum of parts

For example, Adam was just a collection of chemicals until God breathed into him his own breath of life, and Adam became a living spirit (breath). I realize that it is not biblical to create a Cartesian body/soul dualism here. I know that in the Hebrew mind, we do not just have a soul; we are a soul! But when I was in school, I was taught to be objective and just get the facts, as if the more I thought like a cold calculating machine—suppressing all personal feelings, such as intuition and faith, the more likely I was to get at real truth. So ultimate knowledge was found in objective facts (impersonal, measured, and quantified).

But the Bible seems to take the opposite approach. It says real knowledge is passionate personal knowledge. When the Bible speaks of the "imago dei" (or the "image of God"), I believe it is not talking about outward appearance, or even morality or creativity. I believe the image of God is our very personhood and our ability to love. "God created humankind in his image . . . male and female, he created them" (Genesis 1:27). In other words, just as man and woman were made to personally relate to one another, in love, so man was made to personally relate to God and to commune with the one who is *love*! (Agape) "It is not good that man should be alone," said God. The point is that we are social creatures, so real, spiritual truth can only be seen in personal relationships. That is why God sent Jesus as the ideal Adam, the Son of Man, the new "cornerstone" for humanity.

As I see it, on the one hand, Jesus rejected the philosophy of Pilot that truth is merely subjective and relative to personal opinion. But on the other hand, Jesus also challenged the modern worldly philosophy that ultimate truth is something "objective" out there that you can measure and acquire through empirical observation. As if you can actually capture what Immanuel Kant called "the thing in itself." Indeed, there are many well-meaning Christians who also regard all truth as irrefutable hard-nosed facts. Indeed, it was this literalistic and materialistic understanding of truth that, I believe, first gave rise to the fundamentalist movement upward of a century ago. As a consequence, world truth and spiritual truth got all mixed up together like apples and oranges. So, world truth was applied to the Holy Scriptures and God truth was applied to science. After all, if real truth is objective facts, then the Bible must be a book of objective facts. Ergo, the Bible has to be factually accurate and inerrant in all things, from history to science, because the Bible is *true*! Right? QED

One problem with this neat little theory is that Jesus did not teach facts, nor did he hand out tracts full of information saying, "read all about it!" Instead, what Jesus offered was himself as personal truth. "I am the Way the Truth and the life," he said. So he did not just tell the truth, he *was* the truth! In other words, you know his truth, only by entering into a personal relationship with him. In fact, even when he taught truths he did so by telling parables instead of spouting off facts. In short, Jesus found it necessary to tell people stories in order to tell them spiritual truth. Matthew said that this is the only way he ever taught (Matthew 4:34). After all, how else do you describe the infinite personhood of Almighty God to finite beings like us except by metaphor? *It's all about another way of knowing.*

> **For the time is coming when people will not put up with sound doctrine, but having itching ears, they will accumulate for themselves teachers who suit their own desires and will turn away from listening to the *truth* and wonder into myths.**
> **—2 Timothy 4:3–4**

A PERSONAL TESTIMONY

Come to him, a living stone, though rejected by mortals yet chosen and precious in God's sight, and like living stones, let yourselves be built into a spiritual house, to be a holy priesthood, to offer spiritual sacrifices acceptable to God through Jesus Christ. For it stands in the scripture: "See, I am laying in Zion a stone, a cornerstone chosen and precious, and whoever believes in him will not be put to shame." To you then who believe, he is precious, but for those who do not believe, "The stone that the builders rejected has become the very head of the corner," and "a stone that makes them stumble, a rock that makes them fall." They stumble because they disobey the word, as they were destined to do. But you are a chosen race, a royal priesthood, a holy nation, God's own people, in order that you may proclaim the mighty acts of him who called you out of darkness into his marvelous light. Once, you were not a people but now you are God's people; once, you had not received mercy, but now you have received mercy.

—1 Peter 2:1–10

ONCE UPON A time, Jesus appeared to a seminary professor in a dream and said, "Learned doctor, who do you say that I am?" And the professor answered confidently, "You are the soteriological hope of creation, the eschatological manifestation of the ground of being, the essence of the *Kerygma*, and the incarnation of the Eternal Divine Logos!"

And Jesus said, "I am the what?"

Rather than detachment, I believe, truth requires the passionate involvement of the knower. In other words, you will never learn to swim unless you jump into the water. As Saint Augustine said, "I believe, therefore I understand." *So believing is seeing!* As the French philosopher, Pascal once said, "The heart has reasons that reason does not know." What he meant was that beyond cool, calculating logic, there is a more basic kind of knowing. Shall we call it the knowledge of the soul? However, we can be so conditioned by those who shove information at us and tell us what we are supposed to believe—that we lose track of what is innate in our own hearts.

I know because it happened to me! Growing up as a preacher's kid made me a cynic before my time. I was exposed to the cruel ungodly way that hypocritical, nagging church people could behave behind the scenes. Still, I tried to accept my role as a PK and the teachings of the church, as I constructed a rickety scaffolding of faith on a shifting foundation of doubt and other people's opinions. But the lures of the world offered new pleasures, science offered new marvels, technology offered new powers, and *Mad Magazine* offered biting satire, until a quiet rebellion began to rise in me. In fact, sometimes the rebellion was not all that quiet. One thing I knew for certain, whatever my future was to be, I would never become a "preacher."

So at North Carolina Wesleyan College, I got as far from religion as possible, by majoring in experimental psychology. Except for the required freshmen religion classes—that seemed designed to finish off what little faith I had left—I avoided all other religious studies like the plague for two years. I did, however, enjoy debating religion with others—especially with vulnerable freshmen. In short, I was a true sophomore (wise-fool) know-it-all—one who knew just enough to be dangerous. I became a scholastic "wise guy!" and was darn proud of it.

The word psychology literally means "the study of the soul," and my new hero became B. F. Skinner. Skinner devised a way to reduce people to the level of rats and to deny their "psyche" (soul) altogether. He called people "subjects," but treated them more like "objects" as he probed, measured, and analyzed their behavior. I was delighted with this new world of *Walden II* and made good grades. But my balloon burst when an experiment I did on manipulating human retention and learning through trauma and repression" backfired. It so traumatized a girl "subject" that she cried all night and almost left school. Her dad was a sheriff, and I think he was ready to shoot me. Thankfully, however, everything was explained and forgiven. Still, I was haunted by that experience. It reminded me strongly that people are not rats, nor should they be treated as such. They should be loved and not used.

The next semester, I decided to pick up an "easy" elective in religion. It was taught by Dr. James Cox. Dr. Cox had just returned from Germany where he had studied under Friedrich Gogarten. He set the tables in a square-circle so that he could get up close and personal. He wore white bucks with red zigzag soles so he could bounce up to your table and attack. He liked to play the devil's advocate and was so aggressive that students would often leave the class in tears.

"Do you believe in the virgin birth?" he would bark at some poor unsuspecting girl—his face inches from hers.

"Yeees, sir," she would whimper. "I think so."

"Then why did the Gospel writers trace the genealogy of Jesus through Joseph?" he would retort.

Only later did he explain that in Jewish law, the adopted child always inherited the genealogy of the father. "Give it to 'em, Dr. Cox, give it to 'em!" I would say to myself. He made us question everything, but I was doing that already. Only now, for the first time, it was OK. I no longer had to feel like a religious Benedict Arnold. In fact, I got so into his class that the next paper I turned in made Dr. Cox question whether or not I had actually written it. He was about to give me an F but changed it to an A+.

Then right in the middle of my revelry, he said something in class that even made me mad, so mad that I marched right up to his office on the second floor to give him a piece of my mind! Yes, I was scared, but I didn't care. I was mad. The issue doesn't matter, but the point is he had finally gone too far.

I wish you could have been there to see the surprise in my eyes when after I finished my speech, he said, "Denny, I was just about to give up on you. For a while, it looked to me like you didn't believe in anything!"

"What do you mean?" I protested.

"I mean," He said, "that all of us have something way down deep inside to which we are ultimately committed. We may not even know it. It may be covered by layers of things we have been told to believe or feel we are supposed to believe, but now you know the difference. You thought you had rejected God, when all you really rejected was the spurious trappings and hearsay that meant nothing to you. The only thing Jesus ever asked you to believe in is himself. He is the only required foundation. Everything else is just other people's laundry. So let him be your cornerstone and then you will have a solid foundation on which to build your faith. Now get to work! Study theology, pray, read the Bible, and seek to find what God really means to you in your own life."

From that moment on, I was filled with a new excitement and enthusiasm. I began to pour over the Bible and theology books. I was like a hungry wolf. I can't explain it, but that meeting with Dr. Cox changed my life. I felt so free! In fact, I even changed my major. I knew enough about rats in mazes already. Now it was time to love people instead of using them. It was time to know God. And that is how I finally ended up in the ministry—kicking and screaming in spite of myself.

And so I urge you to probe the foundation of your faith to make sure it is built with assurance upon the solid rock. You should never be afraid of truth. Truth will not hurt you. Ignorance is what will hurt you. So boldly scrutinize your beliefs and probe your faith. I say this, not because I want you to fall, but because I want you to stand tall through every storm.

Ponder the prophet Jeremiah: "Thus says the Lord, 'Cursed are those who trust in mere mortals and make mere flesh their strength, whose hearts turn away from the Lord. They shall be like a shrub in the desert, and shall not see when relief comes. They shall live in the parched places of the wilderness, in an uninhabited salt land. Blessed are those who trust in the Lord, whose trust is the Lord. They shall be like a tree planted by water, sending out its roots by the stream. It shall not fear when heat comes, and its leaves shall stay green; in the year of drought it is not anxious, and it does not cease to bear fruit'" (Jeremiah 17:5–8).

I do not believe you are an accident. I believe you are alive today for a reason. I can't tell you what it is, but God has given you unique eyes to see his world. So don't let anyone less than God convince you what is in your own heart. If you construct your faith solely on what others tell you, then your faith will hang by a rope of sand. It took me a long time to figure this out, but I give you this wisdom—with my compliments.

Once upon a time a rich man asked a builder to build a house. "Spare no expense," he said. "I want this house to be perfect." But the builder, in order to increase his profit decided to cut a few corners here and there and used inferior materials where they would not show. Finally, when the beautiful house was finished, the rich man said, "John, I wanted to find a way to thank you for all your many years of service to me and that is why I wanted you to build the best house you could—so I could give it to you as your reward. The house belongs to you!" The builder then remembered all the short cuts, the botched workmanship and the inferior materials that went into the house, because now, he would be living there the rest of his life. Jesus, the good carpenter, is saying to you that your life is like an unfinished house and that by your beliefs and actions, you will build it. No one else is allowed to live in it but you, and you will pay the price for all the flaws you build into it. Furthermore, only Jesus Christ has the blueprints that can make sure your house is built according to specifications.

Over the years, I have learned that I do not believe in Jesus because I first believed in the Bible, but rather I believe in the Bible because I first believed in Jesus. He is the one sure truth that has never failed me. So my faith is no longer built on the shifting sands of hearsay and other people's opinions, but on a personal relationship with Jesus Christ. He is my new cornerstone and now nothing—not even tragedy, new discoveries, doubt, danger, "or anything else in all creation," can sway me from that sure foundation.

Years ago, when my son, Patrick, was a year old, he was sitting in his high chair having lunch when he reached down and picked up a pea. "Ball!" he said. In my high school geometry class, we were required to read a little science fiction book, called *Flatland*. In the country of Flatland, different geometric forms lived in a flat, one-dimensional universe. Then one day a sphere paid them a visit. Imagine a ball sliced into a thousand pieces, and you could only view one slice at a time. That is how a sphere looked to the people of Flatland. To them the sphere was a circle that seemed at first to appear very tiny, then grow larger, only to shrink again and disappear.

"How did you do that?" asked a triangle from the one-dimensional world. "Do what?" asked the sphere. "How did you change sizes and then disappear?"

"Oh, I did not change sizes," said the sphere, "that is only a matter of perspective. I just went up."

"Up, what is up?" asked the triangle. So the sphere picked up the little triangle and stood him on his side. "This is up," said the sphere. "Weee," said the Flatlander, "what a concept."

"Up" was the most exhilarating experience the triangle had ever had. So with excitement, he rushed to tell all of his friends about this wonderful new dimension, "up." But they refused to believe him; instead, they ostracized him and even threatened to put him to death as a false teacher.

Isn't that how Jesus comes to us, like a sphere to our flatland, to help us see above the level of our ordinary existence and seek new wonders and new horizons. He called this new way of seeing the world, "the Kingdom of God." As I look at it, I spent most of my life in Flatland, until that wonderful day when Jesus, through the power of the Holy Spirit, lifted me up, touched my heart, and set me high upon a rock so I could see life from an entirely new perspective.

"Everyone who hears these words of mine and acts on them will be like a wise man who built his house on rock. The rain fell, the floods came and the winds blew and beat on that house, but it did not fall, because it had been founded on rock" (Matthew 7:24–25).

If you follow Jesus and do what he asks you to do, then no doctrines, or creeds, or interpretations, or new discoveries, or anything else in all creation will be able to shake you loose from your sure foundation. For like a tree planted by the waters, you shall not be moved. That is the kind of sure foundation I was hoping to provide for my senior high Sunday school class. I knew what they would face when they went off to college, so I was trying to prepare them for the shock. But I was a stranger to them, and they did not know me enough to trust my intentions. I remember a line from Bishop Asbury, "My discourse on the blind and the lame was very lame, and I left my hearers where I had found them: *blind*."

SIN IS NOT ALL THAT ORIGINAL

Now the serpent was more crafty than any other wild animal that the Lord God had made. He said to the woman, "Did God say, 'You shall not eat from any tree in the garden?'" The woman said to the serpent, "We may eat of the fruit of the trees in the garden, but God said, 'You shall not eat of the fruit of the tree that is in the middle of the garden, nor shall you touch it, or you shall die.'" But the serpent said to the woman, "You will not die; for God knows that when you eat of it, your eyes will be opened, and you will be like God, knowing good and evil." So when the woman saw that the tree was good for food, and that it was a delight to the eyes, and that the tree was to be desired to make one wise, she took of its fruit and ate; and she also gave some to her husband, who was with her, and he ate. Then the eyes of both were opened, and they knew that they were naked; and they sewed fig leaves together and made loincloths for themselves. They heard the sound of the Lord God walking in the garden at the time of the evening breeze, and the man and his wife hid themselves from the presence of the Lord God among the trees of the garden.

—Genesis 3:1–8

WHAT DOES IT mean to understand the Bible relationally? First, of all, it is to realize that the story of Adam and Eve tells—with great clarity—about our own humanity? I told the senior highs: "Only when you see the story in Genesis as your story will you really understand what the Bible is all about." Under the inspiration of the Holy Spirit, thousands of years ago, some very wise men wrestled with our universal human condition. They realized that deep in the heart of humanity, there is a longing for relatedness, a yearning for wholeness and fulfillment, a need for meaning and a need for God. To describe this all-too-common condition of humanity, they told the story of Adam and Eve in a perfect Utopian garden. In the story we see the idyllic life—a garden paradise— where everything is in perfect balance, harmony, and tranquility, where our great creator is intimate and close at hand.

I want you to imagine for a moment that you are a reporter and you have an exclusive interview with Eve in the Garden of Eden. She glows with radiance and happiness. She has close intimate contact with Adam, God, plants, and animals. She is perfectly content. "Eve," you say, "Would you please describe yourself to our audience?"

"Who, me? Why, I am a child of God, made by his own hand and created in his image to love and be loved. I am Adam's life mate, flesh of his flesh and bone of his bones. We belong to one another, and we are all perfectly one! Isn't that the way life should be?"

In other words, Eve knew who she was; not by her own private attributes, but by her relationship with those whom she loved and who loved her. God and Adam called her into being and gave meaning and purpose to her life. But God understood human nature and our strong temptation to find ultimate meaning in material "things" inside of his creation (like forbidden apples). He knew we would be tempted to worship the creature rather than the creator. So God set boundaries and drew the line at a particular forbidden fruit. I have heard people argue over whether this forbidden fruit was an apple, a pomegranate, or a pear. Who cares! What matters is that it was a material thing that was *forbidden*.

Anytime human beings are confronted with rules, whether it is the Ten Commandments or forbidden fruit, our reaction is the same. "Who says I can't do (or have) that?" "I'll show you what I can't do (or have)!" "Just give me one reason why I can't!"

So God said, "Don't," and humankind has been rebelling ever since.

"Don't what?" asked Adam.

"Don't eat from that one tree over there," said God.

"Why not?" said Adam.

"Because it is forbidden!" said God.

"Wow, forbidden fruit!" said Eve. "We have forbidden fruit! Where is it? What's it like? Why can't we eat that fruit if we want to?"

"Because the day you eat it, you will die," said God.

Remember in Exodus how God introduced himself as the Lord of deliverance who first set his people free and then gave laws to keep them free? "Didn't I bring you out of bondage in Egypt and guide you safely through the wilderness? Therefore, keep these laws that your days may be prolonged!"

When God says, "Thou shalt have no other gods besides me," he is not exercising divine vanity or trying to force us to flatter him. Instead, he is telling us that it is utterly dangerous and self-destructive for us to worship anything less than God. Because any part of God's creation that receives our ultimate allegiance can devour us from within. Only a God who is above the world can keep us from being enslaved by it.

Sometimes when we tell our children "No" and they say "Why not?" we answer back, "Because I said so." But God does not do that. Instead, to paraphrase, he says, "I am the God of freedom who made you and who delivered you from bondage; therefore, if you want to stay free, you need to live by the rules I give you. Otherwise, if you wander off the main highway, you are likely to get lost or stuck in a ditch. So, Adam and Eve, this forbidden-fruit rule is for your own good because the *day* you eat that forbidden fruit, you will *die*!"

"Tell me this," I said to the class, "if we all assume that God told the truth, is it also possible that the serpent in the story actually told the truth as well?"

Let's go back to the talking snake and review that conversation. Along comes the tempter with a forked tongue. He says (in effect), "Come on, Eve, you will not die, take a bite, it won't kill you. Doesn't it look delicious and beguiling? Besides, it has special powers. It will make you the center of the universe. Everything will revolve around you, your needs and your desires. So you won't need God or Adam anymore because you will become a God unto yourself. You can decide for yourself what is good or bad for you. Take some, you deserve it, you owe it to yourself. To hell with God's silly rules and regulations. You go, girl! You are in charge now! You show him who's boss. Eat! Be happy! You will not die! You have my word on it."

All of us have tried to snatch meaning and fulfillment in our lives from material things but it always falls flat. The devil promises so much more than he can deliver, because greed is a bottomless pit that can never be satisfied. That is why the prophets were so down on idolatry. To worship anything less than God will only lead to despair—not to mention enslavement, addiction, false pride, and utter emptiness. Like a man on a life raft trying to quench his thirst with sea water, he will only become madder with thirst with every gulp. No wonder "evil" is "live" spelled backward, because it leads to spiritual death.

So Eve ate the tantalizing fruit, and just as the serpent promised, she did not die—(physically, that is!). Yet (just as God promised) spiritually there was a world of difference. For one thing, she lost her innocence and became aware of her own physical appearance and self-importance. Perhaps she caught a glimpse of her own reflection in a pool. What a wonderful weapon her body was! So she covered her nakedness and hid herself from Adam. Thus, she changed from Adam's partner into a little serpent temptress as she beguiled Adam into taking a bite of forbidden fruit. Nothing eases guilt like dragging someone else down with you. Then in shame and rebellion, they both tried to hide themselves not only from each other, but also from God.

In my younger days, I used to think Adam and Eve hid from God because they were afraid they were going to get a spanking, but it was really about a power struggle for authority. Before Eve ate that "apple," her whole life revolved around others—outside of herself. God brought her into being and made her in his own image. He was intimate and close at hand and made her to be one with Adam—flesh of his flesh and bone of his bones. But now, both God and Adam seem like a threat to her self-fulfillment. She wants to be the captain of her own soul. "I'm free at last," she said with pride. But deep inside, she knew that something died!

SPIRITUAL DEATH, NOT MORTALITY, IS THIS THE REAL DEATH THAT GOD WARNED EVE ABOUT

WHAT IS THE QUESTION?

Now and then, I pass a homemade road sign that says, "Christ is the Answer." But answers are only meaningful if we ask the right questions. The book of Genesis simply states the problem, but offers no solution. So what exactly is the concern that the ancient writers of Genesis wanted to address? I do not want to oversimplify, and I certainly do not claim to have all the answers, but surely there is a lot more to salvation than responding to an altar call at some evangelistic crusade! So what is it? I believe the problem is this—the universal human condition of estrangement and alienation from God, from neighbor, and even from ourselves. Thomas Wolf may have overstated it a bit, but he hit a raw nerve when he wrote:

'Naked and alone, we came into exile. In her dark womb, we did not know our mother's face; from the prison of her flesh, have we come into the unspeakable, incommunicable prison of this earth. Which of us has known his brother? Which of us has looked into his father's heart? Which of us has not remained forever prison-pent? Which of us is not forever a stranger and alone? O waste of loss, in the hot mazes; lost, among bright stars on this most weary unbright cinder, lost! Remembering speechlessly, we seek the great forgotten language, the lost lane-end into heaven, a stone, a leaf, an unfound door. Where? When?' *Look Homeward Angel*

Dr. Carl Jung has said, "The central neurosis of our time is a sense of emptiness." Albert Switzer put it this way, "We are all so much together and yet we are all dying of loneliness." Call it jealousy or distrust. Call it insecurity or our innate refusal to be vulnerable. Call it suspicion or even rebellion. Call it fear, bitterness or even anger! Call it original sin! Whatever the label, the effect is the same; it leads to spiritual death.

This strange condition of alienation and estrangement is the root of all sins.

TWO KINDS OF SIN

I was leading a children's sermon one Sunday and I asked the kids, "What is sin?" One little boy raised his hand and said, "I'm not sure what it is, but there's a whole lot of it at the beach." The entire congregation broke out laughing. I think what he really meant was "sand," but out of the mouths of babes the Lord speaks. What often confuses people, however, is that sin has more than one meaning. In relational theology, we make a clear distinction between sin that we do (bad actions) and sin that we are (a condition of estrangement). Sins we do are like spots on our skin when we have chicken pox while the real disease is on the inside. Sin is arrogance, selfish pride, prejudice, jealousy, and hate that consumes and depersonalizes all of us. Sin is both self-destructive and other destructive. It scars the soul, demoralizes the spirit, and breaks the heart. It loves things and uses people instead of the other way around. Sin corrupts our attitudes, warps our desires, dampens our joy, and makes our pleasures empty. It breeds corruption, resentment, jealousy, cynicism, doubt, bitterness, and fear! It betrays our trust in one another because we are deceived by the great deceiver until, like Eve in the garden, we become tempters and deceivers ourselves. That is why those *bad* things that we do are merely an outward, visible sign of an inward sickness of the soul unto spiritual death.

But some people have a hard time distinguishing between sins with a little "s," in the plural and Sin with a capital "S" in the singular. Sins in the plural are simply the outward things we do as a result of the inward state of Original Sin. If the root of Sin were merely an act, perhaps we could fix it ourselves by doing better. But Original Sin is not an action, it is a condition, and overcoming it requires a Savior.

> **Therefore, just as sin came into the world through one man,**
> **so death spread to all because all have sinned."**
> **—Romans 5:12**

UNDERSTANDING SALVATION WITHOUT LEGALISM

> *For if while we were enemies, we were reconciled to God*
> *through the death of his Son, much more surely, having been*
> *reconciled will we be saved by his life. But more than that, we*
> *even boast in God through our Lord Jesus Christ, through whom*
> *we have now received reconciliation.*
>
> —Romans 5:10–11

T HE APOSTLE PAUL was an expert in the Old Testament. He was trained by the great rabbi Gamaliel, one of the greatest teachers of his age. So in reading Genesis (the book of beginnings), Paul immediately saw its universal implications. Paul saw in Jesus the new Adam, the perfect human being—once more made in the image of God. So the Son of Man became our new model for humanity, who by his life, example, death, and resurrection could restore the mold of humankind, put the broken pieces back together again, and reopen the door to wholeness and harmony. "As in Adam all have died; so in Christ shall all be made alive" (1 Corinthians 15:22). In seminary, this is called "recapitulation."

Remember brick X? Well, you might say that Eve was brick X—apart from the wall. But then again, aren't we all? Just imagine what would happen if all the different kinds of bricks (or as Peter put it, "stones") in that wall—different colors, sizes, and shapes—had separated themselves from one another, just like Eve did. The whole wall would come tumbling down.

But wait, suddenly we are confronted with a single stone that is actually a perfect model of the entire wall—as the architect intended that wall to be. That, of course, would be Jesus, the new Adam (the new prototype for humanity, the "cornerstone"). No wonder Jesus insisted on calling himself "Son of Man" instead of "Son of God." The early church was confused by this title and insisted on calling him "Son of God," because the name "Son of Man" can simply mean "human being." That is why it rarely appears in the Gospels outside of the lips of Jesus. Not only was Jesus the exalted Son of Man from the book of Daniel, who was to judge the world in the last days, he was also the ultimate mold for humanity. The stone that the builders rejected had indeed become the stone of the corner! (In ancient times, cornerstones were often used as "sighting stones" to align the foundation correctly.)

But we still have our dilemma. Just what do people really mean when they speak of Jesus paying the price of our salvation? If Jesus purchased our pardon, who sent the ransom note and who did Jesus pay off? Was it Satan? Was it God? Did he save us from the devil, from hell, or from the wrath of God? What?

Once upon a time, a man fell down a deep well. He was hopelessly trapped for many hours and could not escape. Someone finally heard his cries for help and pulled him from the well. Afterward, he was so grateful to be saved and felt so wonderful about his life that he spent the rest of his life pushing people down wells. Just so he could save them; that way, they could experience the same joy in being rescued that he had felt. Is that our goal as Christians—to preach fire and brimstone to scare the "hell" out of people, so that we can rush back in and save them?

That is exactly the impression some evangelistic preachers give when they talk about the atonement. They use the legalistic language of fear and appeasement, as if sin caused such a terrible problem for God, that he is legally bound to burn us all in hell! He is absolutely unable to forgive us until the books are balanced, and the debt is paid in full. In this scenario, Jesus does something to buy God off and change God's mind, so that God will be able to control his temper and forgive an evil humanity.

But Paul says that is wrong. He says our salvation was God's plan from the beginning. Jesus did not have to die on the cross to appease God's anger. The Bible says that God is "slow to anger and abounding in steadfast love." So there was no need for Jesus to calm God's wrath over broken rules.

Consider this parable: A boy was playing ball with his dog on his father's ship when the ball bounced over the railing into the ocean. So the dog jumped in after it. The boy runs to his father, the captain, and says, "Dad, stop the ship, my dog is overboard."

"No," says the father, "I will not turn this ship around to save a dog."

Then says the son, "Would you turn it around to save me?"

At that, the son leaps overboard. Quickly, the captain begins to turn the ship around to save both his son and the dog.

That is a nice story, but it is a terrible parable of the atonement! Why? Because if you compare the ship's captain to God and Jesus to the captain's son and us to the dog, then you have a very confused picture of salvation.

"For *God* so loved the world that *he gave* his only begotten son." So it was the captain, not the son, who initiated the rescue mission and threw his own son in the ocean. Jesus did not pay God back or force God to change God's plans. Those were God's plans! "All of this is from God, who reconciled us to himself through Christ."

In short: "The law is not above God, nor is God subject to it. So Jesus did not have to die in order to buy off the heavenly courts. (What court would that be anyway?) Nor did Jesus need to help God forgive our sins. Why? Because from beginning to end, the work of forgiveness and grace was entirely God's work. Get it? Forgiveness is not, nor has it ever been, a problem for God. We are the ones who have problems with forgiveness, not God!

> **I will forgive their iniquities and**
> **I will remember their sins no more.**
> **—Jeremiah 31:34b**

> **All of this is from God who reconciled us**
> **to himself through Christ.**
> **—2 Corinthians 5:1**

SO WHY DID JESUS HAVE TO DIE ON A CROSS?

Some Greek Pilgrims in Jerusalem, for the Passover, sought out Philip because he had a Greek name and asked if they could meet Jesus! But Jesus knew that his death was very near, so he was too somber to entertain guests. "The hour is come for the Son of Man to be glorified. Now my soul is in turmoil. And what am I to say, 'Father, save me from this hour'? No, it was for this reason that I came to this hour—And I when I am *lifted up* from the earth, will draw all people to myself" (John 12:27 ff).

I have asked many people, "What did Jesus mean by 'if I am lifted up'?" Some would guess the resurrection, or the ascension, or just adoration and praise, but hardly anyone associated that phrase with a cross. But the cross is precisely what Jesus was talking about. Indeed, it must have been a common expression of the day, because even these Greek-speaking foreigners realized immediately that he was talking about dying on a cross. But they saw no glory in it. "We have heard from the law that the Messiah remains forever! How can you say that the Son of Man must be lifted up (crucified)?" What they were asking was, "Why must the Son of God die on a bloody cross?" (Why was the cross necessary? Wasn't there some other way?) What could that horrible cross possibly do that could not have been accomplished without so much blood and senseless cruelty? Why couldn't we just have our sweet gentle Jesus and joy, without that disgustingly *bloody* cross?

WHAT'S BLOOD GOT TO DO WITH IT?

That's a good question! What does blood have to do with it? Indeed, there is a movement afoot by some to have such language purged from the church liturgy and church hymns. The answer, however, is the talk of blood is unavoidable, so it has everything to do with it. We live in a bloodstained world of war, violence, and suffering! We are the ones who made the world "bloody," not God! The shedding of blood was not God's doing; it was humanity's doing. It's our fault! In fact, I can imagine young Jesus going to the temple at the age twelve and seeing the barbaric slaughter of the doves and the lambs (not to mention the awful stench). As the blood-soaked priest raises his knife and shouts, "Except for the shedding of blood, there is no forgiveness of sins."

"Whack!" I can hear Jesus saying to himself. "One day I intend to end that bloody barbaric practice, once and for all, or die trying," and on Mount Calvary, he did.

In ancient times, covenants were often sealed in blood because blood was a symbol of life and mystery, of sacrifice and commitment, of bravery and of bonding. So a covenant sealed in blood was a covenant to be taken seriously. Yes, the sweet lilies of the field are pretty and romantic, but it was the blood of the New Covenant shed for the forgiveness of sins that really gets our attention. The cross reveals the agony of God for the world and drives the message painfully home! "This is my blood of the New Covenant that was shed for you for the forgiveness of sins."

There is a saying among TV journalists, "If it bleeds, it leads." The age of sensitive journalism is long gone, and the age of gross sensationalism is here. Tabloid TV rules because it grabs you by the throat and demands your attention! So whenever violence happens, wide-angle, instant replay cameras are there to capture close-ups of the horror in living color—from plane crashes to terrorists' attacks, from battle scenes to crime scenes.

So when you ask, "Why all this talk about blood in the church?" I say, "Ask that of the families who lost loved ones in the Oklahoma bombing, Newtown, Connecticut, the Twin Towers, or in Iraq and Afghanistan." Surely a God of compassion weeps for the battered, abused, and afflicted. Ask the prisoner of war who witnesses the murder of cellmates or experiences beatings, broken bones, and torture. Ask the homeless refugees who saw loved ones lose legs and lives to land mines or bombs. Ask nurses in crowded hospitals where medical supplies are depleted and wounded men, women, and children clamor for relief, unable even to get a bed or bandage. Ask the victims of muggers, robbers, and terrorists, "Why blood?"

The outdoor passion drama, *Worthy Is the Lamb* used to be located in Cape Carteret, just a few miles from Swansboro, North Carolina, where my late parents retired, so I saw the pageant several times. One evening as we left the show, I overheard a little boy say to his mother, "Mama, I saw some sheep, but which lamb was 'Worthy'?" Oh, the innocence of children—like those who waved their palm branches long ago in Jerusalem. How could they ever understand that just as the sacrificial lambs were about to be slaughtered in the temple, Jesus was about to become the paschal Lamb of God that takes away the sins of the world. "He was wounded for our transgressions . . . bruised for our iniquities, upon him is the punishment that made us whole, and with his stripes we are healed" (Isaiah 53:5 ff).

Yes, these things do sound offensive! Paul said they were foolishness to the Gentiles and a stumbling block to the Jews. They were offensive, because they were supposed to be offensive. No wonder Jesus said, "Blessed is he who takes no offense at me!" He also said, "Greater love has no one than this, than to lay down his life for his friends."

Sometimes love hurts a lot, but it is the pain and sacrifice that keeps love from becoming icky, sticky gooey fluff. Dr. Ted Runyon used to say that one reason for Calvary is our secret desire that God should die. Like Adam and Eve in the garden, we disobey God's rule and hide from his authority over our lives by simply ignoring him altogether. We cast him aside as if he wasn't even there! Like rebellious children, we nail him to the back of our minds and shove him into the parking lots of our lives. We crucify Christ anew by sheer indifference, as well as by the wicked way we treat one another. Instead of loving our neighbor and putting God first, we move ourselves to the center of the universe and try to take God's place. So what does Jesus do? He becomes an extension of God's love, who reaches out his arms in reconciliation, in order to tear down the dividing walls between us, and give us the opportunity to become perfectly one through him. *When the vertical will of God clashes with the horizontal will of man, a cross was formed, and on that cross, Jesus died.*

RECONCILIATION

From now on, therefore, we regard no one from a human point of view; even though we once knew Christ from a human point of view, we know him no longer in that way. So if anyone is in Christ, there is a new creation; everything old has passed away; see, everything has become new! All this is from God, who reconciled us to himself through Christ, and has given us the ministry of reconciliation; that is in Christ God was reconciling the world to himself, not counting their trespasses against them; and entrusting the message of reconciliation to us. So we are ambassadors for Christ, since God is making his appeal through us; we entreat you on behalf of Christ, be reconciled to God. For our sake he made him to be sin who knew no sin, so that in him we might become the righteousness of God

2 Corinthians 5:16–21.

One day a mother caught her teenage daughter coming home from a date with alcohol on her breath, so she grounded her for a month. Two weeks later, Mom and Dad were planning to go to a party, and the mother laid her new party dress on the bed. The bitter daughter came into her mother's room, saw the dress, and said to herself, "That's not fair. If I can't have any fun then neither should she!" In a rage, she slashed her mother's party dress with a pair of scissors. The mother had been taking a shower, and when she came back into the bedroom and saw the mangled dress, she let out a scream and fell upon the remains of her dress, weeping. By now the daughter was feeling very ashamed. She ran to her mother and fell at her feet crying, "O Mother, I am so totally sorry. Please don't hate me. Please forgive me. Please take me back!" There was a long uneasy pause, but eventually mother and daughter embraced and cried together. "You hurt me terribly," her mother said, "but of course, I will forgive you, and of course, I will take you back. After all, I love you and even when you disappoint this much, you are still my daughter."

What that mother and daughter had experienced together that day is what the Bible calls *reconciliation*. Remember the story I told you about my Dad and I? . . . How I spat communion juice all over his new white robe . . . how, when he saw the resentment and defiance in my eyes, he gave me his belt and asked me to change places with him. He let me punish him for what I had done? Remember the impact that act had on me. How in the end, we embraced and were forever bonded in a powerful new way! I believe, that is sort of what God was doing on Calvary.

It is as if, God our Father says to us, "OK, I have given you rules to live by for your own good. However, if you consider my laws to be an unjust threat to your freedom and independence, if you think I am being cruel, harsh, and unfair, if you think that your sin is none of my business—then let's reverse places! Here, you take the cross—that symbol of vengeance, violence, and resentment, and you punish me for what you have done! And finally, when you have hammered the last nail and vented all your hatred and anger against me, even piercing my side, then I will open up my nail pierced hands to you and draw you to myself. I will love you, embrace you, forgive you, and take you back like a prodigal child, just as if you never rebelled at all" (read Luke 15).

I believe, the problem that Jesus came to address was estrangement, rebellion, and spiritual death. But God's answer, in Jesus, was grace, love, and forgiveness. No wonder Jesus prayed in the garden that we should all be perfectly one. To accomplish that oneness, God sent us his spirit to abide in us and to fill that God-shaped void in our souls! God in Jesus took our sin, our loneliness, and our rebellion upon himself. He let us kill him. He let us break his heart, and then he opened up his arms to draw us back to himself. He took that awful bloody cross, a symbol of man's hatred and cruelty to man and transformed it into the instrument of our salvation. His fate should have been our fate; his punishment should have been our punishment, but God took that bloody barbaric instrument of mass torture and transformed it into a symbol of his eternal grace and redeeming love. That is the real meaning of the *atonement*.

THE SONG FROM THE CROSS

When it was noon, darkness came over the whole land until three in the afternoon. At three o'clock, Jesus cried out with a loud voice, "Eloi, Eloi, lama sabachthani?" which means, "My God, my God, why have you forsaken me?" When some of the bystanders heard it, they said, "Listen, he is calling for Elijah." And someone ran, filled a sponge with sour wine, put it on a stick, and gave it to him to drink, saying, "Wait, let us see whether Elijah will come to take him down." Then Jesus gave a loud cry and breathed his last.

—Mark 15:33–37

Did you know that Jesus left all of us a special message on the cross in the form of a hymn? Perhaps because of his weakened state, only a few mumbled phrases were actually discernible to the witnesses. Or perhaps we only have a fragmented shorthand (*Reader's Digest*) version of what actually happened (John 21:25). In either case, this psalm is very important. The psalm was credited to David, but I do not believe that David was predicting the cross when he (or whoever) wrote it. Like all psalms, it was actually set to music. (It even has musical directions for the choirmaster.) So Jesus reached back in his memory and began to sing an old familiar hymn of hope that so eerily fit his dire circumstances. Strangely, Psalm 22 does not begin with hope. On the contrary, it begins as a deeply depressing blues song. Indeed, it sounds more like a requiem or a dirge than a hymn of praise and promise. But as we shall see, that is precisely what it was! Immediately, those who knew the psalm would have picked up on this clue just from hearing the opening verse: "My God, my God, why have you forsaken me?" (Psalm 22:1, see Matthew 27:46, Mark 15:34)

It was very convenient for the adversaries of Jesus that in Aramaic those words do indeed sound a little like he is calling for Elijah, "Eloi, Eloi, lama sabachthani." But instead, they are a secret message meant for believers like us. In order to be our mediator, Jesus had to experience our lostness, but note that even in his darkest hour, Jesus still addresses God as "my God" (someone to whom he still belongs). But now he is surrounded by enemies:

"All who see me, mock at me . . ." Psalm 22:7.
"After mocking him they stripped him," Mark 15:20.

"Commit your cause to the Lord, let him deliver—let him rescue the one in whom he delights," Psalm 22:7.

"But the leaders scoffed at him, saying, 'He saved others; let him save himself if he is the Messiah of God his chosen one!'" Luke 23:35.

"You kept me safe on my mother's breast," Psalm 22:9.

"Here is your mother," John 19:26. As eldest son, Jesus was still responsible for the care of his mother, so he gave her into the protection of John.

"My mouth is dried up like a potsherd, and my tongue sticks to my jaws," Psalm 22:15.

"I am thirsty," John 19:28.

"At once, one of them ran and got a sponge, filled it with sour wine, put it on a stick, and gave it to him to drink," Matthew 27:48.

"They have pierced my hands and feet," Psalm 22:16 RSV.

"Then they crucified him," John 19:18.

"They divide my clothing among themselves, and for my clothing they cast lots," Psalm 22:18.

"So they said to one another, 'Let us not tear it, but cast lots for it to see who will get it,'" John 19:24.

At this point in the psalm, the mood of the music suddenly changes. There is a dramatic shift in its message, as Psalm 22 begins to take on what sounds a lot like praise music (v 22 ff). We no longer hear the groans of Good Friday, as suddenly there is as new song of renewal and hope with a hint of Easter. Can you hear the difference?

> You who fear the Lord, praise him! All you sons of Jacob, glorify him; stand in awe of him, all you offspring of Israel! May your hearts live forever! All the ends of the earth shall remember and turn to the Lord . . . For dominion belongs to the Lord, and he rules over the nations.

Also in verse 24, we find a short message of hope and promise that Jesus wanted us all to hear. It was a message to take heart and not give up! God is aware of your suffering and anguish. He feels your pain. You are not forgotten.

> **For he did not despise or abhor the affliction of the**
> **afflicted . . . but heard when they cried to him.**
> **—Psalm 22:24**

Finally, the psalm ends with what sounds a whole lot like the alleluia chorus or an Easter anthem of hope and victory:

To him shall all who sleep in the earth bow down . . . and I shall live for him. Posterity shall serve him; future generations will be told about the Lord and proclaim his deliverance to a people yet unborn that . . .

"He has done it," Psalm 22:31b. In Hebrew, the word for "done" is *aw saw*. It can also be translated as "finished." He has *finished it*. "It is finished!" (John 19:30) So I am convinced that Jesus was still singing that psalm right to the bitter end!

Now it just happens that, whenever the Passover fell on a Sabbath, (Saturday), the paschal lambs would have to be slaughtered quickly in the temple on Friday morning, because at 6:00 p.m. all work would have to cease as the new day of Passover would officially begin. At that time, according to tradition, the head of every Jewish household would read the same words at the beginning of the Sader meal, "Thus the heavens and the earth were *finished*, and all their multitude. And on the seventh day, God *finished* the work he had done, and he *rested*." MISSION ACCOMPLISHED!

THE SONG FROM THE CROSS

My God why have you forsaken me,
Why are you so far from helping me?
Though I cry and I groan, you have left me all
Alone, to suffer and die on a tree.

My foes surround me with blind deceit,
As blood in a flood flows, they repeat,
"If you're God's only son, then come down chosen
one." They have pierced both my hands and my feet.

CHORUS:
That's the song Jesus sang from the cross,
For a world that is lonely and lost.

Psalm 22 was a song that he knew,
And he sang it for you from the cross.

My heart, like wax, melts within my breast,
I strain at the pain upon my chest,
They cast lots for my clothes, and not one of them
Knows, the hope that I bring them in death.

To all who suffer, don't be deceived,
Your prayers and your cares have been received.
So take heart in your plight, somehow
God will make things right,.
If you trust in His love and believe. (Chorus)

So praise the Lord for what he has done,
Proclaiming his name to everyone,
For the proud shall bow low,
And this wicked world shall know,
The victory Jesus has won.

FINALE:
That's the song Jesus sang from the cross,
For a world that was lonely and lost.
A song of anguish, it's true, but of victory too.
That's the song Jesus sang from the cross.
Psalm 22 was that song that he knew,
And he sang it for you from the cross.

It is finished.

GOD HIMSELF WILL PROVIDE THE LAMB

Isaac said to his father Abraham, "Father!" And he said, "Here I am, my son." He said. "The fire and the wood are here, but where is the Lamb for a burned offering?" Abraham said, "God himself will provide the lamb for a burned offering, my son." So the two of them walked on together.

—Genesis 22:7–8

THINK FOR A moment, what would you do if you lived three thousand years ago in a land where all of your relatives and friends were pagan idol worshipers and you encountered a new God who claimed to be the only one true God! What Abram did was move away from his hometown of Ur. He changed his identity, changed his name and started a new religion, a new life and a new family tree.

At least, that was the plan. His new God had promised him a new nation; but how do you become the father of a new nation when you are old and your wife, Sarah, can't even conceive? Can you imagine the ridicule they both endured?

Surely, poor Sarah was teased unmercifully until finally she wavered and offered Abraham her maid servant Hagar as a surrogate mother. "Look at Abraham; he's called for a 'stand-in,' ha, ha, ha!" Sarah's humiliation only increased when Hagar conceived and bore a son. But Abraham never lost faith in either Sarah or God, and then one night Sarah dreamed that she was finally going to have a son. It struck her so funny that she woke up and laughed out loud.

But Abraham did not laugh. This was no laughing matter to him. In spite of the obvious absurdity of the situation, he believed his prayers had finally been answered. And he was right. After seventy years of longing and faithful expectation, Sarah finally bore a son and Abraham had the last laugh after all. They named the baby Isaac, which means "to laugh."

For some men, dreams come true quickly, but Abraham waited seventy years for his. Try to measure in your mind how deeply Abraham must have loved his son, Isaac. He was his heart and soul. He was more precious to him than life itself. But one night, Abraham had a dream. In that dream, he heard a voice demanding as proof of his loyalty and devotion to God that he must sacrifice his only beloved son as a burned offering.

Remember he once was a pagan and had not known his new God very long! While for our modern ears, the very idea sounds preposterous and barbaric, that was not the case in the time of Abraham—it was tradition. In those primitive days, in the land of Ur, in the pagan culture of Abraham's own ancestors, the slaughter of the firstborn to the moon God Moloch was customary. It was a common practice. I suspect that Abraham's older brother may have been offered, because it was a sign of penitence and appeasement to the gods.

In the Exodus 13, a memory fragment of that ancient tradition still remains, "'Consecrate to me all the firstborn; whatever is first to open the womb among the people of Israel, both man and beast is mine,' saith the Lord." No wonder the Bible warns us that we must test the spirits, because sometimes, our superego can be corrupted by the culture that nurtures it, and our conscience can play cruel tricks on our souls. But Abraham heard an inner voice and he was convinced that it was the voice of Almighty God.

"Abraham, take your son, your only son, Isaac, whom you love, and go to the land of Moriah, and offer him there as a burned offering on one of the mountains that I shall show you" (Genesis 22:2). I doubt that Abraham slept that night. How could he? But the next morning, faithfully he obeyed. He rose before dawn, saddled his donkey, cut wood, woke Isaac and two young servants and told them to come with him. They said goodbye to Sarah and set out for Moriah. It was a three-day journey—three days of cold silence and fearful brooding. Abraham kept his face fixed on the ground; Isaac followed, confused and bewildered. Every step of the way must have been torment to Abraham's soul. Finally, the torturous journey ended. "Then Abraham said to his young men, 'Stay here with the donkey; the boy and I will go over there; we will worship, and then we will come back to you'" (Genesis 22:5). Was he still hoping that this would be the case when he said "we will come back to you?"

Abraham resolutely picked up the firewood, laid it on Isaac's back and took the fire stick in his hand (which had to be brought from home). He tucked his knife into place and started up the hill with his son. On the way, Isaac said in confusion, "The fire and the wood are here, but where is the lamb for a burned offering?" Abraham said, "God himself will provide the lamb for a burned offering, my son" (Genesis 22:8). So they continued up the hill together. Eventually, Abraham finds the spot and begins to place the wood on the ancient altar—perhaps it had been used on other occasions, by other fathers, for the very same purpose. Then suddenly, he grabs Isaac and binds him like a sheep. The boy's eyes are wild with fear. His father's eyes are tearful, but resolute as he lights the fire.

Just imagine for a moment that you are standing there in that desolate place—standing beside the old bloodstained altar as the flames of the sacrificial pyre begin to crackle in the night. You look up at stars that are light years apart and experience the even greater gulf that exists between man and God and man and humanity. And in the deep silence the ancient words of Job come alive, "Man is born to trouble as the sparks fly upward." You watch the sparks scatter and dim out in the darkness and in that moment God seems very far away and you can grasp the loneliness, the utter lostness and dread that sometimes grips the human soul.

Call it original sin or what you will; we yearn to return to Eden, to a paradise lost. In every human being, there is a strange sense of emptiness burned deep within us—we long for a place from which we seem exiled and locked out. Perhaps, as Kierkegaard suggests, Abraham thinks to himself, "Better that he hates me for this terrible thing than for him to hate God."

Poor Abraham, with watery eyes, he resolutely raises his knife. Oh, the agony, the utter despair, as he is about to thrust it into the now screaming and cringing child. "No Daddy, no, no!" Suddenly, there is a sound, a deep voice and a new word, "Abraham, Abraham, do not lay a hand on, the boy!" This was the voice of God. Then there was another sound, a rustling in the thicket. "Baa, baa." It was a small ram. It was a miracle! God himself had indeed provided an offering after all!

If God was testing Abraham, what was the purpose of the test? Don't you think God already knew what was in Abraham's heart? But the real purpose of a test—as teachers well know—is to educate! So who needed educating here, God or Abraham? Abraham learned a powerful lesson that day. No wonder he is called the father of a new religion, because at that precise moment, a new understanding of God was revealed to him for the very first time. And Abraham was forever severed and freed from the savageness and butchery of his pagan past. No longer would he have to cringe before God in terror or have to appease his anger by the primitive traditions and rituals of his ancestors. Instead, he could live by faith. You see, what our modern culture fails to grasp is that the truly shocking part of this story is not that Abraham almost sacrificed his firstborn son. No, that was pagan custom; that was tradition. The shocking thing was that in spite of custom, *he did not do it!*

Listen to the words of the prophet Micah: "With what shall I come before the Lord, and bow myself before God on high? Shall I come before him with burned offerings, with cows a year old? Will the Lord be pleased with thousands of rams? With ten thousands of rivers of oil? Shall I give my 'firstborn' for my transgressions? The fruit of my body for the sin of my soul? He has told you, O mortal what is good; and what does the Lord require of you but to do justice, to love kindness and to walk humbly with your God" (Micah 6:6–8).

So Abraham learned a lesson that day that God desired mercy and not sacrifice. That God does not want us to cower before him in fear to appease his fierce anger! Nor is God a murderer of children. Jesus said, "It is not the will of my heavenly Father that any of his little ones should perish." Listen to what God told Moses, "There shall not be found among you anyone who burns his son or his daughter as an offering" (Deuteronomy 18:10), and Leviticus 18:21 says, "You shall not give any of your offspring to sacrifice them to Moloch and so profane the name of your God." Well, that certainly seems plain enough to me. And yet over the centuries, that same pagan practice of child sacrifice continued to raise its ugly head.

Under King Manasseh, King Ahez, and others, in 800 BC, King Moab slew his own firstborn as a burned offering upon the wall of the city in a mad attempt to save it from destruction (2 Kings 3:37). But in Jeremiah 7:30–31, God speaks, "For the people of Judah have done evil in my sight, says the Lord; they have set their abominations in the house that is called by my name, defiling it. And they go on building the high places of Topheth, which is in the valley of the son of Hinnom, to burn their sons and their daughters in the fire—which I did not command, *nor did it come into my mind.*" Just in case you still didn't get it, he says it again in Jeremiah 19:4–5 and a third time in Jeremiah 32:34–35. It did not even cross his mind! Do you get it now? But here is the irony—that while God did not require that sacrifice from Abraham, God would one day make that very sacrifice for the whole world!

During the Great Depression, jobs were scarce, so John Griffith moved to Missouri and got a job as a bridge operator on the Mississippi River. His job was to raise the bridge at certain hours to allow barges to pass through and to lower it at other times so that the trains could rush across. It was summertime and John invited his only son, eight-year-old, Greg, to come to work with him for the first time. The boy was thrilled. He marveled at the control house with all of its levers and the gigantic gears and pulleys that worked the bridge.

At noon, John raised the bridge for some oncoming barges, and then he and the boy ate lunch out on the observation deck. Time passed quickly as they watched the boats pass below until John was startled by a shrieking whistle in the distance. It was already 1:07 P.M., and he had forgotten to lower the bridge for the passenger express bound for Memphis with four hundred people on board. He leaped to the catwalk—the train was only minutes away. But as he took hold of the lever, he glanced down and saw a sight that brought his heart leaping to his throat. Young Greg had slipped on the catwalk and had fallen on the great gear that operated the bridge. The boy's left leg was pinned between the wheels. John knew what would happen now. If he lowered that bridge, his only son would be crushed by four tons of grinding steel. So what would you do? There was no time left. The train whistle shrieked again. John's mind was in desperate panic. That was his son down there, but there were four hundred souls on that train. He gritted his teeth, closed his eyes and knew what he had to do. He could not allow four hundred people to die.

So with tears of agony streaming down his face, he heaved the lever with all his might, the bridge began to come down with a loud grinding groan. Seconds later, the roaring Memphis Express thundered across the span of tracks as John cried out a scream of agony above the rumble of the express, "I sacrificed my son to save your lousy necks." While on the train, businessmen read their papers and fancy-dressed ladies sipped their tea, totally unaware of the great sacrifice that John had made for them—perhaps even totally indifferent to it. "Is it nothing to you, O you that pass by? Is there any sorrow like unto my sorrow?"

For God so loved the world that he gave his only begotten son, that whosoever believes in him might not perish, but might have everlasting life.

—John 3:16

Corrie Ten Boom, in her book the *Hiding Place*, tells about her life in a Nazi prison camp. She was there for hiding Jews in her Christian home. Every Friday, the Nazi's made the prisoner's undress for medical inspection and decontamination. The humiliated, dehumanized women had to march in shame, stark-naked before the grinning, gawking guards to be sprayed for lice. It was on one of those Friday mornings that Corrie said, "Another truth leaped to life for me, He hung naked on the cross. I had not known, had not thought. The paintings and the carved crucifixes all showed at least a scrap of cloth, but this I suddenly knew was respect and reverence of the artist, but oh, at that time, on that Friday morning, there had been no reverence, no more than I saw from the faces around us. I leaned toward Betsy ahead of me. Her shoulder blades stood sharp and thin beneath her blue matted skin. "Betsy, they took his clothes too!" Ahead of me I heard a gasp, "Oh, Corrie, and I never thanked him." *Have you?*

LIVING IN THE NOW

Very truly, I tell you, anyone who hears my word and believes him who sent me has eternal life, and does not come under judgment, but has passed from death to life. Very truly, I tell you, the hour is coming, and is now here, when the dead will hear the voice of the Son of God, and those who hear will live.

—John 5:24–25

ONE DAY A Sunday school teacher asked, "Boys and girls, what do you think you have to do to go to heaven?" One boy raised his hand and said, "I think the first thing you have to do is die." I seriously challenge that assumption. In fact, I am here to argue that if you wait until your deathbed to find eternal life, the party may have already passed you by!

I grew up on Roanoke Island, coastal North Carolina as a resident alien. I learned in Sunday school that I was a sojourner on this earth and that my true home was in another time and place far, far away! Actually, it was two homes in two different times and places. One home was in the distant past and another was in the distant future. I learned about my two homelands from Bible pictures, and from posters and maps in my Sunday school classroom. I could trace my finger from Jerusalem to Jericho before I knew how to make my way from Manteo to Kitty Hawk. I learned about the architecture of my past homeland from cardboard models built in Bible School. I learned about my proper attire from the annual towel and bathrobe dramas at Christmas and Easter.

But at the same time, I also learned about a future homeland: a New Jerusalem, up high in the sky in the sweet by and by. This was, of course, a strange contradiction for a child to comprehend. My second homeland looked a lot like the inside of a giant oyster shell with mother-of-pearl gates and gold metallic, cobblestone streets. I knew that one day I would leave this wicked world and enter that sweet alabaster city of tomorrow with jasper walls, wearing a long white robe with a halo on my head, wings on my back, and a harp in my hand.

"I will sing you a song of that beautiful land, the far away home of the soul, where no storms ever beat on the glittering strand while the years of eternity roll."

With all the seriousness and innocent determination of a bewildered child, I resolutely set off on my pilgrim journey, trying to resist the world's temptations—lest I should invoke the fierce anger of the Almighty, and be sent to the fiery pits of the "bad place." (We were not allowed to use the word "hell" in those days. Preachers could "damn us to hell," but we had to call it the "bad place.")

I can remember people talking about how evil the world had become and how they knew from the signs of the times that Jesus would be coming at any minute! Is it any wonder then that I developed a kind of spiritual schizophrenia as I looked for God's ideal time in two opposite directions? I either looked backward, before movies, television, rock and roll, cars, and electricity, to that "Golden Age of Yesteryear" when Jesus walked about performing signs and wonders. It was a slow-paced time when the world was quiet enough for God to actually be heard. Or I looked forward toward some unseen celestial Never, Never Land in the far away distant future.

The point I am trying to make is the church seemed to be telling me that the ideal place to be, was always some place I was not. It was either in the primordial past or the unseen future. Because those were the real action places where wonders really happened. But if I was a good boy, then one day I too could meet God! However, as I grew older I began to rebel. I began to lose interest in both of those distant worlds. Instead, I became fascinated by life in the now! So forget the past and to hell with the mysterious future. Just let me have today, thank you, with sports, movies, cars, television, the beach, fishing, swimming, and *girls*! Life was good! I just wanted to wallow in it, taste it, smell it, and experience it in all of its fullness, variety, and wonder. In short, I became a passionate lover of the world!

The truth is that I became the stereotypical rebellious preacher's kid as the church had lost its appeal for me altogether. It no longer seemed to speak to me and my needs. I became more wrapped up in the joys and wonders of today. Bible words like "salvation" and church words like "sanctification" left me cold and indifferent. I regarded them as outdated anachronisms for the aged and dying. Heaven also offered little appeal, as all I could picture was sitting in a church pew from everlasting to everlasting hearing somebody preach. What could be more monotonous and boring than that—even with wings and a harp?

A barber became a new convert to Christ and told his preacher that he was ready to give up barbering and go into the ministry. "There is no need of that," his pastor said. "You can be a fine witness right in your barbershop." So when the next man who sat in his barber chair wanted a shave, the barber was ready. He smiled extra big as he shaved the man's neck, and softly said, "Friend, are you prepared to meet your Maker?" Not only did that poor man jump up and flee from that barbershop, but he never came back there again.

Years ago, I saw a movie about a quarterback who was killed in an accident "before his time." The angels, realizing the error, sent him back in a millionaire's body to finish out his allotted days. The movie was entitled *Heaven Can Wait*. Most of us can identify with that feeling—heaven can wait a while for us as well. Yes, we want to go there "someday," but we are in no hurry right now, thank you! But Jesus said just the opposite. He said it can't even wait until you die! Heaven is an experience that actually begins now. If that seems confusing to you, then perhaps your definition of heaven needs expanding.

One of my favorite stories is about a Catholic missionary who was telling an Eskimo chief about hell. "You are all in danger of going to hell because you even let strangers 'laugh' (sleep) with your wives," he said.

"But what if I had never heard of Jesus Christ?" asked the Eskimo chief. "Would I still be in danger of hell?"

"Oh no!" said the Catholic priest. "We call that 'invincible ignorance.' It would not be your fault if you did not know."

"Then for God's sake, man," said the Eskimo, "why in heaven's name did you tell me?"

I believe that missionary priest got it wrong. Not knowing Jesus is hell already, and knowing Jesus is heaven already. We don't tell people about Jesus in order to make life better for them after they die; we tell them about Jesus to make life better for them now!

When I was a child, I thought of heaven as gold real estate instead of relationships. I thought of immortality as quantitative—a dreary endless existence beyond the grave—rather than qualitative—the fullness of joy in fellowship with Jesus! Yet Jesus defines heaven, not as a time or a place, but as a personal relationship with him. Jesus did not describe heaven as some undiscovered country to be entered into after you croak; rather, Jesus described heaven as an encounter with the Heavenly Father, the Son, and the Holy Spirit—both now and forevermore! In his high priestly prayer, Jesus said, "And this is eternal life, to know you, the one true God and Jesus Christ whom you have sent" (John 17:3).

Therefore, heaven is an indwelling of God in your heart. Remember, in Hebrew, the word "to know" literally means "to be at one with." So Jesus prayed that we would all be perfectly one, he in us and we in him. "I do not pray to take them out of the world," he said. What I am trying to get across is that you don't have to die in order to discover eternal life. The party begins *now!* "He who hears my word," Jesus said, "and believes in me—has eternal life" (John 5:24). He didn't say "will have someday" or "could have someday," but "*has*" in the present tense! "He does not come into judgment, but *has* passed out of death into life."

So the call to eternal life is not just for those who are dead in the grave, it is also for those who are spiritually dead—who know how to exist but not how to experience true joy in Jesus and the indwelling of God abiding in your heart forever. "In this," said John, "the love of God was made manifest among us, that God sent his only Son into the world so that we might live through Him!" (1 John 4:9) "I have come," Jesus said, "that you may have life more abundantly" (John 10:10). He came that our "joy might be complete" (John 16:24). Jesus came to help you discover joy, abundant life, rebirth, regeneration, and renewal right now, not just later! "*Now* is the time of salvation" (2 Corinthians 6:2).

Over the years, I have come to believe that the real danger in life is not what God or the devil is going to do to punish you; the real danger is what you are going to do to punish yourselves. As Pogo put it: "We have seen the enemy and he is us." Jesus came to free us from all of the addictions that enslave us—greed, lust, drugs, alcohol, etc. He did not come to keep you out of hell after you die; he came to welcome you into heaven, even before you die. Heaven comes to us both now and forevermore! *That is why heaven can't wait.*

WHAT PART OF "YES" IS IT YOU DON'T UNDERSTAND?

Do I make my plans according to ordinary human standards, ready to say "yes, yes" and "no, no" at the same time? As surely as God is faithful, our word to you has not been "yes and no," for the Son of God, Jesus Christ, whom we proclaimed among you, Silvanus and Timothy and I, was not "yes and no;" but in him it is always "yes." For in him, every one of God's promises is a "yes." For this reason it is through him that we say the "Amen," to the glory of God. But it is God who establishes us with you in Christ and has anointed us, by putting his seal on us and giving us his Spirit in our hearts as a first installment.
—2 Corinthians 1:17b–22

MY GRANDSON CONNOR used to be into everything—all day long. All we ever seemed to say to him was "No! No! No!" Once, he almost burned down our parsonage by putting a small broom into the pilot light, catching it on fire, and then trying to put the flaming broom out by sweeping it across the living room rug. I think some people's impression of the Christian religion is also about putting out fires and shouting "No! No! No!" To them our faith is negative and confusing, stifling, and restrictive. Their emphasis is on what we are "saved from" rather than what we are "saved for," on what we ought not to do as opposed to what we ought to do. Some see faith as abstaining, denying, and purging, instead of growing, living and loving! But all of this negativity makes the Gospel seem like "bad news" instead of "good news." It makes God a tyrant instead of a redeemer! The emphasis is on guilt, shame, fear, punishment, and divine retribution rather than on hope, love, forgiveness, healing, and kindness. Far too often, that is the message we pass onto our own children and to ourselves as well. We make God sound like a tour guide for guilt trips.

But when Jesus began his ministry, he stood before the people, opened up the book of the prophet Isaiah and began to read, "The Spirit of the Lord is upon me, because he has chosen me to preach the Good

News to the poor; he has sent me to proclaim release to the captives and to set at liberty those who are oppressed." Jesus did not come to be your jailer and tie you up in "Nots!" Instead, he introduced himself as a liberator, the ambassador of freedom. As God's "Yes," his mission was to loosen the chains that bind us, so that we might never be slaves to anything again. Jesus came to free us to be our true selves. So salvation is not God's no; it is God's yes to life. Jesus came to turn us on to life, not off! He came

- to build you up, not break you down
- to turn you into a new creation
- to forgive and forget
- to fulfill your destiny
- to give you hope and assurance
- to heal you and cleanse your soul
- to make you whole and complete
- to give you the power to cope
- to give you inner peace, harmony, and joy
- to show you truth and beauty
- to give you a sense of the sacred and the eternal within *your own soul*

Jesus loved John the Baptist, but *he compared John's ministry* to children in the marketplace playing funeral. John was cold and stern. John weighed people down with guilt and shame. He was the president of the "Misery Squad." He talked judgment. One Sunday a woman met me at the door of the church and said, "Did you know that after all this time preacher? You finally made me cry." I guess she would have loved John the Baptist. But Jesus compared himself to children playing wedding feast, with flowers in their hair, making music and dancing in the streets; not the followers of John the Baptist playing funeral. He told the disciples they did not have to fast, because the bridegroom was still with them. He even compared the kingdom of God to a wedding party. So Jesus was a laughing, dancing God, who loved life and people and taught the way to genuine happiness and fulfillment was through him. "I have set before you an open door that no one can shut" (Revelation 3:8).

So Jesus did not come to enslave us; he came to set us free to be our true *authentic* selves. Today the word "saved" has lost part of its original meaning. It has been reduced to mean "responding to altar calls at revivals." As a result, they have made a perfectly good Bible word into the brunt of jokes. Like the graffiti that says, "Jesus saves and at today's prices, that is a miracle." One reason for such sarcasm is that today we associate being saved only with negatives:

> He got saved and gave up pleasure.
> He got saved and gave up smoking.
> He got saved and gave up liquor!
> He got saved and gave up women!
> He got saved and gave up gambling!
> He got saved and gave up profanity!
> He got saved and gave up fun.

"O Lord," one man prayed, "after I have given up all of these things, please help me to be fit to live with! Amen!" It is true that salvation is not license to do anything. We do have responsibilities. Nevertheless, being saved is not giving up something; so much as it is being pulled out of the mire. It is to be set free from traps (literally to become wide and spacious!). It is to burst loose from chains; like someone escaping from prison. It is like one who moves from the filth and confinement of the big city slums to the wide open spaces where the air is fresh and pure and nothing blots out the light of the sun or fences your soul!

In short, being saved is exactly the opposite from being stifled and constrained by rules and regulations. Rather, it is liberation. It is being released from bondage. It is a beautiful sense of wholeness and healing. It is wonderfully positive experience! That is why Jesus Christ is always God's "Yes" to you!

> In the face of despair, God's "Yes" is joy.
> In the face of darkness, God's "Yes" is light!
> In the face of doubt, God's "Yes" is hope!
> In the face of guilt, God's "Yes" is forgiveness.
> In the face of hate, God's "Yes" is love!
> In the face of sin, God's "Yes" is grace!'
> In the face of death, God's "Yes" is eternal life!
> In the face of rebellion, God's "Yes" is reconciliation!
> In the face of defeat, God's "Yes" is "victory!"

That is why the apostle Paul could say, "Whatever is true, whatever is honorable, whatever is just, whatever is pure, whatever is lovely, whatever is gracious; if there is any excellence; if there is anything worthy of praise, then think on these things and the God who gives us peace will be with you" (Philippians 4:8–9).

You have turned my mourning into dancing, you have taken off my sackcloth and clothed me with joy (Psalms 30:11):

> **The Bridegroom is still with us- so, as the song**
> **goes, "If you have a chance to sit it out or dance,**
> **I hope you'll dance"**

WHY LITERALISM IS SO DARN DIVISIVE

You yourselves are our letter, written on our hearts to be known and read by all and you show that you are a letter of Christ, prepared by us, written not with ink but with the Spirit of the living God, not on tablets of stone but on tablets of human hearts. Such is the confidence that we have through Christ toward God. Not that we are competent of ourselves to claim anything as coming from us; our competence is from God, who has made us competent to be ministers of a new covenant, not of letter but of spirit; for the letter kills, but the Spirit gives life . . . Since then, we have such a hope, we act with great boldness, not like Moses, who put a veil over his face to keep the people of Israel from gazing at the end of the glory that was being set aside. But their minds were hardened. Indeed, to this very day, when they hear the reading of the old covenant, that same veil is still there, since only in Christ is it set aside. Indeed, to this very day whenever Moses is read, a veil lies over their minds; but when one turns to the Lord, the veil is removed. Now the Lord is the Spirit, and where the Spirit of the Lord is, there is freedom. And all of us, with unveiled faces, seeing the glory of the Lord as though reflected in a mirror, are being transformed into the same image from one degree of glory to another; for this comes from the Lord, the Spirit.

—2 Corinthians 3:2–6, 12–18

A BOY WAS READING his Bible and he said to his father, "Dad, is God really in this book?"

"Yes, son," said his father. SLAM! "Got him!" said the boy.

In ancient biblical times, the most sacred object known to the people of Israel was the "Ark of the Covenant." In fact, the people held it in such awe that Uzziah accidentally touched it and literally died of sheer fright. So the people began to worship the Ark, as if the infinite God who ruled the stars had been captured in a box. They even took the Ark into battle with them and used the Ark as a powerful weapon of war. But when the Ark was captured by the Philistines, the people gave up, as if Almighty God himself had been kidnapped! Don't laugh too loud, because some people today feel the same way about the Bible.

Very early in my ministry, I was sent to a little chapel that was located across from an Assembly of God church. As a side note, one of my young members once asked his mother: "Why do we go to the Methodist Church and not to God's church over there?" Anyway, one spring, our little church was feeling very ecumenical, so we asked the people of the Assembly of God if they would like to hold a joint Bible School with us. Now that was pure "culture shock!" Not only did their teachers refuse to wear shorts (that was a sin), but they also refused to use our "Godless" United Methodist literature. So as a compromise, we ordered our VBS materials from some fly-by-night outfit called Standard Publishing. Believe me, it was extremely substandard in almost every category I can think of—including the comic-book quality of the paper. But to make matters worse, the Assembly of God refused to take part, unless we agreed to recite, as "Bible believers," a Pledge of Allegiance to the Bible.

At that point, I felt morally compelled to object. "I do not mind a pledge of allegiance to my Lord and Savior Jesus Christ," I said, "but I refuse to break the second commandment and pledge allegiance to a book, because we do not worship the teachings, we worship the teacher." The Bible serves as a testimony, but it is a means not an end. We cannot capture God or Jesus in a book, but that book can lead us to Jesus. As Jesus told the Pharisees, "You search the scriptures because you believe that in them you have life, (and it is they bear witness to me) and yet, you refuse to come to me that you may have life!" (John 5:40) Did you get that? Read it again!

The point is that, our ultimate goal should be a personal relationship with the living Lord. As the apostle John put it, "These things are written that you may come to believe that Jesus is the Messiah, the Son of God, and that through believing you may have life in his name" (John 20:31). So the purpose of scripture is to lead us on the path to Jesus. He is the one to receive our adoration, not a book. So beware of those who would turn the Bible into a magic icon or an object of worship.

Instead, we must view the Bible as a sacred tool that only under the guidance of the Holy Spirit, can lead us into a right relationship with God. The Bible is like a map that leads us to heaven, but we do not worship the map. The Bible is like a shovel that helps us dig deep for eternal treasures, but we do not worship the shovel. The Bible is like a highway sign that points us to God, but we do not put the sign on the altar between two candles and think that we have already arrived at our destination. Mere words, no matter how eloquent (not even Old Elizabethan English!) can capture the infinite, invisible God of the universe. Words can only point us toward God; they can never define (make finite) God. No wonder Jesus taught with metaphors, parables, and figurative language. "I have said these things to you in figures of speech" (John 16:25). That is why he compared the Kingdom of God to "a mustard seed," "a pearl of great price," a "treasure hidden in a field," and so on.

God help me, I am going to take the gloves off here and challenge one of the most divisive, yet pervasive forms of idolatry in this country today. It is verbal inspiration or biblical literalism. It is the naive assertion that the Bible is not a human book at all, but rather it sprang directly and completely from the mind of God. Therefore, it is without error of any kind. Every word is infallible and inerrant on any subject from history to science. It is as if God grabbed the hand of the writer, who lost all reason and conscientiousness, and was forced to blindly write, word for word, exactly what God dictated (in Elizabethan English, of course). And since God cannot make a mistake, neither can the Bible.

I love the Bible and have given my whole life to teaching its wonderful truth, but the real problem with inerrancy is that even if the Bible were "word perfect," people are not. They manage to interpret the same verses in hundreds of different ways—sometimes very strange ways. That is why we need the guidance of the Holy Spirit to lead us "beyond the sacred page" into the arms of Jesus. So while the Bible is a wonderful book, a sacred book, a holy book, an inspirational book, a powerful book—it is not a magic book with supernatural powers! It is not to be worshiped. It is an instrument that under the guidance of the Holy Spirit leads us to God as God's spirit comes alive and Jesus takes up residence in our hearts.

It was the dream of the Gospel writers that putting their sacred experiences in words would serve as a catalyst to set off the same joyful experience through your own personal encounter with the Holy Spirit. But never in their wildest dreams did they mean to imply that they had captured the Holy Spirit on paper. The holy word of God, "which is alive and active and sharper than any two edged sword," is not a book—it is Jesus. He is the Word that became flesh and dwelt among us. But if we make the Bible an end instead of a means, then that creates all kinds of arguments and diversions as we "nit-pick" God's "word" to pieces. Jesus called that "straining at a gnat and swallowing a camel" (Matthew 23:24).

So you may ask, "How does the letter kill?" I'll tell you! The letter kills because it offers law instead of Grace and ignores the intent of the law, in favor of technicalities. The letter kills because it ties up the spirit in chapter and verse and looks for salvation in a sentence. The letter kills because it divides God's children into factions to argue over this verse or that verse, while the Spirit brings unity. The letter kills because it stifles freedom, limits creativity, and majors in the minors. It dwells on the finite, instead of the infinite. The letter kills because it denies human reason and scientific inquiry, as if God gives us minds and then tells us not to use them. The letter kills because literal language is shallow, naive, stagnant, and earth- bound—while spiritual language soars like an eagle high above this worldly domain to a distant realm far over the horizon. The letter kills because it narrows the window to God and reduces truth to its lowest common denominator. The letter kills because it is manipulative as people use it to look over God's shoulder and predict what God will do next—even though that is none of our business. The letter kills because it reduces revelation to stiff rules and cold regulations, instead of a warm loving personal relationship with the living God. The letter kills because it focuses on the symbol instead of reaching upward toward that which the symbol represents. The letter kills because it emphasizes the outward visible sign, instead of the inward spiritual grace. It clips the wings of the Spirit and chains the soul to the ground. Jesus said the Spirit is like the wind and nothing can pin it down or bind it, instead it blows where it wills. So all we can do is hang on for the ride!

That dynamic Spirit burned for Moses in a burning bush; it spoke to Jeremiah through a potter's wheel; it flashed like lightening before Paul on the Damascus Road. The Spirit is the holy vibrant force of creation; it is the intimate presence of the infinite invisible God. The Bible then is a secondary source that tells us about a primary personal encounter with the Holy Spirit.

Two of the most famous literalists in the New Testament were Rabbi Nicodemus and the Samaritan woman at the well. Nicodemus wanted to know if he had to reenter his mother's womb in order to be "born again," and the woman at the well wanted Jesus to give her his "living water" so that she would not have to come out and draw water from the well anymore. (How quickly she managed to reduce God's "living water" to indoor plumbing!)

Let me ask you a question: "Which came first, the New Testament or the church?" Please think about this carefully. It was not the New Testament that created the church, but rather it was the church, under the influence of the Holy Spirit, that created the New Testament. So the Spirit came first, and the written words were a response, an affirmation, a witness, a testimony to that encounter and not the other way around. Never in their wildest dreams did the Gospel writers ever believe that they had captured Jesus in a book. Instead, they hoped that you would be inspired to join them in the dance and soar with them as that Spirit of wondrous joy tabernacles (pitches tent) in your dancing heart!

Once upon a time, an intelligent man wanted to learn how to dance, so naturally he bought an instruction book on dance and began to read all about it. He memorized the book from cover to cover and practiced each step with detail. When the book said "step left and sway," he did it with precision. He even glued footprints to the floor so that his steps would be exactly as the book said. Then he called his girlfriend over to show her his newfound skills. But his dancing was awful—very mechanical and stiff—although technically perfect. "You killed it," she said. "But I did it exactly by the book," he protested. "Yes you did," said she, "but you forgot to listen to the rhythm of the music." So she puts on a CD. "Now listen with your heart and stop looking at your feet," she said. "Look me in the eye, and we will be able to move as one together, in harmony with the music." The next thing you know, they are flowing across the room with beauty and grace.

That is what I call living by the Spirit instead of the letter. You have to listen for the music of the spirit in your soul. Then you can learn to dance! So would somebody please explain to me why so many good and faithful Christians insist in going back to the rigid Old Wine of the letter instead of the fresh New Wine of the Spirit? Why do those very churches that claim to live by the Spirit remain the most chained and fettered to the legalism and literalism of the letter? Even stranger, these are the churches to which people are flocking? I do not understand. "Where the spirit is, there is freedom," not slavery! So why do chains look so inviting?

Is it because in a complex world of confusion and uncertainty, people are willing to give up their freedom for the security of simplistic answers? Just as the Israelites in the desert pined for the "fleshpots" of Egypt, some people seem to prefer their chains.

> **So if the son makes you free, you will be free indeed.**
> **—John 8:36**

WHAT DOES IT MEAN TO SAY THE BIBLE IS INSPIRED

Then the Spirit said to Philip, "Go over to this chariot and join it." So Phillip ran up to it and heard him reading the prophet Isaiah. He asked, "Do you understand what you are reading?" He replied, "How can I, unless someone guides me?" And he invited Philip to get in and sit beside him.

—Acts 8:29–31

THERE IS AN interesting story in the book of Acts, where Phillip is standing on the street when a carriage ambles by. In it sits a member of the queen's court from the African kingdom of Cyrene or Ethiopia. To put this delicately, since he lives with the queen in her palace, this black envoy has been neutered. Anyway, as the royal carriage passes, Phillip is surprised to hear this eunuch slave reading scripture. In those days, it was not uncommon to read out loud, because the ability to read was so rare. So prized and precious was this gift that it was customary for anyone who could read, to read so that others could hear. This was not, in any way, to show off but was an act of courtesy to share the wisdom.

Two things immediately caught Phillip's attention. First, the eunuch was reading Holy Scripture, even though the Law of Moses clearly stated that all eunuchs were to be cut off from the Covenant of God and denied access to the Holy Temple (Deuteronomy 23:1).

The second thing that struck Phillip was that this foreign infidel was reading the suffering servant passages from the prophet Isaiah. These were Holy Scriptures which Christians from the very beginning have identified with our Lord Jesus Christ, the Lamb of God that takes away the sins of the world.

Phillip began to walk briskly alongside the cart as it moves slowly down the narrow street. In his excitement, he says, "Do you have any idea what you are reading?" The eunuch replied, "How can I, unless someone explains it to me." Whereupon, Phillip seized the day, boarded the wagon and began to interpret the scriptures in the light of the Son of Man, who gave his life as a ransom for all—even black Ethiopian eunuchs. So powerful was Phillip's testimony that this African envoy was converted on the spot—accepting Christ as Lord and Savior. He was even baptized right there in a pool beside the road.

Two things should really speak to us in this story. First of all, it shows that the same scriptures can be interpreted by different people in many different ways. The Christians read Isaiah, and they clearly saw Jesus; while the Jews read the same scripture, and they saw only themselves.

Second, the Spirit bade Phillip to ignore and override the Old Testament Mosaic commandment that cut off eunuchs from access to God. So Phillip baptized the Ethiopian in the name of the Father, the Son, and the Holy Spirit—even though he was breaking an Old Testament Law to do so. Thus, the Spirit was leading him to a new truth and a new direction. Therefore, the question we need to address is not "Is the Bible inspired?" Of course, it is! The question we need to address is "How is the Bible inspired?" Is the Spirit above the letter or subject to the letter? Does God inspire words in a book or does God inspire people? Who, in response to his encounter, bear witness to that inspiration—by writing words in a book?

Imagine, for example, Saint Luke as he sits at his desk with quill in hand, is suddenly emptied of his intelligence and prejudice, as God uses him as a writing instrument to record his absolute immutable truth. Losing all consciousness, God compels Luke to write every single word, perfectly and automatically—without study, without preparation, without fore knowledge, and without one single mistake. That sounds pretty dramatic and powerful, doesn't it!? The problem is, it just didn't happen that way!

How do I know this? Because Luke told me so. In the opening chapter of his Gospel, Luke clearly says that he compiled his Gospel only after reading other less satisfactory accounts which he wanted to correct. So he did his own research and even interviewed eyewitnesses. He admits that writing his Gospel took serious human effort on his part. So does that mean that the Gospel of Luke was not inspired? Of course not! If I thought that, I would have left the ministry. But what it does mean is that some people need to be a little more open minded as to how the Bible was inspired. I believe God works through a personal relationship with people. God inspires people; and people write books.

Let me offer a parable: Suppose a man fell head-over-heels in love with a beautiful woman named Judy. (It happened to me!) Then in the height of his ecstasy, he composes a poem entitled "An Ode to Judy—Floating on Cloud Nine." Now suppose that some news reporter is so struck by the beauty of this fine piece of literature that he conducts this interview:

Reporter: Good day, sir, I have just concluded an interview with an old boyfriend of hers that she rejected, and he paints an entirely different picture of her. What do you have to say about that?

Author: Then let him write his own poem. I can only speak for myself—from my own experience—but I believe she is wonderful beyond compare.

Reporter: Well, tell our audience, did she coach you on what to say? Were you coerced by her into writing this glowing tribute?

Author: Certainly not! Well, not exactly! I couldn't help myself, but she didn't force me. The words just flowed out from inside my soul. She was merely the source, the catalyst of my inspiration. What I wrote, I wrote of my own free will. If I had not known her, of course, I could not have written it; but precisely because I do know her, I felt drawn to express how I feel! But I was never manipulated or controlled in what I wrote. You see, she just isn't that kind of person! You need to understand that. Nevertheless, this poem welled up from the deep conversations and sweet communion we shared together in love.

Reporter: So you feel pretty good about the results of your work. Do you feel like you have captured her essence?

Author: Are you crazy! No, I did not capture her essence. How could I put her soul in a poem? I couldn't do that in a thousand poems. What I feel for her transcends any description. Our love is beyond words. How can you describe a symphony to a deaf man or a rainbow to a blind man; that is how hard it would be to capture who she really is in words. But what I tried to do was paint a picture of what she means to me and the relationship of love we share together—as well as my limited inadequate words allow!

Reporter: Well, I have read the poem several times over, and I feel that I know her pretty well myself now.

Author: Man, you must be kidding me! You can't know Judy just by reading words about her in a poem. You have to get to know her personally yourself. You must meet her face to face, for only she can reveal herself to you. Words could never do that! Your souls have to touch. Like ours did!"

Reporter: One more question, I don't believe there are any numbers on clouds. So how do I know for sure you two were really on *Cloud Nine,* and not, say, on cloud six? Just give me the facts.

Author: Come on, man, give me a break! Who cares what number the cloud was—eight, nine or ten? Do not sweat the details! All I know is that she has brought more joy to my soul than I have ever known before and I shall love her forever and ever!"

That, my friends, is a parable of how I believe the Bible was inspired. In other words, God works through people, not "word processors." I regard the Bible as the most sacred and holy book ever written. It is a book like no other. It has touched billions of lives, including mine. It has blessed my soul and that is why I write to you today. But I do not regard it as inerrant or infallible, because it was written by imperfect people and people make mistakes. So it is a human book as well as a Holy Book. As Paul put it, "We have this treasure in earthen vessels." Only God is 100 percent perfect; people are not. People can interpret the very same passage in an amazing variety of ways. How many senseless divisions have occurred, even wars, over conflicting interpretations of the same verse?

Think of the Bible as a road map! You can spend a thousand hours memorizing every city, town, and county seat on the map and how far it is from one town to another, but if you never go there, what good was the map? Don't you see! A map is not something you argue over. A map is a guide to keep you moving in the right direction. So pilgrims, the point is that life is a journey and the Bible is your road map to the kingdom of God. Still, there are people who feel that God has called them to be his personal road blocks, and to keep some people off the path and exclude them—especially if they do not think like they think. Instead, we are called to lead people home, not to bar the door, just because they have yet to achieve their exalted "level of holiness." We are not supposed to use the Bible like a club to beat people, threaten and intimidate those who may not interpret it quite the way we do. Our job is not to separate Christians from Christians or churches from churches. Not a single time did Jesus say, "Believe in the Bible, and you will be saved."

He said, *"Believe (into) in me."* (The Greek translation in parenthesis is mine.)

The Bible offers you more than a list of things you need to memorize. Or a list of regulations you must follow. It tells you how to meet the Master. It offers more than a book of words; it offers the *Living Word*. Remember what the men on the road to Emmaus said, "Did not our hearts burn within us, when 'he' opened to us the scriptures." And so it is that when the Holy Spirit comes to us, the scriptures spring alive with new transforming power and the message of the Bible takes on shades of the "Hallelujah Chorus!" The Holy Spirit stands above everything, to clarify our scripture, our traditions, our reason, and our experience.

For this reason in 1877, Mary Lathbury wrote a poem about the living word entitled, "Break Thou the Bread of Life." Many people think it is a communion hymn, but it is not. Mary was praying that the Holy Spirit would open the Bible to give her spiritual wings in order for her to see the Living Word. Words alone cannot do that, but the Spirit can! "Beyond the sacred page," she wrote, "I see Thee Lord. My spirit pants for Thee, O Living Word."

Before he died, Jesus told the disciples that there were so many wonderful truths he wanted to share with them, but they would be incomprehensible to their time and place and culture, and they would not be able to take them in. But the Holy Spirit would guide them. Indeed, it was by the inspiration of the Holy Spirit that the church was formed and the New Testament written. And it is by the inspiration of the Holy Spirit that the church has spread all over the world and is alive and active in our modern age. The Holy Spirit has continued throughout the ages to inspire heroes, saints, and sages. They, in turn, have introduced the Gospel to the world.

A woman in her eighties decided to go back to college by enrolling in a course in Hebrew. As the end of the course approached, her professor asked if she was cramming for her finals. "In a manner of speaking," she said, "I just thought it would be nice to address God in his native tongue." Almost everyone who reads the Bible is reading a translation of a foreign language. Even the New Testament would be Greek to us! Yet the powerful truth of the Gospel still shines forth through the inspiration of the Holy Spirit.

The Lord is my light and my salvation.
—Psalm 27:1a

LIVING AMONG THE WEEDS

> *He put before them another parable: "The kingdom of heaven may be compared to someone who sowed good seed in his field; but while everybody was asleep, an enemy came and sowed weeds among the wheat and then went away. So when the plants came up and bore grain, then the weeds appeared as well. And the slaves of the householder came and said to him, 'Master, did you not sow good seed in your field? Where then did these weeds come from?' He answered, 'An enemy has done this.' The slaves said to him, 'Then do you want us to go and gather them?' But he replied, 'No; for in gathering the weeds you, would uproot the wheat along with them. Let both of them grow together until the harvest; and at harvest time, I will tell the reapers, "Collect the weeds first and bind them in bundles to be burned, but gather the wheat into my barn."*
>
> —Matthew 13:24–30

THAT SCRIPTURE IS hard for me because many of those weeds that hide under the umbrella of Christianity bring so much ugly baggage with them. It often brings shame to the Christian name. There are narrow-minded people, haters, fear mongers, doomsday prognosticators, pistol-packing preachers, judgmental holier-than-thou hypocrites, weird cult leaders, KKK chaplains, and crazy fanatics—all of whom call themselves Christians. Jesus said, "If a blind man leads a blind man, both will fall." So who is in charge here? Who sets the standard, and who is minding the store?

That dilemma was a real concern to the early church as well, especially when certain religious nuts began to come up with more and more crazy ideas under the guise of Christianity. So the church fathers organized great conferences (like the Council of Nicaea in Turkey in AD 325) to develop standard statements of faith that all Christians could hold in common and support together. Those who adopted and followed these creeds were regarded as orthodox; those who rejected these guidelines were regarded as "unorthodox," even heretical.

But even that did not work. The fear of heretics eventually led to such horrible atrocities as the Inquisition, where people with "unorthodox" beliefs were tortured—even burned at the stake! If a woman was accused of being a witch, she was bound and tossed into a pond. If she managed to float to the surface, this was considered a rejection of her baptism, so she was burned. If, however, she drowned, she was considered vindicated and would receive her just reward in heaven. In short, fear and hate only breeds more fear and hate, and division only breeds more division. It just does not work.

Jesus must have seen all of this coming because he told a strange parable about an enemy who maliciously sowed a poisonous bearded darnel weed into a neighbor's field. This weed looks a lot like grain but is bad. So the workers go to the owner of the field, tell him that this nasty weed is now growing up among the good plants. "Shall we go through the fields and try to pull up all those weeds?"

"No," says the landowner, "because in pulling up the weeds, you will also pull up the good plants as well. Just let them comingle together until the harvest, and then we will separate the wheat from the weeds!"

No wonder then that so many passages of the Bible, including 1 and 2 Timothy, were specifically written to warn about the weeds growing among us and to counter such false teachers that threaten the faith. And even in our day, strange cults and weird groups are out there, seeking to win over the hearts and minds of our children with exotic schemes and bizarre ideas.

My own sister was caught up in such a cult for a while. The first thing a cult leader must do is make you afraid, very afraid. The more paranoia he can instill in you, the better. Fear is a great motivator. It also weakens reason. Once you have learned to fear, whether it be Satan, the government, or whatever ; you are ripe for the picking. Next the cult leader cuts you off from your family, isolates you from old friends, and limits all outside communication in order to make you totally dependent on him.

So now let us pretend that I am your new spiritual master. Are you ready for your formal initiation? This is roughly how it works:

Step 1: I must convince my followers that the Bible or some holy book is infallible and without any error, from history to science.

Step 2: I must convince my followers that my interpretation of the holy book is also infallible and must never be questioned.

Step 3: My followers must believe that I am also holy, infallible, and inerrant and that my way is the only true way. Trust no one but me! I will protect you from the enemy!

Congratulations, and welcome to my new cult! I am now your awesome holy master guru!

So how do we live among this kind of evil weed and still protect our own loved ones from its life-choking influence? First, we must teach our children well, and then we must trust them to be as "wise as serpents and as gentle as doves" (Matthew 10:16). Then we must try as best we can to live among the weeds in peace and harmony (but always with caution). As much as possible, we must try to "love our enemies and do good to those who persecute us." Some people think that is being far too open and tolerant. They may even call it wishy-washy. But fear can easily turn us into ugly weeds! We cannot defeat our enemy by becoming what he is. If that happens, he has already won. Is this a cop-out? No, I don't think so. I believe that is simply doing what the Lord Jesus taught us to do—to cautiously and diligently live among the weeds. Yet we must forever stay alert to protect our own from so many "wolves in sheep's clothing" that move among us (Matthew 7:15).

A publisher went to visit the late Harry S. Truman after his retirement. It was well into the day, and Mr. Truman was still sitting on the bed between two large stacks of books.

"Mr. President, as a publisher, I am pleased to see that you have been buying all of those fine books. You must read yourself to sleep every night."

"No," said the former president. "I read myself *awake!*"

There is no fear in love, but perfect love casts out fear, for fear has to do with punishment, and whoever fears has not reached perfection in love.

—John 4:18

Almighty God, you have said to us, "Fear not!" You have said, "Come, let us reason together." So we come to you, not as elitists or know-it-alls but with troubled hearts. Please heal our blind eyes and our anxieties. We humbly seek a broader vision. Wean us off spiritual milk and give us "solid food." Help us be more mature in our thinking and bold in our beliefs, lest we wander into myths. Give us clear direction so that we do not lose our own stability. Forgive us for all the petty unimportant things that we use to distance ourselves from you and one another .Bring all of your wayward children together as one. Help us ignore the little squabbles that divide us, and by your grace, help us build our faith only on the solid rock of Jesus rather than upon the shifting sands of fads, fools, fanatics, and far-out religion. Lord, have mercy! Christ, have mercy! In the blessed name of the Holy Trinity—Father, Son, and Holy Spirit! *Amen.*

> **Paul wrote to you, according to the wisdom given him**
> **. . . There are some things in them that are hard to**
> **understand, which the ignorant and unstable twist to**
> **their own destruction . . . Do not be carried away . . . and**
> **lose your own stability.**
> **—2 Peter 3:15–17**

BEYOND THE SACRED PAGE

In the beginning was the Word, and the Word was with God, and the Word was God. He was in the beginning with God. All things came into being through him, and without him not one thing came into being. What has come into being in him was life, and the life was the light of all people. The light shines in the darkness, and the darkness did not overcome it. There was a man sent from God, whose name was John. He came as a witness to testify to the light, so that all might believe through him. He himself was not the light, but he came to testify to the light. The true light, which enlightens everyone, was coming into the world. He was in the world, and the world came into being through him; yet the world did not know him. He came to what was his own, and his own people did not accept him. But to all who received him, who believed in his name, he gave power to become children of God, who were born not of blood or of the will of the flesh or of the will of man but of God. And the Word became flesh and lived among us, and we have seen his glory, the glory as of a Father's only Son, full of grace and truth. (John testified to him and cried out, "This was he of whom I said, 'He who comes after me ranks ahead of me because he was before me.'") From his fullness, we have all received grace upon grace. The law indeed was given through Moses; grace and truth came through Jesus Christ. No one has ever seen God. It is God the only Son, who is close to the Father's heart, who has made him known.

—John 1:1–18

IN THE FULLNESS of time, when time was ripe, the love of God, which was from the beginning, appeared to us in the person, nature, and personality of Jesus. "In this," wrote John, "the love of God was made manifest among us—that God sent his only Son into the world so that we might live through him" (1 John 4:9). The real message of Jesus is not what he taught but who he was. There have been lots of great teachers: Confucius, Buddha, Moses, Mohammad. But they were not the "Living Word."

I believe that in his person, Jesus is the ultimate revelation of God. First, God gave us the law in the Torah, which we either broke or nitpicked to death. Then God gave us the prophets, which we killed or ignored or reduced to fortune-tellers. So finally, in the fullness of time, God reveals himself personally through Jesus—the Word made flesh. Therefore, we no longer view the Word as symbols on paper. The Word lives! Jesus did not write about the way; he was the way. He didn't just tell about the truth; he was the truth. Long ago, the prophet Jeremiah spoke of a time when men would no longer depend on a written code, but God would give them a new covenant—written in the human heart. I believe that prophesy was fulfilled in Jesus. He is the *logos* or the "meaning," the ultimate revealer of God (Jeremiah 31:31 ff).

We are not saved by what we read but by who we know, not by great literature but by a great Savior! The truth is that we have filled the trash baskets of the world with billions of dollars' worth of old church publications. But they will not save us. Nor are we saved by how many Bible verses we can quote. Rather, we are saved by a personal relationship with Jesus Christ. So Jesus is the truth that sets us free, not information we read in a book. We are *not* Bible believers who follow Jesus, but rather, we are Jesus believers who follow the Bible. That is an important distinction that Jesus directed at the first-century fundamentalists of his day: the scribes, the Pharisees, and the Sadducees. Remember?

> **You search the scriptures because you believe that in them you have life and they do bear witness to me—yet you refuse to come to me that you may have life.**
> **—John 5:39**

To me, that says it all! The Gospels are not book reports on the beliefs of Jesus or even a summation of his views. Rather, the Gospels are an invitation for *you* to come to the Living Word.

Consider this:

- Moses pointed to the law.
- Mohammad pointed to the Koran.
- Confucius pointed to the analects.
- Buddha pointed to the eight-fold path.
- But Jesus, and Jesus alone, pointed to himself as the way. Only Jesus dared call himself equal with God, "I and the Father are one."

C. S. Lewis put it bluntly when he said that anyone else who dared say what Jesus said would either be a deceiver or a nut. "He would either be a lunatic on the level with a man who says he is a poached egg or else he would be the devil from hell" (mere Christianity). I agree, either Jesus was right or else he was insane; there is no middle ground on this point.

There is a Greek pronoun that is almost never properly translated into English. It is the Greek word *eis* or "into." Jesus calls us to believe not "in" him but *eis*, "into" him. That means we are to become totally involved with our whole person—body, soul, and mind—in complete self-surrender. We are not to remain aloof or detached like some disinterested observer. In order to know Jesus, we have to totally immerse ourselves in the community of faith as we join together to seek a personal encounter with his life-giving Spirit.

> **I was born to bear witness to the truth and everyone who belongs to the truth listens to me.**
>
> **—John 18:37**

PRAYER IS LIKE A WHISTLING SURFER

I live, and yet no longer I but Christ lives in me.
—Galatians 2:20

I USED TO THINK that prayer was a special skill that only a very few holy people could ever possess. I thought the more eloquent you were with words, the better you prayed. I did not consider myself to be one of those people. So I was very tempted to write the whole thing off. I even used to wonder if there was really someone up there who had enough time to waste to ever bother with the likes of me anyway. But then everyone kept insisting on its value, and so reluctantly, I began to take it up. I usually did this in a nonverbal fashion late at night. As I began to try it, I became more and more convinced that I was not delusional. I felt that I was making some kind of connection. So this is my conclusion: Real prayer takes two subjects, not one. We do not pray "to whom it may concern." Prayer is more than self-reflection. It is not talking to yourself. Prayer is making yourself available to be moved by the Spirit. It is listening for that still small voice that is both above and beyond you and yet intimate and close at hand. I have learned to be a believer in prayer.

My father used to be an avid duck hunter, and he used to say that praying was a lot like duck hunting. If you make too much noise, you scare away the ducks. Wait quietly upon the Lord and the wings of the Spirit will descend upon you. Some people's understanding of prayer is about on the level of Mark Twain's *Huckleberry Finn*. Huck prayed for things like fishing hooks to no avail, so he concluded, "There ain't nothing to it." But prayer is not like presenting Santa with your list of demands. It is not like the little girl who prayed for a flat tire on the school bus so she wouldn't have to go to school. It is not getting your way at the expense of someone else.

There is an old Jewish saying that goes, "Heed not, O Lord, the prayer of the traveler in the rain." We do not always get our way through prayer. I know preachers who have seriously injured people's faith by implying that they could get anything they wanted if they prayed hard enough. But the Bible says, "You shall not tempt the Lord your God." The truth is that even Jesus and Paul prayed for things they wanted but did not get it. What they gained was the power to endure. If every prayer was answered, then the world as we know it could no longer exist. The farmer prays for rain, while a mother nearby prays for a sunny day for her daughter's wedding. Can you imagine the chaos if everybody got his or her own way all the time?

So God, in his wisdom, provided that our prayers will not turn summer into winter or make the sun rise backward. Because God is faithful and good, Jesus said, "The rain falls upon the just and the unjust" without partiality (Matthew 5:45). This means that God made our universe to be consistent and orderly. Thanks be to God!

I am not rejecting the idea of miracles. But Jesus said that we must prayerfully petition "in his name." That means that our prayers are answered according to his will, his nature, his purpose, and his character—not "in our name," not according to our will, our purpose, and our character. Therefore, in real prayer, we don't just run our mouths or try to force our words up to heaven. We do not give God directions, we receive direction. As Soren Kierkegaard put it, "Prayer is mostly attending."

Did you know that the word *obedience* comes from two Greek words, *ob audio*, which literally translates as "to hear toward"? When we open ourselves up to God and make ourselves available to be moved by the Spirit, then prayer becomes obedience or "a hearing toward" God. However, when we try to tell God what to do, then prayer becomes "disobedience" or "not hearing toward" God. God is not our private genie to be manipulated at our convenience. In prayer, we do not move the arm of God or bring God around to our way of thinking. We do not change God's mind. As Jesus said, "Your Father knows what you need before you ask it" (Matthew 6:8).

Some people think that the most important thing in prayer is to make sure God hears what they have to say. But it is just the opposite! Over and over, the Bible says, "Wait upon the Lord!" Prayer then is not cluing God in; rather, it is patiently attending and then responding as the Spirit tells us what we need to hear. Then like vibrating strings on a piano, we become instruments of God's purpose as we move in resonance with his divine will.

> **Then said I, "Here am I, send me."**
> **—Isaiah 6:8b**

HOW PRAYER IS LIKE WINDSURFING

One day while I was at the beach, a new image for prayer hit me. I saw those surfboards with sails flying on the waves. It was a spectacular sight with their brightly striped sails. The Hebrew word for wind also means spirit, and seeing the wind fill those sails reminded me of the nature of prayer as we catch the wind of the Spirit on the wave of God's will. That's it—that's what prayer is like!

Once upon a time, there was a king who would on occasion go down to the ocean and command the waves in order to keep himself from getting too bigheaded. "Halt. I command you in the name of the king." Of course, the waves refused to listen and knocked him down. Only Jesus could command the elements, not us. You can't control the waves, and you can't control God either, but you can learn how to move in harmony and ride the waves like a surfer. You can also learn to ride with the winds of God like a windsurfer. "Nevertheless," Jesus prayed, "*not my will but thine be done!*" (Luke 22:42)

The Methodist Church has a nice-sounding little slogan, "Catch the Spirit." But Jesus said the wind blows where it wills. No one can catch it! Prayer is not like a fishhook, a butterfly net, or a baseball glove. You can't catch the Spirit; instead, the Spirit catches you as you are swept up by the powerful current of the rising tide. All you can do is what a surfer does—hang on for dear life and experience the powerful energy of the incoming wave!

Prayer is also like surfing because surfing takes patience, practice, and perseverance. Surfing requires discipline and determination. So does prayer! You cannot ride a surfboard the first time you try; you must work at it. The same thing can be said for prayer! Many people think that surfing is a frivolous waste of time; some people feel the same way about prayer. Surfing is for recreation. Prayer is for re-creation. And just as surfing is exhilarating, prayer should also be a joyful experience. Surfers love to hang ten during very rough weather, and in the stormiest times in their lives, those who pray will gladly offer God their adoration and praise!

Finally, every good surfer knows that when you get out of sync with the wave, you will wipe out, as the wave knocks you down and pulls you under! "Lord," said the psalmist, "you overwhelm me with all your waves" (Psalm 88:7). But if you study the wind and the currents and have enough discipline to stay in the groove, your prayers will sustain you. Yes, and even when you wipe out or fail completely, you do not give up. You try again. God is still there. "When you pass through the waters I will be with you, and through the rivers they will not overwhelm you" (Isaiah 43:2).

So take heart, prayer is not a skills test. "We do not know how to pray as we ought," said Paul, "but the Spirit intercedes on our behalf with sighs too deep for words" (Romans 8:26). In that rare and precious moment, when you feel that soaring connection in your life as the Spirit picks you up and rings you like a bell, then oh, what a wonder! Oh, what a power! Oh, what a glorious ride!

One day Jesus came foot-surfing on the water and impetuous Peter became envious. So in his usual brash way, Peter began barking orders. "Lord," he commanded, "bid me to come to you on the water." Jesus said to him, "Come." At first, Peter did fine. But then he looked down, and oops, he began to drop like Wile E. Coyote. Poor Peter! The name *Peter* means "rock" in Greek, so "the rock" forgot his power source and sank like a rock! Now instead of making demands, he pleads, "Lord, save me!" So Jesus reached down, held him up, and returned him to the safety of the boat. The point is that in real prayer, we do not control God's hand. Instead, we learn new power as we receive our marching orders from him.

However, the phrase "Wait upon the Lord" also has an entirely different meaning. In the book of the Acts, the deacons (servants) "waited upon" tables and then distributed the leftovers to "wait upon" the widows, orphans, and others who were needy. So when we get up from our knees, it is time to go to work (See Deuteronomy 15:7–11). *So let's catch the wave and start surfing!*

PRAYER IS ALSO LIKE WHISTLING

Then another metaphor hit me: Prayer is also a lot like whistling. There are many occasions when we whistle and when we pray. We whistle when we are doubtful, in danger, or afraid. We pray for the same reasons. We whistle to hail a taxi or call a friend. In prayer, we invoke God's presence. We whistle when we are happy and full of joy. In prayer, we praise God for the same reasons. We whistle as a sense of relief—"Boy that was close!" In prayer, we thank God for deliverance—"Thank God that is over!" We whistle after a great speech or a beautiful concert to show our approval. In prayer, we offer God our thanks and praise. In my younger days, it was not considered politically incorrect to whistle when a pretty girl walked by; even adulation and adoration was also a vital part of prayer. We also whistle a tune from the music that is in our souls. Just as in prayer, we seek to get in tune with God. Like whistling, prayer works best on the out-breath. Try saying a prayer by pausing between phrases on the out-breath as you exhale slowly. You breathe in for energy, but you breathe out to relax. Try it. It works!

Did you know that the word for spirit means "breath" and the name for God was two out-breaths put together, "Yah-weh"? So in a sense, every time you exhale, you are praying God's name. What really brought whistling to mind for me as a paradigm for prayer was Paul's injunction to "pray without ceasing." In other words, we should not only pray in sanctuaries or shelters, but we should also pray on the go, as we learn to "whistle while we work."

Over six hundred years ago, Meister Elkhart pinned these words:

> A man may go into a field and say his prayer and be aware of God or he may be in church and be aware of God, but if he is more aware of God because he is in a quiet place, that is his own deficiency and it is not due to God. For he who knows God rightly, knows him to be everywhere.

Prayer then is like trail mix; you take it with you. It releases its energy wherever you go. It is not like a tire jack to be hidden away until needed. "Prayer" is an action word. There is a direct correlation between what you pray to God and what you do for your neighbor. The Puritans had a saying, "Pray as if everything depended upon God, but work as if everything depended upon you." The best prayers are not the ones prayed in seclusion but the ones that are acted out on the battlefronts of the world—against sin, injustice, and evil—as we seek to become doers of the word and not hearers only.

I once read a poem by Edgar Frank entitled "Altars." A man I know has made an altar of his factory bench; and one has turned the counter of his store into a place of sacrifice and holy ministry. Another still has changed his office desk into a pulpit desk from which to speak and write, transforming commonplace affairs into the business of the King. A Martha in our midst has made her kitchen table into a communion table; a postman makes his daily round a walk in the temple of God. Each separate task, a listening post, and every common circumstance a wayside shrine.

I love to sing the hymn, "Lord, Prepare Me to Be a Sanctuary," but I would prefer to sing "Lord, Prepare Me to Be a *Missionary*." The word "sanctuary" implies a place of refuge, safety, or hiding. Churches have often provided sanctuary for people from their enemies. But that is not at all what the apostle Paul meant when he exhorted us "to put on the whole armor of God." He was talking about going into battle, not retreating from it. He was calling us to enter the danger zone, not hide. Just look at what happened to him: "Five times I received at the hands of the Jews the forty lashes less one. Three times I have been beaten with rods. Once I was stoned. Three times I have been shipwrecked, a night and a day I have been adrift at sea . . . in danger from rivers, danger from robbers, danger from my own people, danger from Gentiles . . ." (2 Corinthians 11:24-26) *If safety and protection were the purpose of prayer, Paul never discovered its worth.*

ARE YOU THE ANSWER
TO SOMEONE ELSE'S PRAYER?

Just a few miles from my first appointment was another fishing village called Davis. I am told that the tale I am about to relate is true. It was the bitter winter of 1898, one of the coldest in North Carolina history. It was so cold, in fact, that the salty waters of Core Sound froze over solid, and no boats could go in or out. There is not a lot of good land around Davis. It is mostly marshland. A few people had small gardens, but no one grew crops. There were no bridges and no roads to reach the nearest town some twenty miles away. All travel to purchase food and supplies had to be done by boat. With the sound locked solid in ice, that was imposable. So what were the poor people of Davis, whose survival depended on fishing, shrimping, and seafood, supposed to do when the food ran out?

In desperation, a few Methodists decided to pray. They had no meeting house, so they bundled up and gathered on Oyster Creek bank.

A black man named Moses Davis was the class leader, so he began to pray, "Lord, we remember how you delivered your people and led them by pillar of fire. We are gathered here today to ask your help out of our troubles. We are willing to work hard if you can just open up a way and free our boats from—"

Before he could say another word, a little boy shouted, "Look! Uncle Moses, there's somebody out there on them banks."

Sure enough, there was a thin spiral of smoke rising on the ocean side of Core Banks. Now let me explain—in those days, nobody in his right mind lived on the ocean side. So any smoke from there was a sign of real trouble.

One woman holding her bundled-up baby said, "That's just too bad for them, we can't help them anyhow."

"Shame on you!" said Moses. "Here we are asking God to help us in our distress and we are not willing to help someone who is worse off than we are."

"But what can we do for them, Moses, when we can't even take care of ourselves?" asked an old man.

Moses pondered that question for a moment and then said, "Here is what we will do—first, I'll need some young strong volunteers—you, you, and you. Here is the plan. We will break loose this twenty-foot skiff up here on the bank and slide it on to the ice. You fellows will tie ropes to your waists and to the boat so that you can pull it like a sled. Take oars with you to punch the ice for soft spots, and hopefully, even if one of you falls through, you will be able to pull him out by his rope before he freezes to death."

So they did exactly as Moses directed. They walked gingerly on the ice for upward of two miles across the sound. When the brave "volunteers" finally reached the other side and crested the dunes, there they found a group of shivering wet seamen huddled together. They were the survivors of a shipwreck who had somehow managed to start a driftwood fire. And it just so happened that all up and down the beach, barrels of wheat and molasses were washed ashore. It was salvage from the shipwreck, and it was that food that kept the people of Davis and the sailors they rescued alive during that bitter winter of 1898. There's a lesson here about finding your life by losing it and casting your bread upon the waters: *"Then said I, 'Here am I, send me!'" (Isaiah 68)*

**So just perhaps before you petition God to do you a favor,
you just might be called out to be the answer
to someone else's prayer!**

HONEST PRAYER IS AN ACTION WORD

I once read about a Catholic priest who dreaded hearing confessions at a convent. The nuns spent hours of his time brooding over petty little incidents. "It was like being 'stoned to death with popcorn,'" he said. His point was that, in isolating themselves from real life, they negated a part of what prayer is really all about. How can people who have hidden from life have life in their prayers? Some people's prayers never get beyond thanking God for the pretty flowers and trees. Like Jacob, we sometimes need to do a little arm wrestling with God. Like the psalmist of old, if you are angry, lay it on the table—God knows it anyway! If you secretly blame God for a loss, a death, an illness, or some desperate predicament, bring it out in the open and clear the air. "I cry with my voice to the Lord; I pour out my complaint before him. I tell my trouble before him" (Psalm 142:2). "Evening and morning and at noon, I utter my complaint and moan" (Psalm 55:17). The prophets were not immune to pity parties either. They confronted God head on and did not sugarcoat their angry feelings: "O Lord, how long shall I cry for help, and you will not listen? Or cry to you 'Violence!' And you will not save? Why do you make me see wrongdoing and look at trouble? Destruction and violence are before me; strife and contention arise, so the law becomes slack and justice never prevails. The wicked surround the righteous—therefore judgment comes forth perverted" (Habakkuk 1:2–4).

Wouldn't it be phony and dishonest if we didn't show a little outrage now and then? Don't gloss over your prayers or cover up your ugly feelings. Let the negative demons of fear, hate, bitterness, and pent-up frustrations pour out like water before the holy throne of God. (After all, they represent your honest feelings, ugly as they are.) How else can God help you grow beyond these bad feelings if you refuse to confront them? In prayer, you sharpen your focus, realign your priorities, gain new insight, and then go to work to get better.

In 1775, a delegation of women met with a captain in the Colonial Army and asked what they might do to advance the cause of liberty. "Ladies," he replied, "you may pray." Now I ask you, when these able-bodied women could have done a thousand things from sewing uniforms and providing medical care to cooking for the troops and assisting in weapons production, even bearing or loading arms, could those high-sounding words be regarded as anything short of a slap in the face? That's what I mean when I say sometimes our best prayers are prayed on the battlefronts of the world and not closets.

Moses did not want to return to Egypt "to set his people free," but honest prayer drove him into action. Jesus did not want to die on a cross, but real prayer led him boldly to Calvary. Authentic prayer recharges our batteries and energizes our souls. It is not an escape from life. In real prayer, we do not cower in a corner or hunker in a bunker. Prayer in action is like the young men who challenged the hijackers on September 11, 2001. They whispered a prayer and then shouted, "Let's roll!" The church is not a lounging pad for comfort but a launching pad for service. Bishop Asbury said he came to America "to reform the continent and to spread scriptural holiness across the land." Shouldn't we also put our life where our prayer is? Let us boldly seek to do justice, resist evil, lift the fallen, and carry out God's purposes in the world. If Jesus had us pray "Thy will be done," shouldn't we be out there doing it? *Go thou and do likewise.*

IN SEARCH OF THE PERFECT PRAYER

There was a time when prayer meant something entirely different. The prayers of the Pharisees were very long, very complex, and strenuous exercise. They were also very loud (as if prayer needed to be loud enough to irritate God and get his full attention). Loud, long, and flowery prayers could also be better heard by others. The Pharisees were experts at prayer technique. They had "being religious" down to a science, as they loved to hear the sound of their own pious poetic voices. They even wore prayers on their clothes. Prayer was often reduced to empty elocution, as they would string together lofty-sounding but meaningless phrases as if they were trying to filibuster God (Matthew 6:5–7). Such phony prayers were often as meaningless and insincere as the boy who mumbled, "Our Father, who aren't in heaven, Howard be thy name. Give us this day our jelly bread. Forgive us our trash baskets and deliver us from e-mail." Not very cute, was it?

But Jesus said that our prayers should not be loud or wordy or overblown. He offered, instead, a wonderfully succinct and simple model. "Pray like this," he said. He did not say, "Memorize this or recite this or pray only these words every time." He did not offer a discourse on prayer technique or memorization, and yet in that short simple prayer, he gave us a wonderful example of what true prayer ought to be. That beautiful little prayer shines as a paradigm for all of our spontaneous communications with God. Therefore, let us carefully examine it phrase by phrase:

>**OUR FATHER**—Right off the bat, in two words, Jesus tells us not only about our relationship with God but also about our relationship with one another. He is not "my" father—the word "my" is not mentioned in this prayer. Instead, he is "Our Father," or more correctly, we are his children. In two words, Jesus establishes a sense of humility and community, as we are all brothers and sisters under God. Jesus lets us know from the start that prayer is not exclusive but inclusive. You can't ask God for anything without including others in the petition.

>**WHO ART IN HEAVEN**—That tells us that God is transcendent. He is above us and beyond us. He has the big picture. He knows more than we do. He can see over the horizon. He can see a way out of a maze when we feel completely trapped by present difficulties. Isn't it great that we worship a God who is not limited like us, who is exalted in the heavens? So prayer is not a little chat with God to bring him down to our level like our own secret pal. After all, he is the infinite, sovereign Lord of creation. He is a lot bigger than you!

>**HALLOWED BE THY NAME**—Our modern society has lost any sense of the sacred and the holy. Our kids lightly toss out words like "awesome" to describe a new soft drink flavor, but they are rarely awed by anything anymore. The Bible says that true wisdom begins with "fear of the Lord." So let us

never lose sight of the majesty, glory, and wonder of Almighty God, for he "has made us and not we ourselves."

THY KINGDOM COME, THY WILL BE DONE ON EARTH AS IT IS IN HEAVEN—Over and over, Jesus kept saying how important the kingdom was. So the questions we need to ask ourselves are these: Am I helping the rule of God or hindering it? Am I letting my petty selfish problems stand in the way of the kingdom's progress? Am I building a way or blocking the way? Am I willing to accept God's rule in my life? Our job is not to chase God down like a hound dog to do our bidding. It is to wait for God's spirit to descend like a dove and then move us into action as we do his bidding and help bring about his heavenly will on earth.

GIVE US THIS DAY OUR DAILY BREAD—There is another kind of bread, there is also "Spiritual Bread." Jesus said, "You cannot live by bread alone." Again, he said, "Is not life more than food? Therefore, be not anxious, saying 'What shall we eat or what shall we drink?' But seek ye first the kingdom of God, and these things shall be yours as well." Remember, Jesus called himself the Bread of Life. "For the bread of God," he said, "is that which comes down from heaven to give life to the world." This is why the monks of Qumran prayed for the great messianic banquet at the end of time: "Our bread for tomorrow, give us today." But Jesus also said, "I was hungry and you fed me." Therefore, one of the instruments that God uses to feed the hungry "daily bread" is those of us who share our abundance (Deuteronomy 15:7–11). After all, how can we pray for the hungry and withhold our bread or pray for starving people or do nothing while people starve? So true prayer is bound to mission. Your prayer cannot be two-faced. There has to be a direct correlation between what you say to God and what you do to your neighbor. Your life has to square with your prayer.

FORGIVE US OUR TRESSPASSES AS WE FORGIVE THOSE WHO TRESSPASS AGAINST US—George

Carlin used to say that he hated going to McDonald's because every time the girl would say "Have a nice day," it placed far too much responsibility on him. But that pales in comparison to the responsibility this prayer puts on us! We actually ask God only to forgive us to the extent that we can forgive others who have wronged us. Now that is a scary thought! I bet you harbor a grudge against someone right now. But Jesus did not tell us to forgive others just to help them; getting over anger, bitterness, hate, and resentment can save our insides from headache, heartache, ulcers, and turmoil by restoring inner peace to our souls.

LEAD US NOT INTO TEMPTATION—One of the great mysteries in life is why temptation had to be so darn tempting, enticing, and attractive. But let us not forget what Paul told the Corinthians, "No temptation has overtaken you that is not common to everyone" (1 Corinthians 10–13). God is faithful and will not let you be tested beyond your strength. It still doesn't seem that way at the time, does it?

BUT DELIVER US FROM EVIL—How can anyone look at the ravages of terror, war, violence, hatred, and racism all over our world and not believe that evil is a real force? We see it in drug addiction, alcohol abuse, child abuse, pornography, political corruption, and exploitation of the weak and the poor. As Paul told the Ephesians, "We are not contending against flesh and blood but against principalities, against the powers, against the rulers of this present darkness, against the spiritual host of wickedness; therefore put on the whole armor of God that you may be able to stand in the evil day" (Ephesians 6:12–13). He also said, "Do not be overcome by evil, but overcome evil with good" (Romans 12:21).

Now wasn't that a wonderful prayer? But I know what you are thinking. I have left something off, haven't I? Scholars tell us that the doxology at the end of the Lord's Prayer is not found in the oldest manuscripts. They believe that it was actually added later by the early church as a lay response to the Lord 's Prayer during the Easter ritual. We know, for example, that by the second century, this doxology was included as such a response in a second-century book of worship called the *Dediche* (attributed to the disciples). It is also echoed in 2 Timothy 4:18, "To him be glory forever and ever." An even more dramatic parallel can be seen in a prayer attributed to David:

> Thine, O Lord, is the greatness, and the power, and the glory, and the victory, and the majesty, for all that is in the heavens and the earth is thine. Thine is the kingdom . . . in thy hand are power and might and now O Lord, we give thanks to you and praise your glorious name. (1 Chronicles 29:11)

FOR THINE IS THE KINGDOM, THE POWER, THE GLORY, FOREVER—This, of course, brings us right back to where we started, which was adoration, praise, and glory to God. So all our petitions are merely footnotes to our praise. His will and glory always comes first! Only then do we add our final word. As the captain of the *Starship Enterprise* used to say, *"Make it so."* Or as the Beatles sang it, *"Let it be."* Or as I would say it, *"I believe it is so!"* All of which means *"Amen."*

POSTSCRIPT

Have you ever heard of a "turkey trap"? It's just a box with a very low doorway on one end. The farmer scatters corn down the path and into the box. The turkey follows the corn through the low door, nibbling at the corn all the way. When the corn runs out, he raises his head and he is trapped. We know that all he has to do to get free is to bow his head, but somehow, he never seems to understand that. So he remains trapped. Now listen to me all you turkeys, sometimes you may feel overwhelmed and snared by the difficulties of life and you feel trapped and boxed in by unfortunate events in this life. If so, try bowing your head and just possibly doors will open and you can stand tall against anything this world can throw at you. Move with the Spirit on the wave of God's will. Prayer whistlers and Spirit surfers unite. Hoist your sails! *Surf's up! Start surfing!*

"SEARCH ME, O GOD"

A Paraphrase of Psalm 139

Lord, you have searched me and known me,
You discern all my thoughts from afar.
And even before my lips can say more,
You already know what they are.

CHORUS:

So search me, O God,
Please unwrap my heart, I pray.
Just try me and see if I'm pleasing to thee,
And lead me in thy holy way.

Where shall I flee from thy spirit?
If I walk through heaven or hell,
You're still with me there to show that you care.
No wonder you know me so well. (Chorus)

If I take the wings of the morning,
Or dwell in the depths of the sea,
You still hold my hand, I don't understand,
Why you should care about me? (Chorus)

More than the sands on the beaches,
More than the stars up above,
How precious shall be your thoughts, Lord, to me.
You formed me and filled me with love. (Chorus)

IN SEARCH OF HIGHER TRUTH

Let love be genuine; hate what is evil, hold fast to what is good; love one another with brotherly affection; outdo one another in showing honor. Never flag in zeal, be aglow with the Spirit, serve the Lord. Rejoice in your hope, be patient in tribulation, be constant in prayer. Contribute to the needs of the saints, practice hospitality. Bless those who persecute you; bless and do not curse them. Rejoice with those who rejoice, weep with those who weep. Live in harmony with one another; do not be haughty, but associate with the lowly; never be conceited. Repay no one evil for evil, but take thought for what is noble in the sight of all. If possible, so far as it depends upon you, live peaceably with all. Beloved, never avenge yourselves, but leave it to the wrath of God, for it is written, "Vengeance is mine, I will repay, say the Lord." No, "if your enemy is hungry, feed him; if he is thirsty, give him drink; for by so doing you will heap burning coals upon his head." Do not be overcome by evil, but overcome evil with good.

—Romans 12:9–21

WHAT DO YOU suppose Paul meant when he said, "If your enemy is hungry, feed him . . . For by so doing you will heap burning coals upon his head"? Does that make sense to you? I once heard a radio preacher preach on that text, and he insisted that doing good to your enemy was the ultimate form of sweet revenge. After all, God said, "Vengeance is mine, I will repay." So surely, the punishment of a wrathful God is far more awful and horrible than any puny punishment we could dole out. "For God will turn him over to Satan," the preacher said, "and he will be thrown into the everlasting lake of fire where he will weep and wail and gnash his teeth as the devil shovels hot burning coals upon his lousy head, forever and ever." But somehow, to me, that mean-spirited attitude does not reflect at all the nature of Jesus nor the teachings of Paul. So that radio preacher's hateful interpretation left me with cold chills down my spine. Who knows, by his interpretation, perhaps the more kindly thing to do would be to be nasty to my enemy and thereby save him from the unquenchable fires of eternal torment. Seriously though, that radio preacher's point of view is so unlike Jesus that I dismiss his vile interpretation totally.

But what did Paul mean when he said, "You will heap burning coals upon his head"? In my opinion, he had several levels of meaning in mind all at once. One useful thing I learned in seminary is that the Bible, like all great literature, is written on many different levels. In other words, what we read in one verse one day may be entirely different from the understanding we discern from the exact same verse the next day because as our needs, circumstances, and perceptions change, so does our insight into God's eternal truth.

Therefore, today I wish to share with you on three different levels of interpretation what I believe to be the real meaning of this text (the radio preacher's version not included). Each level will be a little closer to God and a little further away from the primitive perspective of hate, revenge, and hellfire. For Jesus said, "It is not the will of my Father that any of my little ones should perish." So from that perspective, let me offer three interpretations:

The first and most primitive level has to do with what used to be called killing them with kindness. When we are kind and good to those who have been mean to us, sometimes—not always but sometimes—we bring so much embarrassment and shame upon them that we make their necks burn and their faces blush red as if someone had poured hot coals upon their heads. In other words, if you do something nasty to me, wouldn't you feel a whole lot better about it if I turned around and did something even worse to you? That would serve to reinforce and vindicate your original low opinion of me. This would justify your cruel actions. But on the other hand, if after you have been so bad to me, I turn around and do something really nice to you, boy, would you blush. You would feel and look like a real jerk.

A marine drill sergeant was particularly harsh with a young black private. But every time the gunny came down on him hard or forced him to clean the latrine, the young solder would mumble, "Someday you may regret this." Time passed, and on the battlefield, that same sergeant was seriously wounded and the same buck private risked his life to carry the gunny away from danger. "Sir," the young soldier said, "I told you that one day you would be sorry!" Mahatma Gandhi used the tactic of passive resistance to shame the mighty British Empire and bring them to their knees. But while on the lowest level, "murder by kindness" is an effective weapon for revenge. I do not believe that this is what Jesus intended when he told us to love our enemies. For that would not be genuine forgiveness at all but rather a sneaky backdoor form of revenge. Surely, Paul had more noble intentions in mind than that.

This brings us to the second level of meaning for our scripture. In order to help you understand this level, I must tell you a story: One of the duties of every woman in first-century Israel was to keep the home fires burning. There were no matches, and starting a new fire was not easy. So if your fire did go out, what would you do? You would go over to your neighbor's house to borrow some hot coals. Your neighbor would help you fill a clay pot half full of sand, and then you would fill the other half with hot burning coals. So how would you take home these fresh hot burning coals? Why, you would place a doughnut-shaped pad upon your head for carrying the hot coals. Therefore, a higher and nobler reason for loving one's enemy and returning good for ill is because it is clearly the right and neighborly thing to do. "If your enemy is hungry, feed him. If his fire goes out, share some of your hot coals!" So it is simply an act of being a good neighbor and setting a good example because virtue is its own reward, and two wrongs do not a right make. After all, are you merely a pawn of your enemy? Is your conduct only determined by a reaction to what other people do to you?

Once upon a time, a Hindu yogi was mediating under a tree when he saw a scorpion with its leg trapped in a root. The yogi tried to free the scorpion, but all the while, the scorpion kept stinging his hand until it was badly swollen.

"You stupid man," the people said, laughing, "That scorpion does not appreciate what you are doing for him."

"Yes," the yogi replied, "but because it is the scorpion's nature to sting, should I change my nature, which is to be kind?"

Are you merely an echo? Do you drift with every tide and let your enemy decide how you are going to act? Sure, the world is full of meanness and hate, but does adding more hate help the situation? Certainly not! Such negative emotions merely diminish the humanity of us all. Let's be honest—doesn't our hate actually say more about us than about the person we hate?

For example, when you spend your time brooding and holding a grudge about what someone else has done to you or to someone you love, in the long run, you will be the loser! Hate can cause hypertension, colitis, heart problems, or worse; it causes subtle changes in your own personality. I know because it has happened to me. It starts when someone hurts you very badly, and so what do you do? You begin to generalize that newfound mistrust to everybody, and it becomes harder for you go give yourself to anybody. It walls you up in an unbreakable shell that no one can penetrate. So distrust leads to doubt and doubt to cynicism and cynicism to loneliness and despair until you become withdrawn, self-pitying, and just generally obnoxious to everyone. Then like Rodney Dangerfield, you begin to pout about not being appreciated. "I don't get no respect, the postman even thinks my name is 'occupant,' poor pitiful me! People treat me so lousy—boo-hoo." And you know what, the more like that you become, the more self-fulfilling your own prophesy will be. After all, who wants to associate with a sad self-centered grouch?

Unfortunately, many people will act just like that scorpion. The more you reach out to be kind to them, the more they will sting you. The more you try to help them, the more you will get hurt! But don't let that discourage you. Isn't that what also happened to your Master on Calvary. The Lord Jesus Christ said, "Blessed are those who are persecuted for righteousness's sake; for theirs is the kingdom of heaven." Yes, a higher reason for returning good for evil is because it is the right and noble thing to do. If your enemy is hungry, feed him, for by so doing, you will heap burning coals of kindness upon his head—just like a good neighbor should.

But there is a still a far higher level meaning. In ancient biblical times, fire was a symbol for the presence of God. Moses met God in a burning bush. Mount Sinai was a volcano. The holy of holies had a pit of red hot stones. Something like flaming tongues of fire descended upon the apostles at Pentecost. So when I am kind, forgiving, and loving toward my enemy, I become a conduit for the Holy Spirit as Pentecostal tongues of fire rain down upon my foe. In other words, I act in the same manner that Jesus acted toward me when I was a sinner. So as I forgive my enemy, by God's help, I heap the hot coals from the holy of holies and the flaming tongues of Pentecost upon his head.

A woman came up to Abraham Lincoln in anger, saying "Why are you so nice to our enemies in the South when they killed my son?"

"But, madam," said Lincoln, "when we love our enemies, can we not transform them into our friends?"

Paul said, "Do not be overcome by evil, but overcome evil with good!" Yes, I still believe that the powers of good are stronger than the powers of evil. I believe in light over darkness and love over hate. As the old saying goes, "You catch more flies with honey than you do with vinegar." So the best way to defeat your enemy is to transform him into a friend. Repaying evil with good has the power to be a spiritually enriching experience for both you and the evildoer—it can transform you both. And even if your enemy is not redeemed and transformed, you can be spiritually strengthened by acting under the power of the Holy Spirit to do that by which, by your own nature and character, would be impossible for you to do. This is living at the very highest level of humanity. It is not in my nature to love those who hurt me, but it is in God's nature. "Not I, but Christ in me."

I knew a lady in one of my churches who was abused by her drug-addicted father as a child, and when she became an adult, she cut off all contact with him. If he sent gifts to her children, she sent them back—unopened. He was both a drug user and an alcoholic and did some very, very bad things. But one day he got cancer, and it was terminal. He begged me to try and bring them together one more time, and so I did. Finally, just before he died, they had an amazing reconciliation. Later, after the funeral, she said to me, "Thank you for giving me back my daddy. I had so much hate, but now it is healed."

Once, a husband confessed to his wife, "Honey, I have betrayed you. I have committed adultery, and I am so sorry!" The wife fell back against the wall with tears in her eyes and deep anguish in her heart as her outstretched arms formed a cross. "You have hurt me badly," she cried, "but I love you, and somehow, by God's help, I am going to forgive you." That was a God-like act, for God forgives us, even when we hurt him badly and do not deserve forgiveness. He does this so that we will be able to forgive those who have hurt us.

Sir Francis Bacon once said, "Taking revenge makes you even with your enemy, but forgiving him makes you superior; for only a prince can pardon." Well, Jesus is our Prince of Peace, and he came to pardon all our sins, and he asks us to do likewise with his help and for his sake. As they say, "To err is human, but to forgive is divine." This is because forgiveness is such a hard thing to do, that only by the grace of God are we able to do it. After all, isn't forgiveness the central act of God's salvation? "For I will forgive their iniquity, and remember their sin no more" (Jeremiah 31:34). That is the strange forgetfulness of God.

So Paul urged us to be kind to our enemy, not to punish him with hellfire nor make him blush with embarrassment. It is not just because it is the neighborly and right thing to do. It was not even just because of Pentecost. It is because that is what Calvary was all about! As John put it, "Beloved, if we love one another, God abides in us and his love is perfected in us! But he who says he loves God and hates his brother is a liar!" (1 John 4:20) So to love our enemies is to share in the very nature of God! As the flaming tongues of Pentecostal move through us to melt the cold hearts of our enemies and transform them into our friends, Jesus said, "Love your enemies that you may be the children of your Father which is in heaven." *So go ahead and shovel some piping hot coals of Pentecost on your enemy's head! He just might thank you for it!*

GUYS JUST WANT
TO HAVE FUN

Then Jesus said to the Jews who had believed in him, "If you continue in my word you are truly my disciples, and you will know the truth, and the truth will make you free." They answered him, "We are the descendants of Abraham and have never been slaves to anyone. What do you mean by saying, 'You will make us free'?" Then Jesus answered, "Very truly I tell you, everyone who commits sin is a slave to sin . . . So if the Son makes you free, you are free indeed."

—John 8:31–34, 36

A S STRANGE AS it may seem, while we worry about what school or courthouse displays the Ten Commandments, Jesus talks about freedom from legalism. The rabbis called the Old Testament law, the yoke of obedience, but Jesus said, "My yoke is easy and my burden is light." In ancient times, the yoke of an ox was a heavy wooden device, and when the ox became mired in the mud, the kind wagoner would often get down in the mud with the ox to lift the yoke and ease the animal's burden in order to help him get out of the mire. Jesus's namesake Hosea put it this way, "I led them with cords of compassion, with bands of love. I became to them like one who eases the yoke on their jaws, and I bent down to them and fed them" (Hosea 11:4 RSV).

One of the hardest things for some Christians to understand is why Jesus picked on "law-abiding good people" like the Pharisees. He criticized them unmercifully. I think one thing that Jesus was getting at was religious legalism. In other words, some people become so heavenly minded that they are no earthly good. And that is what happened to the Pharisees. They got so wrapped up in "purity" that they were no longer

125

fit to live with. Jesus said, "Woe unto you who shut the kingdom of God against men and then refuse to go in yourselves" (Matthew 23:13).

He told this parable: "When an unclean spirit has gone out of a person, it wanders through waterless regions looking for a resting place, but not finding any, it says, 'I will return to my house from which I come.' When it comes, it finds it swept and put in order. Then it goes and brings seven other spirits more evil than itself, and they enter and live there; and the last state of that person is worse than the first" (Luke 11:24–26).

I am told that when Texas Christian University was founded in 1873 in a little village south of Fort Worth, they proudly advertised that they were forty miles from every form of sin. However, that didn't last long, for the administrators soon found that the students were quick to bring their own supply with them. Today some call it a party school. It's like the woman who had a skunk in her cellar. She called animal control, and they advised her to make a trail of bread crumbs from the cellar out to the garden to draw the skunk away from the house. The next day the woman called in a panic, "I took your advice and now I have three skunks in my cellar."

The Pharisees remind me of the greedy slum lord who blatantly overcharges his poor tenants and then gets all upset when he hears profanity on TV. Jesus said the Pharisees were so meticulous about obeying the letter of the law that they even measured out 10 percent of their spices and yet they neglected the weightier matters of the law, such as justice and mercy and love.

In America during the eighteenth century, that kind of self-righteous piety was still very much in vogue. Indeed, Benjamin Rush reported that in the colonies, the most common sins were drinking, smoking, dancing, gaming, horse racing, and having too much fun on Sunday. But once people realized that a lightning bolt was not going to strike them dead if they danced or wore makeup or kissed or listened to rock-and-roll or shopped on Sunday, they began to grow more and more tolerant of many other so-called sins until they threw out the proverbial baby with the bath water. So to them, it all became relative as the whole notion of sinfulness itself was called into question. "We are sinking deep in sin." Weeeee!

As I said before, all of this was made worse by certain church groups who railed out at the petty sins, like drinking and chewing tobacco, but who remained amazingly silent about the more serious sins like prejudice, violence, racism, war, oppression of the poor, child abuse, drug abuse, spousal abuse, political corruption, vicious gossip, and hate. Yet these are the real obscenities of every age—including ours. In fact, everything that degrades the human spirit is a reflection of *sin*!

I heard that a certain TV evangelist once announced to his listeners that the topic of his next sermon would be the seven deadly sins. So all week long, the TV station was deluged with phone calls from people who wanted an advance copy of that list. I suppose they did not want to waste another whole week to find out what it was they were missing! Folks, with attitudes like that toward sin, no wonder people did not get too excited about being saved from *it*. No wonder they are confused by the cross and wonder why it was necessary for Jesus to die such a horrible death just to save them from something they had just as soon not be saved from in the first place. After all, they enjoy sin too much to give it up. The French have a saying, "Thank God for the church, it made sin a lot more fun." But Jesus wasn't against having fun. Didn't he provide 160 gallons of wine at the wedding reception? Didn't he say he came to give us joy and abundant living? And yet somehow this notion has gotten around that God sent Jesus to "poop your party" and take away all of your good times. So much for "Good News."

The problem with pleasure is not that it is bad. On the contrary, the problem is that it is often too darn good to be true. In other words, Satan offers a false hope of fulfillment. Pleasure will not make you happy. It will not bring ultimate meaning to your life. You may think it will because it is attractive, seductive, and addictive, but in the end, you will find it gravely disappointing, unfulfilling, and even downright dangerous. It is a trap! Just look at some of the swinging lifestyles of the rich and famous that often end with drug addiction, divorce, suicide, depression, venereal disease—all due to a twisted lifestyle built around empty pleasures! But is pleasure bad? Certainly *not*! God created pleasure, and everything that God created is good—*unless* it is abused and you begin to worship pleasure instead of God. Then pleasure will turn on you like a snake and devour you from within like a stage 4 cancer.

But Jesus did not come to take away your fun. On the contrary, he came to make your life fuller, happier, richer, and more beautiful than ever before! In short, Jesus was "not" against sin because he was narrow-minded and prudish. He was "not" against sin because he was backward, behind the times, or uncool. He was against sin because he knew it hurts both you and others. It corrodes the heart and kills the spirit and enslaves the soul.

One winter, a hunter observed an eagle sitting on a limb beside a waterfall. At any moment, that eagle could have turned loose of that perch and soared up into the blue sky. But it refused to let go. The eagle stayed so long that, eventually, the spray from the falls began to gradually freeze on the giant bird's talons on that icy limb until the bird became trapped and could no longer fly. At first, the eagle had the branch, but then the branch had the eagle. And that majestic creature, created to soar, sadly perished. Sin is like that! The Bible says that the wages of sin is spiritual death. I don't know what holds you captive. It could be a thousand things: jealousy, envy, lust, fear, hate, loneliness, drugs, power, resentment, doubt. But all of us know what it is like to be that eagle on the icy branch—and be trapped by those self-destructive impulses and desires that drag us down, enslave our very souls, and crush our spirits. *That is the real problem with pleasure.*

IN SEARCH OF THE NEW COVENANT

The days are surely coming, says the Lord, when I will make a new covenant with the house of Israel and the house of Judah. It will not be like the covenant that I made with their ancestors when I took them by the hand to bring them out of the land of Egypt—a covenant that they broke, though I was their husband, says the Lord. But this is the covenant that I will make with the house of Israel after those days, says the Lord; I will put my law within them, and I will write it on their hearts; and I will be their God, and they shall be my people. No longer shall they teach one another, or say to each other, "Know the Lord," for they shall all know me, from the least of them to the greatest, says the Lord; for I will forgive their iniquity, and remember their sin no more.

—Jeremiah 31:31–34

I USED TO HAVE an aunt named Grace, so when our parents would say "Say grace," we would reply, "Grace ain't here." Those are about the only times I can recall hearing the word grace mentioned. It certainly never made an impression. Why wasn't I told as a boy about grace and the strange forgetfulness of God? It turns out that God can even erase those bad things I did, right out of his big black book. I had hope after all! Actually, the absence of an emphasis on grace is only one reason why I believe that the most serious cause for division in the family of God is legalism. While I was a part-time student pastor at Centenary United Methodist Church in Macon, Georgia, a Jewish rabbi came and spoke to our congregation on Judaism. After the meeting, I overheard two men talking and one said to the other in amazement, "I can't believe it, he actually believes the same things we do." And do you know what, he was right. The fact of the matter is that while he regarded himself as a Christian, his religion was so steeped in Old Testament Jewish legalism that for all intents and purposes, he and the rabbi were very much on the same page. In fact, I recall that at almost every evening service, the two hymns most frequently requested at that church were "Yield Not to Temptation" and "Trust and Obey." Now don't get me wrong, those are fine old hymns, but their main emphasis was on the *law* and not grace. So in effect, that gentleman from Georgia had abandoned the grace and freedom of the New Testament and had submitted himself again to the yoke and tyranny of Mosaic Law.

By law, the Hebrews meant the first five books of the Bible and everything in them. It was called the Torah or Pentateuch. Indeed, that same narrow-minded emphasis on law, gave the apostle Paul fits among the Christians in Galatia. People, like the men from Macon, who could not distinguish the Old Covenant from the New Covenant or separate the legalism of Judaism from the liberation of Jesus. I know, for a fact, that racism flourished in that old church. They even passed a resolution that if a black person entered their sanctuary, he or she would be permitted to stay as long as that person was sincere! Of course, they were never able to explain how they would determine sincerity. My point is that sin was reduced to breaking rules instead of ruining lives. The message was "Don't drink, don't smoke, don't cuss, don't chew, or burn in hell if you do."

But John said, "The law was given through Moses, but grace and truth came through Jesus Christ!" So what exactly does John mean? In other words, "What was the matter with Moses?" After all, wasn't he a pretty remarkable guy—the leader of his people, the giver of the law, an oracle for God? To make matters worse, the name *Moses* means not only "Moses," the man, but also "Moses," the five books, the "Law of Moses." So while some people still think that the law refers to the Ten Commandments, in reality, it refers to every rule in the Torah.

So what was the matter with Moses? Well, for one thing, while Abraham lived by faith, Moses introduced law. But the problem was not the law itself; the problem was legalism (the same legalism Jesus confronted the Pharisees with). Paul later faced it from the Jerusalem council. The saints faced it in the Inquisition. Martin Luther faced it from an angry pope. In America, it came across the sea as Puritanism and later evolved into extreme fundamentalism.

I heard a story once about a woman who went to UPS to mail a large family Bible to her son. "Ma'am," said the clerk, "is there anything in this package that is breakable?"

"Well, yes," she said, "as a matter of fact there is. It is chocked full of commandments, and they are very breakable."

Nine times out of ten, when I ask someone what sin is, they will reply, "disobeying God's laws," even though the one thing that the apostle Paul struggled against in all of his letters was "the law." Was circumcision necessary? Was eating pork a sin? What Paul tried to tell us was that God is not as concerned about broken regulations as much as broken hearts, broken relationships and broken promises. Therefore, our main concern should not be about broken rules but broken souls and fractured spirits. The real sin that worried Jesus was not the violation of some statute but a sickness of soul unto spiritual death.

No wonder the apostle Paul warned the Galatians, "We ourselves are Jews by birth and not Gentile sinners; yet we know that a person is justified, not by the works of the law but through faith in Jesus Christ. And not by doing the works of the law, because no one will be justified by the works of the law . . . For through the law I died to the law, so that I might live to God. I have been crucified with Christ; and it is no longer I who live, but it is Christ who lives in me. And the life I now live in the flesh, I live by faith in the Son of God, who loved me and gave himself for me. I do not nullify the grace of God; *for if justification comes through the law, then Christ died for nothing* (Galatians 2:15-16, 19-21).

Paul said the law actually put bad ideas in his head—to be told not to covet made him covet all the more. Have you ever heard of the "rule of paradoxical effect"? It states that there is always a danger of your becoming that which you most passionately despise. For example, consider the case of Eric Rudolph, who hated abortion so much that he blew up people and abortion clinics in protest. Then there is the man who hated child pornography so much that he kept collecting hundreds of examples to show everybody just how bad that filth really was. Perhaps that is what the apostle Paul meant when he said, "The law came in to increase the trespass, but where sin increased, grace abounded all the more."

In other words, the law does not always make us better, sometimes it simply reminds us of how far from the mark we are, and the higher the climb up the ladder, the further the fall. So sometimes, rather than making us better, all the law does is make us despair, as we simply stop trying and give up on ourselves. Kierkegaard called that the sin of despairing over sin. But Martin Luther said, "Sin boldly but, more boldly still, believe"—that is to say live by grace, for even when you fail, God is still with you to pick you up. That's another problem with legalism—intolerance of those who stumble. Jesus became frustrated with the Pharisees because they nitpicked the law to death, dwelling on petty rules and regulations like healing on the Sabbath but ignoring injustice and the giving of alms to the poor. "You strain at gnats and swallow camels," he said (Matthew 23:24).

I once knew a reformed drunk in Macon, Georgia, who "got religion" and "got on the wagon." After that, she had zero tolerance for anybody who drank anything. In fact, she would go back to the same jail where she used to be an inmate herself for drunkenness and demand that those "no-good bums" straighten up and sober up or burn in hell! In fact, she became so intolerant and judgmental that some of her friends said she was actually a much nicer person when she used to be a drunk.

One day the Pharisees approached Jesus with a trick question (Mark 10:2 ff). "Is it lawful for a man to divorce his wife?" they inquired. Jesus answered them, "What did Moses command you?" Notice he did not ask them "What did God command?" but Moses. They said, "Moses allowed a man to write a certificate of dismissal and to divorce her." But Jesus said to them, "Because of your hardness of heart, he (Moses) wrote this commandment for you. But from the beginning of creation, 'God made them male and female. (Notice the distinction.) For this reason, a man shall leave his father and mother and be joined to his wife, and the two shall become one flesh.' Therefore, what God has joined together, let no 'man' (meaning Moses) separate" (Matthew 19:6). The two words in parentheses are mine.

Again, to correct Moses, Jesus said, "You have heard it said of old, an eye for an eye, but I say unto you . . ." Actually, Moses went even further in Exodus and Deuteronomy, saying, "A life for a life, a hand for a hand, and a foot for a foot!" So my question is if some argue the Holy Bible is inerrant, then why did our Lord and Master have to fix it? I'll tell you why—because until the coming of Jesus, the revelation of the Bible was fragmented, imperfect, and incomplete. Only Jesus put all of the pieces of the puzzle together so that all was fulfilled in him. For example, listen to the opening verses of Hebrews, "Long ago God spoke to our ancestors, in many and various ways by the prophets, but in these last days he has spoken to us by a Son, whom he appointed heir of all things, through whom he also created the world" (Hebrews 1:1–2). "For the whole law is summed up_in a single commandment, 'You shall love your neighbor as yourself'" (Galatians 5:14).

So to those who believe that God dictated every word of the Bible to human drones like Moses, I ask, "Why would Jesus feel the need to correct Moses?" For example, in one sentence, Jesus erased all of the rigid dietary laws of the Old Testament when he said, "It's not what goes into a man that defiles him, but what comes out of the man." In another sentence, he erased the rigid Sabbath rules: "The Sabbath was made for man, not man for the Sabbath." On a trip to Israel some years ago, I noticed that on Saturday, no planes flew and all elevators stopped on each and every floor because pushing a button might be construed as work!

Now think, aren't you glad we have gone beyond Mosaic Law? Aren't you glad that instead we have Jesus and his grace? Aren't you glad that you don't have to slaughter bulls and sheep for sacrifice—as Moses commanded? Aren't you glad that women are no longer declared unclean just because God created a biological function? (Leviticus 12:1–8) Aren't you glad that incorrigible children and unfaithful women are no longer stoned to death as Moses commanded? (Leviticus 20:10) Aren't you glad that fathers can no longer turn over their incorrigible children to be stoned to death as Moses allowed? (Deuteronomy 21:18–21) Aren't you glad that slavery is no longer legal as Moses declared in Leviticus 25? Aren't you glad that you will not be put to death for mowing your grass on Saturday as Moses commanded? (Exodus 35:2) Aren't you glad that children can no longer be executed for talking back to their parents as Moses ordered? Aren't you glad that girls are no longer considered inferior to boys as Moses suggested? (Leviticus 12) Aren't you glad that it is no longer illegal to eat oysters, lobster, shrimp and, barbecued pork as Moses commanded? (Deuteronomy 14:3–9) And aren't you glad that all people are welcome in God's house, which Moses forbade? (Deuteronomy 23:1–3) And aren't you glad that we no longer utterly destroy our enemies—men, women, children, and pets—as Moses ordained? (Deuteronomy 7) Aren't you glad we now live by grace and not by law? I certainly am.

"Yes," we respond, "but what will it cost me?"

"Nothing," says Jesus. "I have already paid the price!"

This is why Paul says to us, "If we are justified by obeying the law, then Christ died for a purpose. I do not nullify the grace of God. A man is not justified by works of the law but through faith in Christ."

By the way, do you know what the word "justification" literally means? It means "to be put right," that is to be restored to a right relationship with God. This new relationship with God is the cornerstone of the Gospel— not rules and regulations! So thanks be to God, we are not bound by the law. That is why Saint Augustine could say, "Love God and do as you please." Because if you truly love God, then you will freely want to do what is pleasing to God—not because you have to, not because of obligation or duty, *but* because you want to simply out of love and eternal gratitude. So thanks be to God for grace and for the strange forgetfulness of God!

> **Then he took a cup, and after giving thanks, he gave it to them, saying, "Drink from it, all of you; for this is my blood of the (new) covenant (testament) which was poured out for many for the forgiveness of sins."**
> **—Matthew 26:27–28**

THE FLIGHT HOME

Heard over the speaker system as passenger enters pulling luggage: May I have your attention, please? All Celestial Airlines passengers at Pearly Gate no. 7 for angelic flight no. 144 to the Heavenly Realms must have your identification available and your baggage ready for inspection. Do not accept any items from unknown people. Please report any unattended luggage or suspicious behavior. Control your own carry-on bags at all times. All bags are subject to search. Passengers are invited to board at this time. Please be ready to pass through our final inspection station as soon as possible. Expect some delays. Rows A and B may begin boarding now.

Peter: Hello, my name is Simon Peter. I am here for your final screening to make sure everything is in order? Are you ready to pass over into Paradise?

Passenger: Of course, you silly man. Just check your roster, I know I have already earned my wings!

Peter: Excellent, sir, that means that you have already laid up for yourself treasures in heaven just as you were commanded. However, for the purpose of verification, security clearance requires that I find at least five thousand of such credits in your carry-on bag before you may enter. Do you have any treasures of eternal value that you wish now to declare?

Passenger: Certainly. I have lots of good stuff. Why, I have been an angel. For one thing, I had very good habits. I did not curse or drink in excess or smoke or do drugs. I washed my hands and brushed regularly and always said grace before meals. In fact, I prayed quite well and often received compliments for my efforts.

Peter: You really need to work on that "humility" thing. But that will be one credit!

Passenger: Good heavens! Only one credit for all of that? But wait, there's more. I was married to the same woman for over forty years, and I never cheated on her once—except perhaps in my heart! (Winks to audience) See, here is my ring! (Passenger proudly waves wedding band in Peter's face) That's what I'm talking about!

Peter: Good for you, for doing your duty as you promised you would, one credit!

Passenger: Wait one minute! I attended church and Sunday school all of my life. Here's my perfect attendance pin. I'll bet that counts for something!

Peter: Impressive. On behalf of God and the holy angels, I wish to thank you for the honor of your visits. That will be another point for you.

Passenger: Hold on! I also tithed all of my income (except capital gains and offshore accounts, of course). Here is my pledge card, see!

Peter: Yes, indeed. That is certainly worth another point. Congratulations!

Passenger: Only one credit for that? How about my help on a mission work team (pulls out a stack of photos) and Habitat for Humanity (shows tee shirt).

Peter: That's definitely another point for you. So far, you have five credits out of five thousand!

Passenger: Jesus Christ! I am in serious trouble here! God, help me. At this rate, I don't stand a chance. I'm not going to make it, am I? Lord, have mercy!

Peter: Well, why didn't you say so in the first place? If you call on the name of the Lord Jesus Christ and the mercy of God, then your ticket is prepaid. (Stamps ticket) Here is your first-class saved-by-grace flight pass! Welcome aboard, my friend, and have a heavenly flight!

NOT THE END BUT A NEW BEGINNING

Enough said—grace is what separates Jesus from Moses, and the difference is heavenly.

NOW THAT IS WHAT I CALL A CHURCH

> *Now in the church at Antioch there were prophets and teachers; Barnabas, Simeon who was called Niger, Lucius of Cyrene, Manaen a member of the court of Herod the ruler, and Saul. While they were worshiping the Lord and fasting, the Holy Spirit said, "Set apart for me Barnabas and Saul for the work to which I have called them." Then after fasting and praying they laid their hands on them and sent them off.*
>
> —Acts 13:1–3

WHEN JIM COLLINS wrote his famous book *Good To Great*, about how "good" enterprises can became "great" enterprises, he could have been talking about a little church in first-century Syria. Mr. Collins saw three principles that lead to greatness:

Rule no. 1: Get the right people on the bus—motivated, disciplined, dedicated, driven, positive, honest, humble, selfless, "servant leaders" with strong values.

Rule no. 2: Be a hedgehog. Simplify! Don't meander like foxes. Hedgehogs don't run around in circles; they focus on one great passion and then pursue it doggedly. What can we do best? What is our passion? What drives us?

Rule no. 3: The Flywheel effect: Turn the flywheel slowly—let it gradually build momentum. No flashy programs. No time lines. No hoopla. No campaigns. The magic of momentum will authenticate itself.

With those three Collins concepts in mind, I would like to tell you the amazing story of how a tiny outpost in Syria, in the pagan port of Antioch, gradually outgrew Jerusalem as the epicenter of the Christian movement. Honestly, who would have ever suspected Antioch—the head of Apollo worship where hedonism, debauchery, and temple prostitutes abounded? But in this bustling prosperous place, a group of dedicated Christians with the "right stuff" set off a revolution that changed the world. No, it wasn't any of the twelve apostles that got on the bus at Antioch but Luke the Gospel writer, Paul the self-proclaimed apostle, Mark, Barnabas, Silas, and others. But their "hedgehog" focus was on the great commission of Jesus—to go into all the world and preach the Gospel. And as they stayed on point, slowly, the flywheel began to spin until the whole world was turned upside down by its force.

Luke, apparently being a member of that church, tells its story in the book of the Acts. Antioch was the third largest city in the Greco-Roman world located in what is today Turkey. It was a cultural melting pot where people of different nations and religions rubbed elbows with one another daily, providing a rich cosmopolitan atmosphere for the exchange of ideas. As a result, there arose a large colony of Greek-speaking converts to Judaism in Antioch—former pagans—who were evidently attracted to the idea of one God and high values over the loose morals of paganism. So at Pentecost, some of those very same Greek-speaking Jewish proselytes were still visiting as pilgrims to Jerusalem. That is how they heard Peter preach his famous sermon. Among them were Lucius of Cyrene (North Africa), Nicholas of Antioch, and Simeon who was called Niger (black). By the way, some scholars suggest that this "prophet and teacher" at the Antioch church, may well have been the very same black "Simon" of Cyrene (Ethiopia) who carried the cross for Jesus to Calvary.

At any rate, when the altar call was given, those three were among the three thousand souls to come forward and accept Jesus Christ as Lord and Savior. Shortly thereafter, Lucius, or Luke as we know him, tells us that a controversy arose between these new Greek-speaking foreigners and native Jerusalem Christians. The Greek proselytes complained that their people were being neglected in the daily distribution (*koinonia*) of food and funds to the poor and the needy—blatant discrimination! So the apostles astutely put some of those very same Greek-speaking Christians in charge of the whole project. I call that good diplomacy.

They appointed seven young Greek-speaking men, including Stephen, Phillip, and Nicholas of Antioch, to be "deacons" (servants) in the church. But these young men with Greek names were an energetic and ambitious bunch who wanted to do more than run the food pantry or wait upon tables. They wanted to proclaim God's word as well. So in addition to running the soup kitchen, they also began to lead prayer meetings and preach. Eventually, such a great revival broke out that even a few Jewish priests were converted to the faith. How about that for effective evangelism?

Unfortunately, however, success breeds jealousy and jealousy breeds opposition. And so a counterassault was mounted by the Jewish authorities to nix this great awakening in the bud. That is how the deacon Stephen became the first Christian martyr. But didn't he give a fine account of himself, dying with dignity, praying like his master did before him, for the forgiveness of those who stoned him to death as he shared a vision of his Risen Lord coming to meet him on clouds of glory, to take him home? Among those who witnessed that tragic death was a zealous Pharisee named Saul of Tarsus. Gleefully, he held the coats of the mob as they murdered Stephen with stones. Saul and the other Pharisees eventually succeeded in driving most of the foreign Greek-speaking Christians out of Jerusalem. Consequently, they scattered everywhere, fleeing for their lives. Phillip went to Samaria and founded a church there, and apparently, Nicholas, Luke, and Simeon returned to Antioch to start a church there. Meanwhile, Saul of Tarsus was deeply impressed by the great faith of those brave Christian martyrs, and his inner struggle with his own conscience finally came to a climax with a great vision on the Damascus Road. You know the story—it was a vision so powerful that it left him hysterically blind for days and drove him into spiritual contemplation in seclusion.

It was during that brooding time that God spoke to a disciple named Ananias and told him to seek out Saul of Tarsus and restore his sight. "But, Lord," Ananias said, "I know this man is evil, he murdered the saints in Jerusalem!"

But God said, "He is a chosen instrument of mine to carry my name to the Gentiles, to the kings, and to the sons of Israel."

So Ananias found Saul, and he laid his hands upon him, baptized him in the name of Jesus, and restored his sight. Now Saul went back to Jerusalem, and he wanted to tell everybody about his experience! He asked the disciples for permission to preach to the Gentiles. But the disciples were suspicious of this Christian killer and sent him packing back to Tarsus. No deal, Saul! We don't want you, and we don't trust you.

Meanwhile, news reached Jerusalem that Gentiles were already being admitted to the church in Antioch without having to first become Jews! Shocking! Dreadful! Remember, the apostles still considered themselves to be Jews. So they sent Barnabas as a troubleshooter to clear up the whole mess. Ironically, the name Barnabas means "son of encouragement"—not discouragement—so he was delighted with what he found. Instead of chastising the Jewish Christians at Antioch for taking in non-Jewish converts, Barnabas actually encouraged them to do so! In fact, he remembered Saul and how Saul had told the leaders in Jerusalem about his divine call to convert Gentiles. So Barnabas went up to Tarsus, found Saul, and took him to Antioch. Besides, it was time for Saul to come out of the prayer closet, anyway, before he turned into another one of those isolated religious hermits. So now the right men were on the bus, and the stage was set for the creation of the most amazing and progressive churches in history!

No church of any size, in any age, has ever had a greater vision than did that little outpost congregation at Antioch. Those bold resident aliens had established a beachhead right in the middle of pagan territory! In fact, all Barnabas had to do was bring Saul to them, and these Spirit-filled believers at Antioch charged Saul's batteries, set him on fire for the Lord, and then turned him loose into service. You see, unlike the leaders in Jerusalem, these believers in Antioch had no trouble accepting Saul as a changed man because they had been reborn into new creatures themselves! So they embraced Saul warmly into their fellowship and celebrated his new life by christening him with a new name, "Paul the Apostle of Christ." And it was this same loving congregation that collected the resources and the support necessary to send Paul and Barnabas out as missionaries to tackle the known world with the good news of Christ.

Now if you wonder how one small congregation could accomplish so much, I offer these suggestions: First, it was a compassionate and caring church—a church with heart where Saul, a persecutor of

Christians, could be loved, forgiven, and transformed into an apostle. Furthermore, when a severe famine broke out in Jerusalem, who was the first to take up a collection in their behalf? The Gentile-turned-Christians in Antioch. Surely, they could have ignored the plight of their Jerusalem brothers and sisters who had already rejected them, but because of their love, they reached deep into their pockets and took up a love offering anyway. No wonder the followers of Jesus were first called Christians of Antioch.

Second, the church was led by a committed and prayerful laity under the direction of the Holy Spirit. Luke tells us in the book of the Acts that as they were worshiping the Lord and fasting, the Holy Spirit led them into action. Offering God your praise is cheap, but being obedient do his will—that takes real commitment, dedication, and discipleship. The church at Antioch was the first church to be founded, controlled, and led entirely by the laity. In other words, at Antioch, the people didn't wait around for the apostles or the church hierarchy to tell them what to do. They did not have to be pushed or prodded into service; they took the initiative. They did it on their own, and the flywheel began to turn. Indeed, it was the laity at Antioch who kept pushing and prodding the leaders to keep up! They considered everyone to be a minister. So they trained and persuaded Paul, Barnabas, Silas, John, Mark, and Luke to become world evangelists and missionaries.

Third, it was an open, inclusive, and classless church, as the believers at Antioch boldly followed the Spirit and the dictates of their own conscience to let everybody on the bus—even non-Jews without the prerequisite that they first became Jews. Let me remind you that over the temple door in Jerusalem, there was a sign that read, "Let no Gentile pass this place on pain of death." Yet those Spirit-filled Gentile-turned-Christians were so changed and charged by the love of Christ that they became the first congregation to truly be "a house of prayer for all nations." At any rate, Antioch church was an inclusive church, a classless church, where slaves and aristocrats, Jews and Gentiles, could worship side by side. Can you imagine the social stir this must have caused in Jerusalem? The truth is that, throughout history, the Jewish people have been a very exclusive and intolerant lot, hating foreigners and Gentiles with a passion.

Finally, this was a hedgehog church with a clear and simple vision for open-hearted evangelism centered in the name of the Lord Jesus Christ.

So we Gentile Americans owe our Christianity to a small group of Greeks, Syrians, and North Africans, who, without the apostles' permission or approval, stumbled into tolerance and universality. Thanks be to God. They were not only interested in their own community. They had global concerns! I ask you, what would have happened if the church at Antioch had said, "We believe missions should begin at home. So first let's convert all the sinners here in Antioch, and then we'll take on the world"? Paul would have made no journeys, and we would all be pagans.

He who has ears let him hear what the Spirit says to the churches. My Christian friends, as I see it, the primary mission of the church is "outreach" and not "in-reach"! And yet somewhere along the line, the church became a hitching post instead of an outpost, a lounging pad instead of a launching pad. Organizations are always in danger of becoming institutions. Organizations exist to accomplish a goal, while institutions exist mainly to perpetuate themselves, whether they accomplish anything or not. But Jesus did not found an institution; he started a movement. We are the ones who turned it into an institution—not Jesus. All Jesus ever asked us to do was keep the movement moving. No wonder Saint Luke called his book the book of the "Acts" and not the book of the "Meetings."

I too have a dream. I dream of a dynamic church on fire for Jesus Christ with dedicated prayerful members instead of casual tourists. I dream of a vibrant church involved in mission both at home and abroad. I dream of an excited happy church where the fellowship is warm and the worship is enthusiastic. I envision a united church, a loving inclusive church, a church that opens its doors to rich and poor, saints and sinners, saved and lost, all races and nationalities. I see a compassionate committed church, a caring church, a redeeming church, a church that seeks out not only the successful but also the disenfranchised and unloved. I see a self-giving church, a self-sacrificing church, a servant church—full of willing workers who gladly volunteer to serve others before they are begged! I see a church where a charging laity finally take charge and drag the minister along just so that he can keep up. I see a team-building church, a cooperative church, an excited church where everyone feels welcome on the same bus. I see an accepting assimilating church where each person feels involved and has ownership in its ministries, its mission, and its fellowship.

Our job is not to be selective so that only the "right people" get on the bus; rather, our job is to gather all people (even those we do not like) on God's bus! So let's pack this bus in his name. Let's focus on clear and common goals. Let's reach out and join hands as one family of faith. And let's work in beautiful harmony together in spite of our differences. If we can do that, then the church as the Body of Christ, even in our troubled times, can finally leap forward to reach the mark. *With the help of the Holy Spirit, we can move from great to greater!*

THE CHURCH AS RELATIONSHIPS

Beloved, let us love one another, because love is from God; everyone who loves is born of God and knows God. Whoever does not love does not know God, for God is love. God's love was revealed among us in this way: God sent his only Son into the world so that we might live through him. In this is love, not that we loved God but that he loved us and sent his Son to be the atoning sacrifice for our sins. Beloved, since God loved us so much, we also ought to love one another. No one has ever seen God, if we love one another, God lives in us and his love is perfected in us.

—1 John 4:7–12

MORE THAN ANY other letter, 1 John centers the message to the church on "the relationship of love," not just ordinary love but a rare and extraordinary love that God has for us when he gave his only begotten Son. "We know we have passed out of death into life because we love the brethren," he said. The early Christians resurrected an old Greek word for love that had fallen into disuse. They filled it with new meaning and called it agape. Out of that agape love came the church. Then the Christians also decided to coin a new Greek name for the church *koinonia*. The word *koinonia* was to remind them that the church was far more than a Christian institution; it was a caring community!

But of course, we do not read Greek, do we? So we translate the Greek word *koinonia* into English as "fellowship," which falls flat on its proverbial face! Have you ever heard the phrase "It loses something in translation"? Well, that is especially true in this case. Like the word agape, *koinonia* is filled with a lot of meaning. After Pentecost, in the book of the Acts, we are told that, immediately, the disciples began to devote themselves to four things: teaching, Holy Communion, praying, and *koinonia*. But *koinonia* is a complex word with multiple meanings. It implies not only social intercourse but also soul action. It can mean "distribution," as in giving food or funds to the poor. Altruism, charity, benevolence, benefaction, caring—all are implied in *koinonia*. It also implies involvement, commitment, group participation, cooperation, partnership, community, communion, and communication—in short, "bearing fruit." So *koinonia* is what it means to be Christian. It is so much more than a coffee-and-donuts kind of word. It's a let's-roll-up-our-sleeves-and-work-together-for-good kind of word.

Remember how, after the love feast, the deacons gathered up the leftovers and made a "distribution" or *koinonia* to the poor, the widows, and orphans? How sad then that we take this rich word *koinonia* and call it fellowship? How dull! There is, however, an interesting story behind that old Anglo-Saxon word "fellowship." Originally, it was pronounced fee-lo-ship because *fee* meant cow. It was a custom in ancient Britain that when neighbors really trusted one another, they would tear down the stone walls between them to make openings so that their cattle could mingle freely and graze where they wanted. As Robert Frost said, "Something there is that does not love a wall!" So "fee-lo-ship" came to mean cooperation among friendly neighbors who chose to take down their fences and live in trust and harmony together. "But now, in Christ Jesus you who were far off have been brought near . . . in his flesh he has broken down the dividing wall, that is, the hostility between us" (Ephesians 2:13–14).

No wonder then that one of the most high and holy moments of fellowship with Christ is Holy Communion, or we could call it Holy Koinonia. If there is one place that we should take down the walls and fences that divide us and come together in oneness, fellowship, openness, trust, and love, it is at the table of our Lord, as he prepares a table before us in the presence of our enemies. Indeed, it is no accident that the word "communion" comes from the Latin roots *com unio*, which means "union with." Remember how Jesus prayed in the Garden of Gethsemane that we all be perfectly one? (John 17) "He in us and we in him." So Eucharist is God's fellowship meal, where the people of God come together family-style in a common bond of koinonia and where the walls of disunity come tumbling down like the walls of Jericho.

Unfortunately, in some churches, communion is a cold and somber affair with absolutely no *koinonia* about it. The mood is mournful, formal, and austere like a funeral service. Furthermore, those who are not a part of their elite group are not welcome. They are "walled off."

I am reminded of a Victorian home where the servants, of course, are not allowed to sit at the table and where both host and guests remain prim, proper, and aloof while dressed to the nines for dinner. On the outside, everyone seems so perfectly polite and well mannered, but underneath, there remains an atmosphere of cold indifference and isolation. Everyone is forced to pay strict attention to his or her manners while completely wrapped up in private thoughts. Each seems more concerned about personal appearance and prosperity than one another as they stare hushed at their reflection in the crystal and all is quiet, except for an occasional snub from a child forced to eat spinach before leaving the table.

Some people seem to have adapted that same sort of imagery for the Lord's Supper. Gathering around the feast of the bridegroom for his bride, the church has often become a somber ceremony of formality, performed out of austere obligation and sheer duty because the Lord commanded it. In such cases, there is no real *koinonia*—no real sharing of the Spirit, no community, no fellowship, no love!

On the other hand, there are those who have made Holy Communion resemble a wild high school pep rally or a soup kitchen bread line where people collect bread like everyone is in such a big hurry to get it over with. But Jesus said that whether you play wedding or funeral, "Wisdom is justified by all of her children." In other words, "There is a time to mourn and a time to dance." But in either case, if we as the people of God are to finally to come together, the spiritual glue that will bring this about is *koinonia*.

IT ALL BEGINS WITH CIVILITY

In everything do to others as you would have them do to you;
for this is the law and the prophets.

—Matthew 7:12

WHEN JUDY AND I first got married, all we had to eat on was a hand-me-down set of melamine, so when my ever-observant wife saw a Black Friday ad in the local paper for a set of beautiful blue dishes, she sent me on a crusade.

"It's right on your way to Duke," she said. "You should have no trouble at all, but you need to be there by 6:00 AM to stand a chance to get those dishes at that price."

My name is Wise, like the wise old owl, and daybreak is not my best time of the day. "Why so early?" I protested.

"Because it's an early bird special, silly. The doors open promptly at 7:00 AM."

"Wait," I said. "I thought you said 6:00 AM! Why should I stand around in front of that store for an hour all by myself?"

"Don't worry, dear, you won't be alone," she said, and she was right!

At first, the parking lot was empty, but by the time I got to the door, other cars began to arrive, and soon, there were women everywhere— all women. I followed her exact instructions and stood at the door, determined not to move. I could look through the glass doors and actually see the area where the dishes were.

This will be a piece of cake, I thought. *I don't know why she had to be so melodramatic about it.*

At about ten minutes to seven o'clock, they turned the lights on, and as soon as the lights flashed, a horde of female bodies surged forward, pushing me against the door—from every possible direction at the same time but with no modesty whatsoever. I don't think I have ever smelled so many different kinds of perfume at once.

The man came to unlock the door, and as the door swung open, I felt myself surging forward like a surfer riding a huge wave. *This is ridiculous*, I thought as I tried to turn around, but that didn't work at all. The next thing I knew, I was sitting in the floor. Bam! My head hit the bargain table, and my arm slammed against a cardboard box on the shelf. But there, to my surprise, were the very dishes that Judy sent me after. Gasping for air, I grabbed the dishes like a defensive lineman going after a fumbled football. I sprang to my feet, swinging my elbows like I was holding the lost treasure of the Incas, and smiled with satisfaction. By now, the crowd had dispersed a bit and a long line was already forming at the checkout. Just then, a sweet matronly lady smiled at me and said, "You look like you've about had it, son."

"Yes, ma'am," I said. "But at least I got what I came after—I got these dishes for my wife."

"Aww," she said. "It's a shame you got the uglier pattern, these over here are much prettier."

Of course, I didn't want to get Judy an ugly set, so I laid the box of dishes on the corner of the counter, with my left hand still on the box, and bent over to see where she was pointing on the shelf. Indeed, they were lovely dishes, but they were not the ones on sale. All of a sudden, before I knew what had happened, that dear lady snatched "my dishes" from under my left hand and scampered for the checkout line. My first reaction was to go and grab them back, but how would that look? *This woman was old enough to be my mother*, so who would ever believe that I had them first? I did go to the manager and told him. He said he was sorry, but he only had one set of dishes at that price. That afternoon, after my last class, I returned home empty-handed, a little sadder, but a whole lot wiser—wondering whatever had ever happened to the golden rule!

Being in a big hurry because she is late for work, a stressed-out woman is following right on the bumper of the car in front of her when the light turns yellow. Instead of trying to beat the light, the man in front stops dead, and the tailgating woman behind has to slam on brakes just to avoid a rear-end collision. She is enraged. She yells and screams and toots her horn and flips him off because she knows that if the man up front had just accelerated a bit, they both would have made it through that intersection. Suddenly, there is a tap on her window. It is a police officer, and he orders her to get out of her car. Since she has no driver's license or registration, the officer escorts her to the police station where she is searched, fingerprinted, photographed, and placed in a cell. Later, when her lawyer arrives, the arresting officer apologizes. "I am very sorry for the mistake, ma'am," he says, "but I saw you blowing your horn, cussing up a blue streak, and flipping the guy off. Then I noticed the chrome Jesus fish and your 'Follow Me to Sunday School' bumper sticker, so naturally, I assumed you must be driving a stolen car!"

The problem with humor is that, far too often, it is based on painful truth. This is indeed an apparent decline in courtesy and good manners these days. It may surprise you to know that civility was the only thing that kept the Civil War from ending in a huge bloodbath. You see, the leaders on both sides had been nurtured by the golden rule.

On April 9, 1865, one of Lee's closest advisers suggested that the whole Confederate Army should "scatter like partridges and rabbits" and become guerrilla fighters hiding in the forests and the hills to rain down terror. That was Lincoln's worst fear. But like the gentleman he was, Robert E. Lee said no. Instead, he put on his best uniform and sent a message to General Grant, offering total surrender and peace. Northern newspapers at the time called for blood. They wanted General Lee humiliated, punished, and hanged. But instead, General Grant, guided by Abraham Lincoln's vision of a magnanimous peace, set Lee and his staff free—after receiving Lee's promise never to take up arms again. Later, General Lee was to remark, "I surrendered as much to Lincoln's goodness as to Grant's army." So there was a time in days long passed when courtesy and civility actually mattered a lot.

But what happened? I wonder what those genteel giants from the past would think of our brash, me-centered, rude culture today. When I was a kid, we had to recite the golden rule in public school: "Whatever you wish that men would do to you, do so to them, for this is the law of the prophets. Enter by the narrow gate, for the gate is wide and the way is easy, that leads to destruction and those who find it are many. But the gate is narrow and the way is hard that leads to life and those who find it are few."

Do you remember the old song "School days, school days, dear old golden rule days, reading and 'riting and 'rithmetic taught to the tune of a hickory stick"? Well, gone is the hickory stick, gone is the golden rule, and Johnny isn't doing too well on his reading, writing, and arithmetic either!

In short, we have misplaced those essential basic values and acts of common courtesy and kindness that holds the fabric of society together, and in their place, we have crudeness, rudeness, short tempers, road rage, violence, poor manners, and plain old corruption. We have returned to the days of the judges in Old Testament times, when everyone did what was pleasing in his own eyes! But don't take my word for it, just look around you and weep. Today, apparently, many discourteous people think they are better than anyone else. They must! You can see it as cars joust rudely for spaces in parking lots or as one driver, who is obviously better than anyone else, parks diagonally in the last two spaces to keep his car from being "dinged." You can see it on our highways where some inconsiderate driver passes you like Road Runner and then pulls back in front of you, slows down, and makes a right turn. Courtesy and civility have vanished from our sight like the smiling Cheshire Cat.

Sometime ago, I was on the interstate, and for a mile or two, big flashing arrows and orange signs gave out the warning to "SLOW, LEFT LANE CLOSED AHEAD" and "MERGE RIGHT." So obediently, I slipped over into the right lane. Already, a line of cars had begun to form as the right lane was getting slower and slower until we came to a complete stop. Meanwhile, cars, vans, and eighteen-wheelers continued to fly by in the left lane, ignoring the signs. The end result was that the honest, law-abiding drivers had to sit and wait at the back of the line, while the rude drivers, who ignored the signs, were accommodated one by one at the front. Whatever happened to the golden rule? We pollute our highways with garbage and our airways with trash—not to mention our minds, our ears, and our mouths.

It was not that long ago when the foul language you hear in the media today would not be heard even in bars, not in the presence of women and children and certainly not by women and children. But today a new culture has risen in America, and it is not a pretty sight. We have essentially erased the values, customs, and traditions of the past that held our society together and have been set adrift in a sea of self-indulgence and moral relativism. Gone are the common courtesies that are necessary in a civilized society. For example, today news announcers with differing opinions no longer debate or listen to one another. Instead, they viciously bark and tease and shout one another down—as customs and rules of decency, propriety, and order have been discarded in favor of rude arrogance and blatant brashness.

On another occasion, I was in the supermarket checkout line, and the line was so long that it had to bend into an L shape when, lo and behold, this woman (notice I said woman and not lady) came down the aisle and pushed her cart right into the elbow of that long line and eventually forcing her way into the third space while a long line of us waited behind. She was very careful to ignore all of our intense stares. Whatever happened to the golden rule? The answer is simply this: the golden rule is a religious principle, and the more religion is pushed into the corner of this secular society and the corner of our lives, the less evidence of the golden rule you are likely to see. Thank God I came along before it became necessary in the noble name of inclusiveness to banish religion from the public school system and the golden rule from the curriculum. I understand fully the need to remove Christianity from its lofty throne, but isn't secularism also a kind of religion? It is a real dilemma. I recall the warning of Longfellow, "Morality without religion is only a kind of dead reckoning on a cloudy sea." After all, how can you navigate in the darkness without a point of reference to guide you? So to eliminate all reference to God in education, ethics and morality is like taking away a sailor's compass or blocking out the North Star. You are left to flounder in a dark empty sea of moral relativity. By the way, the golden rule is not really the private possession of Christians. This universal truth is found in almost every major religion, from Judaism to Confucianism, in some form. You could even see it in Kant's nonreligious categorical imperative which roughly states that whatever rule you follow should apply equally to everybody everywhere.

From a religious perspective, there are two major differences between the Christian version of the golden rule and others: First, almost all other versions state what we ought *not* (negative) to do to our neighbor instead of what we ought to do (positive). Second, only Jesus offered himself as the power source to make it work. The power of the golden rule for Christians comes not from the rule itself but from the teacher of the rule (Jesus) and from the teacher's own example. Jesus said, "This is my commandment that you love one another *as I have loved you!*" Again, he prayed, "I made your name known to them, and I will make it known, so that the love with which you have loved me may be in them *and I in them*" (John 17:26).

One day a little boy was being examined by a doctor with a stethoscope. "What is that for?" he asked.

"It is for listening to your heart," she said. "Do you want to hear?"

"My mother always said Jesus was in my heart, and now I hear him knocking."

The gym was crowded to capacity and the noise was deafening. Two high school basketball teams were taking it right down to the wire. The visiting Trojans were leading by one point with thirty seconds left on the clock, and they had possession of the ball. A Trojan shot and missed. The hometown Tigers rebounded and pushed the ball up the court, but the shot bounced off the rim, but suddenly, another player leaped into the air and tapped the ball in. The house rocked. The home crowd went berserk! The roar of the jubilation was deafening. In the frenzy, no one heard the final buzzer.

The son of the Tigers' coach was the person manning the clock, and as the coaches and referees gathered around the score table, the lad looked at his dad and said, "I'm sorry, Dad, but time ran out before the final basket. We lost!"

His dad looked very disappointed at first, but then his face lit up, and he smiled. "That's OK, son. Thanks for making a tough call! You did what you had to do, and I'm very proud of you."

There were a lot of angry and disgruntled home fans that left the gymnasium that night, but two of the losers walked out with heads held high, looking and smiling more like winners—the home team coach and his son. Once again, the golden rule ruled.

One December long ago, my son Patrick said as he came home from school, "We need to buy another present for the Christmas gift exchange."

"But we have already bought a gift for that," his mother said. "You only need one."

"But I have to get one for Jimmy too," Patrick said.

"Why is that?" we asked.

"Because he and I are the only two kids who don't have a gift under the tree, and I don't want him to feel bad."

I don't think I have ever been more proud of Patrick than I was that day. When it came to the golden rule, *he got it!* So we bought a gift for Jimmy—and Patrick and put them both under the tree.

So whatever happened to the golden rule, you ask? I'll tell you what happened to it—NOTHING! It is still there, shining like a beacon before us, calling us to be the righteous neighbors we ought to be. So open your ears and hear Jesus knocking at your heart. He has called you to be a light to the world. So crawl out from under your tubs and shine! When Gen. George Washington was leading the Colonial Army, Mark Anthony Wayne said, "General Washington, sir, lay out the plans and give us the orders and we are prepared to storm the gates of hell for you." Jesus Christ has already showed us the plans and has given the orders. *We call it the golden rule.*

HELL—WHAT IS IT GOOD FOR?

Indeed, God did not send the Son into the world to condemn the world, but in order that the world might be saved through him.
—John 3:17

"PREACHER, DO YOU know how people go to hell?" asked the little boy. The pastor paused to put together—on a child's level—an answer about judgment. Again, the lad repeated impatiently, "I said, do you know how people go to hell?"

"Why don't you tell me?" the minister finally said, trying to be nondirective.

"They go in a helicopter, silly," thus ended the deep discourse on the consequences of sin.

Years ago, there was a nonprescription medical jelly called arnica salve. This petroleum preparation was sold vigorously by door-to-door salesmen as a cure for countless ills. One day a religious zealot painted a message on a small billboard that read "What will you do on judgment day?" Some enterprising salesman painted this message underneath: "Use arnica salve, it's good for burns!"

When I retired, I volunteered to teach an ecumenical Bible study in my new neighborhood. I was excited about the opportunity, and things went very well until we got into a discussion of hell. In order to stimulate the debate, I made the mistake of mentioning a certain minister who had openly questioned why the loving God we know in Jesus would be so cruel and intolerant that he would fry sinners in hell for eternity with no chance for parole. I heard that this one minister boldly preached a sermon on the subject and half of his congregation quit the church.

"But was his concern legitimate?" I asked. "After all, isn't the real purpose of punishment reform and not revenge—or shouldn't it be?"

Jesus said, "It is not the desire of your Heavenly Father that any of his little ones should perish."

I certainly do not know for sure, one way or the other, only God knows, but I do know that according to Peter, Jesus descended into hell to preach to the dead. So wasn't that a chance for parole? Besides, when he said, "Whoever speaks against the Holy Spirit will not be forgiven either in this age or in the age to come," does that mean some sins might eventually be forgiven in the age to come?

"Only God knows the answer," I said. "I don't know nor do you. I am just asking the question."

Well, believe me, I set off a hellfire storm. Some were so defensive and intense in their beliefs about hell and their argument so cocksure that I gave up even trying to continue. I see no point in arguing with people over faith. I suppose teaching something to people who already have all the answers is an exercise in futility. Know-it-alls should always be encouraged to teach themselves, whatever it is that they already know.

When I was a boy, I remember how Dad would sometimes mope around the house for hours, pondering, *"What shall I preach on this Sunday?"* Remember, he was new to the ministry and had no old cold-turkey sermons he could warm up. So Mother would always give him the same answer: "Honey, why don't you preach on hell?"

So one Sunday Dad announced to the congregation, "Next week, my wife will preach, and her subject will be on hell."

All week long, my mother plowed through the Bible and Bible commentaries. The more she studied, the more frustrated she got. Finally, she went to Dad for help.

"I can't find a whole lot of material to work with on hell!" she said. "Where is it?"

"I tried to tell you," Dad said. "Most of the ideas we get about hell come from non-biblical sources like *Paradise Lost* and Dante's *Inferno.* That is why I devote about the same percentage of my sermons to the subject of hell as the Bible does—which is not a whole lot."

I am not trying to be cute or trivialize hell. In a world with so much evil, where the innocent are bombed, raped, robbed, and persecuted, I can certainly understand our deep need for God's justice. The prophet Isaiah promised a time when the mountains of injustice would be brought down, the valleys of despair would be lifted, and the rough places made smooth. I believe that too. I believe that somehow God will balance the books. They certainly do need balancing. But how God does that is God's concern and not mine. It is none of my business. Ironically, the desert people pictured hell as fire because they knew the terror of heat, but the Eskimos pictured hell as ice because they fear the terror of the bitter cold. I prefer, however, to think of hell in relational terms—as the absence of God.

So like sin, hell has a social context, hell is to be cut off and separated from God and alienated from everyone else. It is to be spiritually dead long before your physical death. So as I said before, the real question the Bible addresses is not is there life after death, but is there abundant life before death! The real danger is not losing your soul after you die, the real danger is losing your soul bit by bit until you are little more than an empty shell, and by the time you die, there is no soul left to lose. After all, how can you lose what you have never found? And the more you try to fill that empty void with the things of this world, the more emaciated your soul will become! "What does it profit a man to gain the whole world and forfeit his own soul?" That is why I do not take much stock in death-bed confessions. Heaven is not a reality to put off until just before you croak. What a waste! Heaven is a reality to come to terms with now in the midst of the struggle not just at the end of it. So if we miss God's presence in your life now, one day he may say to you, "Depart from me, I never knew you!" *Who knows, perhaps hell is more of a spiritual condition than real estate.*

DO WE LOOK TO BIOLOGY OR RELATIONSHIPS?

Jesus said to them, "Very truly, I tell you, the Son can do nothing on his own, but only what he sees the Father doing; for whatever the Father does, the Son does likewise. The Father loves the Son and shows him all that he himself is doing; and he will show him greater works than these, so that you will be astonished . . ."

—John 5:19–20

I T IS TIME to stick my neck out a bit and come to the defense of doubters by bringing up a very sensitive subject. I have been faithfully reciting the Apostles Creed since I was four years old and have never had any problem joining the saints of the ages in this historic affirmation. So for years, it never occurred to me that other dedicated Christians would have serious problems with it. But the truth is that while nobody has wanted to talk about it in public over the years, a number of troubled followers have secretly confessed to me serious concerns about the doctrine of the virgin birth. "Do I have to believe that to be a Christian?" they ask. Far too embarrassed, they refuse to admit their doubt out loud because "proper Christians" are not supposed to feel that way. So they often hide their disbelief and shame from fellow Christians, their pastor, and even from their best friends. I prefer to help them rather than condemn them.

Ironically, while most modern Christians have little trouble accepting the humanity of Jesus but struggle with his divinity, most first-century Christians had the opposite problem. They had very little trouble believing that Jesus was divine, but they had a hard time accepting his humanity. Groups such as the Gnostics, for example, never believed in the humanity of Jesus because they regarded all flesh as evil! That is why John wrote, "By this you will know the spirit of God, every spirit that confesses that Jesus Christ has come in the *flesh* is from God" (1 John 4:2).

Strange as it may seem, the birth narratives actually served to challenge the Gnostics as an affirmation of the *physical* humanity of Jesus. You also need to understand that in those days strange stories of mystical births abounded. So in ancient times, the idea of a virgin birth was not that hard for the ancients to accept. For example, Hercules, Osiris, Krishna, Romulus, Dionysus, and Zoroaster (among others) were all said to have been born in a strange and miraculous manner. Indeed, the pagan God Mithra was supposedly born of a virgin on December 25.

Personally, that coincidence does not bother me in the least since the real birth date of Jesus is not recorded in the Bible, anyway, and remains unknown. Regardless, I still love to celebrate our Lord's birth without hesitation every year on December 25. My concern, however, is for those troubled doubters with scientific minds in our modern era. They have serious personal difficulty with the nativity story. To them, it only serves to push them farther and further away from God. In short, they regard the idea of a virgin birth as a stumbling block to their faith rather than a building block. Most of us, of course, have no such qualms. Just think of all of the priceless inspirational carols and sacred hymns about the Virgin Mary that we love to sing every Christmas. Who wants to give all of that up? Not me!

Sadly, however, many well-meaning believers insist that the doctrine of the virgin birth should be the absolute litmus test for salvation. In other words, for them, this affirmation is what separates true believers from nonbelievers. But just because most of us are delighted with the beautiful story of Christmas, does that mean we should use it as a hammer to bash good and faithful followers over the head who are not so comfortable? After all, Jesus never said, "Believe in parthenogenesis and you will be saved." He said, "Believe in me."

Let us also not forget that sex is not inherently evil! Indeed, it was God who invented sex and commanded us to "be fruitful and multiply" (the one commandment we have happily obeyed). But some of these troubled modern Christians have expressed particular concern that an overemphasis on virginity as an absolute virtue has led to some very serious abuses inside the church. (That, however, would make another book in itself.) They also emphasize that the prophesy in Isaiah 7:14 uses the word *almah* in Hebrew which was translated in Greek as "virgin" but literally means "a young woman of marriageable age."

So the question arises: "Is there a way to stop all of the division and bridge this highly controversial theological gap?"

Yes, I believe there is, if we are willing to shift the focus from a biological anomaly to relationships. In that context, most of the differences of opinion will become moot. There is, after all, more than one way to affirm the incarnation and divinity of our Lord. That is why we have four Gospels instead of one. Besides, doesn't the church have room for both strong believers and doubters alike? As the apostle Paul said, "Those parts of the body that seem to be weaker are indispensable" (1 Corinthians 12:22). In other words, "If we are to be an inclusive church, shouldn't the so-called weaker ones also be included?" So as long as we can still profess together a common affirmation that Jesus Christ is Lord, are we not all a part of the Body of Christ? Indeed, one of the most powerful confessions of faith was made by a "doubter" named Thomas as he fell to his knees and cried, "My Lord and my God!" Yet the mystery remains, how could a real human being truly be God and still be a real human being? That is the common conundrum of faith that we all need to address together if we are to call ourselves Christian.

Long ago, in Old Testament times, the author of the book of Job pondered that very God/man mystery. "He (God) is not a mortal as I am that I might answer him, that we could come to trial together. There is no umpire between us, who might lay his hand on us both . . . Then I would speak without fear of him . . ." (Job 9:32–33, 35) In other words, Job's asking, "Is there no one to step between us to judge us both? Is there no arbitrator in heaven to take my side and plead my case?"

For two thousand years, the church has proclaimed that the very "redeemer" Job dreamed of was fulfilled in Jesus. Listen to the words of John in his first letter—almost as if he is writing directly to Job: "If anyone sins, we have an advocate—Jesus Christ the righteous and Christ himself is this means by which our sins are forgiven and not our sins only, but the sins of the whole world" (1 John 2:1–2).

So just imagine poor Job when he arrives in heaven. He is scared to death as he stands before the awesome judgment seat of Almighty God as a defendant. His knees shake and quiver before the fiery throne when suddenly Job is aware of someone else standing by his side. He turns to look. It is an attorney for the defense appointed by the court to plead his case—pro bono. The attorney's name is Jesus Christ the Righteous—the judge's own Son. *But we still have our dilemma—how could a man be God?*

From the very beginning, the church has proclaimed that our redeemer, mediator, and savior would have to be at the same time "fully God and fully man," representing the best of humanity to God and the best of God to humanity, no matter how paradoxical that may sound. But how could he be fully man without sacrificing his divinity or fully God without sacrificing his humanity? The apostle Paul tries to answer that question by seeing the Risen Christ as highly exulted and transformed to a higher level after his resurrection (Philippians 2:9), but the church has also taught the doctrine that Jesus did not just become God when he rose, but somehow, he was God already! "And the Word became flesh and dwelt among us." But how could a man be God? How could he join holiness and humanity—the finite and the infinite?

When Leo Tolstoy was a boy, he used to love to play with the poor serfs behind the big mansion where he lived. Often he even ate with them in their little cottages. Until one day one of them said to him, "You eat in our house, you play our games, but you can never really be one of us because you can always go back up to the big house anytime you wish, and we cannot. So you will always remain different from us."

The question is, can Jesus really be one of us and still be God? That is why one of the ancient heresies of the Christian church was the belief that since Jesus was divine, he could not really be human. Instead, as God's Son, he was supernatural. Therefore, he couldn't suffer like you and I suffer because he came from the big house.

On the contrary, from the beginning, the church has rejected that idea. Jesus was one of us. He had a temper; he was afraid; he cried real tears; he experienced hunger, thirst, temptation, and intense pain; he felt loneliness and grief. He was a mortal human being. Don't you see, if Jesus was not in every way a complete human being with all the frailty that our fool flesh is heir to, then he could not truly be our mediator! In other words, he was not like a carton of Half & Half. He was not like Hercules, half God and half man. Nor was he an alien from outer space like Superman. Of course, some groups refused to accept this. As I said before, the Gnostics absolutely rejected the idea of the incarnation. They regarded Jesus as some kind of phantom spirit that only appeared to be human. That is why John said "The Word became flesh." In fact, the shocking Greek word that John used actually means "meat." Indeed, that is precisely why we take Holy Communion and affirm the virgin birth. It is to remember he was flesh and blood and to challenge the ancient heresy that denied the physical humanity of Jesus. As the book of Hebrews put it, "He had to be made like his brethren in every respect" (Hebrews 2:7).

So throughout the history of the church, one of the paradoxes of the faith has been this dual nature of Christ. "For this we stone you," the Pharisees said, "that you being a man make yourself equal with God" (John 10:33). I, for one, can sympathize with how the conservative Pharisees felt. After all, for centuries, they had been taught to believe in only one God—"Thou shalt have no other gods before me." So how could a man be God? Two Gospel writers said it was by the unique nature of his physical birth, but my question is, *how did some of those other guys answer this conundrum?*

Did you know that the Muslim Koran reveres Jesus, quotes him extensively, and teaches that Jesus was born of a "virgin"? Yet not one single true Muslim has ever believed that Jesus is or was divine. So that affirmation alone proves nothing at all, at least not to the people of Islam. The point is that, since God is an infinite nonphysical being, is the manner of Christ's physical conception, a sufficient source to explain his divinity? In short, should we not also consider the divine nature of Jesus in the spiritual realm as well? After all, that is what almost every other New Testament writer has done. What I mean is that parthenogenesis is briefly mentioned in only two places in the entire New Testament (Matthew and Luke). Neither Paul nor Mark nor John nor Peter nor anyone else in the entire New Testament ever said one word about it! Yet every New Testament writer has boldly affirmed the lordship of Jesus. So my question is, how did those other New Testament writers manage to arrive at the same God/man conclusion, apart from biology? *I believe the answer is through relationships.*

For example, John, who makes no mention of Bethlehem and yet he has the most exalted Christology of any Gospel writer. "These things were written that you may believe that Jesus is the Messiah, the Son of God, and that believing you may have life in his name" (John 20:31). John believed that all miracles are supposed to be signs to make it easier—not harder—for us to believe in Jesus. In other words, signs and wonders are not supposed to push people away from faith but rather toward it. Signs are to encourage faith and not to be used as a weapon for punishing nonbelievers. Miracles are supposed to pull us all together into one body. So John, in his Gospel, points us to a spiritual (nonphysical) basis for the divinity of the man Jesus.

First of all, like Paul and the writer of Hebrews, John sees the divinity of Jesus as predating Bethlehem. "In the beginning was the Word, the Word was with God, and the Word was God . . . all things were made through him . . ." (John 1:1–3) That is to say the divine part of Jesus was already "with God" in a relationship that goes back before time. No wonder Jesus said, "Before Abraham was, I Am" (John 8:58). Indeed, he is the agent in creation (John 1:3). Paul, in his letters (our earliest writings), echoed that same concept of the preexistent Jesus: "For in him all things were created . . . He is before all things, and in him all things are held together" (Colossians 1:16–17).

Second, John sees the divinity of Jesus in the unique relationship that existed between the human Son and the Heavenly Father. So once again, the answer is found in relationships. As a physical man, Jesus was as weak as other men. Oh, he had special gifts. He had charisma, talent, charm, great wisdom, a keen spiritual insight, and heightened potential. He was a great orator, and the people heard him gladly, but his personal relationship with God was so deep, so richly intense, and so passionate that God worked directly through him. Jesus acted like God's spiritual conduit to heal the sick and to accomplish great wonders.

Folks, I'm not making this up, that is precisely how Jesus, in the book of John, described himself—from his own experience! "I am in the Father, and the Father in me," he said. "The words that I say to you, I do not speak on my own authority, but the Father in me, does his works" (John 14:10). Isn't it ironic that while most of us have lived our lives as if we needed no one but ourselves and reject dependence in favor of independence, taking great pride in our own personal accomplishments, Jesus, on the other hand, does not? Instead, the man from God said, "I can do nothing of my own authority, as I hear, I judge and my judgment is just, because I seek not my own will, but the will of him who sent me" (John 5:30). "Why do you call me good, no one is good but the Father" (Mark 10:18). "If I bear witness to myself, then my testimony is not true" (John 5:31).

Well, how about that? Talk about humility. Jesus is saying that as a human being, he takes no credit for his accomplishments whatsoever. He claims nothing for himself and everything for God! "Jesus said to them, 'Truly, truly, I say to you, the Son can do nothing of his own accord, but only what he sees the Father doing; for whatever he does, that the Son does likewise. For the Father loves the Son, and shows him all that he himself is doing; and greater works than these will he show him, that you may marvel.'" (John 5:19–20) Let me tell you what I think he meant by that: To some extent, all of you receive your personhood from relationships with those people who are closest to you, such as family, guardians, your mate, your mentor, or your friends.

Remember the story about the boy who was raised in a dark closet and fed through a slot in the door. He was like a wild animal. He never really became human because it is our relationships with other human beings that make us who we are as people. Only children who are loved are able to love. How else would a child know what love is? Just as a child is an extension of his or her parents' love, so Jesus became an extension of his Heavenly Father's love. It is as if somehow Jesus connected in a deep and personal way with the very glue of the universe. And in that divine-human encounter, this lowly carpenter was transformed and filled with the fullness of God until he took on the very personality of God. Through the person of Jesus, our loving, compassionate Creator became flesh and dwelt among us, as the will of Jesus was no longer his own. Jesus still had a will, but he freely gave it over to God! He was not, however, like a puppet or a slave, but instead, he experienced the very highest kind of freedom—the freedom to give himself away.

"Nevertheless, not my will, but thine be done," he prayed. "The Father loves me," Jesus said, "because I am willing to give up my life, in order that I might receive it back again. No one takes my life away from me; I give it up of my own free will" (John 10:18). Again he said, "The world must know that I love the Father. That is why I do everything as he commands me." So Jesus freely yielded to the power of God deep within himself and allowed himself to be molded and moved by God's own spirit. So as God loved, Jesus loved, and as God wept for the world, Jesus wept, and as God forgave, Jesus forgave, and as God reached out to draw us to himself, Jesus reached out at Calvary. In other words, Jesus was completely filled with the fullness of God's presence and love.

Remember, love cannot be measured, captured, or quantified. If a woman has a child, she does not divide her love in half between her husband and her new baby. Each one of them receives all of her love completely. In fact, no matter how many children she has, she loves them all with her whole heart. That may not compute, but that is the way it is with love. So that is how God's love could fully dwell in the heart of Jesus, and in turn, God could feel the "pain of the world" through him. So the apostle Paul could say to the Colossians, "In him, the fullness of God was pleased to dwell" (Colossians 1:19), and Jesus, the great I Am could say, "Before Abraham was, *I AM*" (John 8:58). That's just the way he rolls!

> **Dogmas and doctrines are steel spikes in the coffins of hypocrites, but love is the angel that rolled away the stone.**

LOVE MAKES THE WORLD GO ROUND

If then there is any encouragement in Christ, any consolation from love, any sharing in the Spirit, any compassion and sympathy, make my joy complete: be of the same mind, having the same love, being in full accord and of one mind. Do nothing from selfish ambition or conceit, but in humility regard others as better than yourselves. Let each of you look not to your own interests, but to the interests of others. Let the same mind be in you that was in Jesus Christ, who though he was in the form of God, did not regard equality with God as something to be exploited, but emptied himself, taking the form of a slave, being born in human likeness. And being found in human form, he humbled himself and became obedient to the point of death—even death on a cross. Therefore God also highly exalted him and gave him the name that is above every name, so that at the name of Jesus every knee should bend, in heaven and on earth and under the earth, and every tongue should confess that Jesus Christ is Lord, to the glory of God the Father.

—Philippians 2:1–11

REAL AGAPE LOVE *is not schmaltzy.* What if what we learned as children was really what it's all about? What if God really is love? Forget about philosophical terms like omnipotence, omniscience, omnipresence; think of this world as created and run by love—that love really does make the world go round literally. Remember the words from John's first letter, "God's love was revealed among us in this way: God sent his only Son into the world so that we might live through him" (1 John 4:9). So what became incarnate in Jesus was not the mighty infinite power of God that moves the stars but rather the intent, compassion, and personality of the Creator God who agonizes over his handiwork and who feels the pain of the world. Like our slowly dying star, the sun, that gives us light, only by reaching out to give itself away, that is the sacrificial kind of love that "became flesh and dwelt among us" in the person of Jesus Christ.

I believe there is a message in the way God chose to reveal himself. From the time we are children, we learn to compete for the top—to be number one. So like chickens in a barnyard, we try to establish our highest niche in the pecking order. We deal with one another from a position of superiority, in a kind of personality arms race. We try to project an image of power, competence, and self-sufficiency. After all, why admit that I have weaknesses when everyone else seems to be so self-assured? Why confess my fears and doubts? Thus, we keep our real selves hidden behind a smiley face as we deal with one another from a façade of self-assured arrogance. No wonder we are confused by a God who empties himself and comes to us washing his disciple's feet. How demeaning that is for the sovereign King of Creation who rules the universe with power and might. But that is only the extrinsic side of God which is beyond our comprehension anyway. What Jesus reveals to us is the intimate, innermost heart of God.

So we as Christians affirm that in the fullness of time, when God chose to tell us who he was, he chose the person and nature of Jesus Christ. After all, who can better reveal God than God? So God, in Jesus, taught us a secret about human relationships, that real sharing and divine love only happens when we dare risk being open and vulnerable to one another. So God, in Christ, emptied himself of his power and limited his own freedom in order to reach us and draw us to himself! "No one has ever seen God, but the only son, who is close to the Father's heart, has made him known" (John 1:18).

The Logos (or Word) means the very essence, the underlying reality, the nature and meaning of a thing. So John is saying, "Hey, get this, the true nature and personality of the living God who created the universe became one of us. That self-giving love, that compassionate Spirit, that presence, that very nature became flesh and dwelt among us." So Jesus did not give us God's secret blueprint for the cosmos or a detailed description to be filed under "G." What God gave us in Jesus was himself. "Lord, show us the Father," said Phillip. "Phillip, have you been with me so long and yet do not know me? I and the Father are one. He who has seen me has seen the Father" (John 14:9).

And we will come to him and make our home in him.
—John 14:23b

EASTER AS RELATIONSHIPS

After this, he appeared in another form to two of them as they were walking into the country.

—Mark 16:12

WHEN JUDY AND I started dating, I was so broke that we would often just sneak into church at night to talk for hours on the floor by candlelight. Believe it or not, but we mostly talked about religion. No joke! In other words, she was first attracted to my theology and not my charming personality and striking good looks, LOL! I confess that in those days, I was almost too enthusiastic. I just knew I was going to change the world. It never happened, of course, but somehow, I managed to convince her that I just might actually be able to pull it off. *Lucky me.* So soon after that, we were married.

Now I am not sure why, but the thing we talked about the most was Easter. I told her that most people had a grossly materialistic understanding of a highly spiritual event. Some people almost seem to view Resurrection morning as something akin to Ezekiel's barren bones, rising on an old battlefield (but that was merely an allegory of the conquered nation of Israel rising from utter defeat). I do agree with Paul, however, that if there was no resurrection of the body, then we as Christians are most pitiful (1 Corinthians 15:12 ff). But I believe that something far more dramatic than the physical took place on Easter morning, something far more powerful than a big stone being rolled away, something transfiguring like Mark (9:2 ff). I believe that the very metamorphosis of what really happened that Easter was so unspeakably mysterious and so complex that there was no real way to describe an event that profound in ordinary words. No wonder their "eyewitness accounts" seemed to be so jumbled, confused, and contradictory. That is just how honest they were. They did not try to doctor their accounts in order to make them match. There was no collaboration. Perhaps the need to stay on point is also why they stuck mainly to the physical aspects of the account. Some experts even regard the transfiguration and the story of Jesus walking on water as resurrection accounts that somehow got out of context. Just imagine how you would tell such a story!

In other words, there is a difference between what happened to Lazarus (resuscitation) and what happened to Jesus (resurrection). Lazarus was only reanimated and went on to die again later on, just like you and me but not Jesus. Why? Because he had no need of a physical body anymore! Now he was Christmas in reverse! Instead of the Word becoming flesh, he was flesh becoming Word! He was no longer bound by space and time. He was *God*! (Philippians 2:9)

As Peter put it at Pentecost, quoting the prophet Joel, "I will pour out my spirit on all flesh." Indeed, it seems as if the Risen Jesus could be everywhere at once or change form at will or walk right through locked doors or even vanish from their sight. He could even appear out of nowhere. The early church, however, tended to emphasize the physical aspects, such as the fact that he ate fish and, apparently, though this is not clear, let Thomas touch him, strangely not Mary Magdalene. Very mysterious. Paul later cut the women out of the Easter story altogether (1 Corinthians 15:5 ff), even though they clearly saw the Risen Lord first. Shame on him.

Remember this, however, Mary failed to even know him until he called her by name, and two close friends walking together slowly on the road to Emmaus did not recognize him at all, that is until they entered into a personal fellowship with him and they once again broke bread together. Then—bingo!—a light went off. "Hey, that was not a stranger—that was Jesus!" Then puff! Just like that, the image was gone. It is interesting to note that, later, the disciples refused to believe their story (or the women's story either), that is until almost the same thing happened to them.

> **Were not our hearts burning within us**
> **while he was talking to us on the road and**
> **while he was opening the scriptures to us?**
> **—Luke 24:32**

Later, Jesus appeared again to Peter and invited him to a friendly little breakfast of fish, fellowship, and forgiveness on the beach. Notice the personal connections here. This is not a scene of some kind of cold impersonal reanimation movie or a late-night horror flick. The warm happy presence of the risen Lord comes alive to them, almost playfully, as he freely moves about from place to place with almost childlike joy and abandon! And once again, they discover the same rich and wonderful relationship with him that they had before, only better, much better!

So it wasn't his physical body that thrilled them so much. It was his real presence as a person. This was not an illusion. It was really *him!*

You see, many ancient religious people viewed salvation as escaping the bounds of earth and body to be swallowed up into the great light of *God*. For them, true bliss was to let their individual little sparks of light escape from this evil flesh to rejoin the great eternal radiance of an infinite being. But others held on to the hope that they would not be swallowed up, but (even after death) somehow, they would still be in a personal relationship with God.. After death, they hoped to still be able to relate I/ thou (person to person) and not just be assimilated like the *borg*. As the Hebrews saw it, their soul was not some pure speck of light trapped deep inside their evil body, from which they needed to escape. It was who they were! There was no body/soul dualism here. They were both body and soul. In short, they did not have a soul. They were a soul.

Even in the presence of God, they would still maintain their identity; they would still be themselves (only better). So when the disciples began to talk about the resurrection, they meant that even in heaven, they would still be entering into personal relationships with Jesus, God, and one another! So the question is—what do we make of that affirmation we all profess?

I BELIEVE IN THE RESURRECTION OF THE BODY?

The apostle Paul tried to get around that kind of language by pointing out that there are different kinds of "bodies." He used the analogy of heavenly bodies. I would have preferred talking about the student body of a school or the church as the Body of Christ.

But someone will ask, "How are the dead raised? With what kind of body do they come?" Fool! . . . You do not sow the body that is to be, but a bare seed . . . So it is with the resurrection of the body. What is sown is perishable, what is raised is imperishable . . . It is sown a physical body, it is raised a *spiritual* body . . . What I am saying, brothers and sisters is this: flesh and blood cannot inherit the kingdom of God, not, nor does the perishable inherit the imperishable (1 Corinthians 15:35 ff).

That was Paul's answer and mine, there is also a spiritual body. But to compare the physical body to the spiritual body is like comparing a mustard seed to a tree! You may recall that when Paul encountered the

Risen Lord, he saw no physical body at all. Instead, what he saw was "a light from heaven that flashed around him." Then the light spoke. "Saul, Saul, why do you persecute me?" So Paul entered into personal dialogue with a blinding flash of light rather than a mere physical body.

I believe there is an important message here for us all. Paul is saying that the resurrection is not about "flesh and blood." It is really about relationships. So perhaps whenever two or three of us are gathered together in his name to feed the hungry or to welcome a stranger, the Risen Lord does indeed appear among us.

Remember the beautiful Christmas story of Martin the Cobbler? I think Tolstoy was on to something! An astute little girl once remarked, "Sometimes Jesus comes to us as somebody else, but you never know for sure who that will be!" As Mark put it, He comes to us "in another form" (Mark 16:12).

I once came across a poem that shocked me a bit. But it also opened my eyes. The more I thought about it, the more it rang true. I do not know who wrote it, but it went something like this:

O Christ, who is beaten on street corners, who is unemployed, O Christ, who knows the sting of the needle and the taste of cheap wine, Help us to see you, make your presence known among us.

> **Truly I say unto you, just as you did it to one of the least
> of my family, you did it to me.**
> **—Matthew 25:40**

MAKING SENSE OF SIGNS AND WONDERS

Jesus answered them, "Very truly, I tell you, you are looking for me, not because you saw signs, but because you ate your fill of the loaves. Do not work for the food that perishes, but for the food that endures for eternal life, which the Son of Man will give you. For it is on him that God the Father has set his seal." Then they said to him, "What must we do to perform the works of God?" Jesus answered them, "This is the work of God, that you believe in him whom he has sent." So they said to him, "What sign are you going to give us then, so that we may see it and believe you?
—John 6:26–30

A FEW YEARS AGO, I preached a sermon on Elijah the Tishbite, and in passing, I mentioned that both Elijah and Elisha used mouth-to-mouth resuscitation to restore a dead child to life: "When Elisha came to the house, he saw the dead child, so he got up on the bed and lay upon the child, putting his mouth upon his mouth, and the flesh of the child became warm" (2 Kings 4:32).

After church, an angry lady met me at the door and said, "Do you know what you have done? You have desecrated that beautiful story by taking the miracle completely out of it."

"Actually," I said, "I thought using CPR three thousand years before it was invented was pretty miraculous, and furthermore, I think you and I have a different understanding as to what a miracle actually is. To me, a miracle is a sign of God's presence, not a proof of God's presence."

It seems to me that when it comes to understanding miracles, part of our problem is that we have divided the world into two distinct layers: One is the natural world; the other is the supernatural world. God dwells above in the supernatural world, while we live below in the

171

natural world. So the belief is that whenever the supernatural is present, the natural is ruled out and vice versa. So if there is a natural explanation for something, there cannot be anything truly miraculous about it. The result is the incredible shrinking God who grows smaller and smaller as scientific knowledge continues to fill in the blanks! Does that mean that God has abandoned creation and only comes back from time to time to do what science hasn't gotten around to figuring out yet? I certainly hope not!

So if God created the heavens and the earth and if God is the uniting force of all creation and if in him we live and move and have our being, then the world is not Godless, and God is at work in it constantly and not just occasionally! Unfortunately, most people go through life blind to that truth and blind to God's eternal presence. But a miracle happens whenever some event in their lives opens them up to the God who is already in their midst. "Earth is crammed with God," wrote Robert Browning, "and every bush is a holy place, but only he who sees takes off his shoes. The rest just pick blackberries."

My point is that miracles do not take place between you and nature but rather between you and God because God is already in nature, whether you are aware of him or not! Therefore, I believe the purpose of a miracle is not found in its natural or supernatural bases but rather in its ability to draw you into a relationship with God and to afford you spiritual communion with him! So miracles are really about relationships.

That is why John, in his Gospel, was very careful to substitute the word "sign" everywhere that Matthew, Mark, and Luke would have said "miracle" because a sign points you to something beyond itself. Remember the parable about a rich man who died and went to hell? But he could see across the abyss into heaven, so he called out, "I beg you, Father Abraham, send Lazarus back from the dead to my father's house, for I have five brothers. Let him warn them, lest they also come to this place of torment."

To that, Abraham replied, "Your brothers have Moses and the prophets to listen to."

"But, Father Abraham," cries the rich man from hell, "if someone comes to them from the dead, then they surely will believe."

To that, Abraham responded, "If they refuse to hear Moses and the prophets, neither will they be convinced should someone rise from the dead." (Get it?)

The point is that God never gives supernatural proofs that make faith unnecessary! Some believe in Easter, others do not. There is no proof. Wasn't that the temptation that Jesus faced in the wilderness when Satan tempted him to leap off tall buildings with a single bound and turn stones into bread? God offers signs—not proofs!

The poet William Blake once said, "The man who does not believe in miracles surely makes it certain that he will never see one."

Indeed, I contend that apart from faith, no one can perceive miracles. You see, the Pharisees almost never questioned the ability of Jesus to work wonders; what they questioned was by whose power and authority did he do them. Was he in league with God or the devil? They chose to believe the devil, for the Jews have always believed in lying miracles and false signs and wonders—as did the New Testament Christians. For. example, in 2 Thessalonians 2:9, Paul warns us that Satan comes with signs and wonders. In Mark 13:22, Jesus warns of signs and wonders that will lead men astray. Revelation 16:24 speaks of demonic spirits that perform signs and wonders.

I used to do a lot of magic as object lessons in my children's sermons. One reason that I stopped was because they began to ask "What trick will you do for us today, Preacher?" The "tricks" were not supposed to be the message, only the medium—a way of getting their attention in order to teach them a truth about God or our relationship to God. For that same reason, Jesus had to stop doing miracles because people came to see the "magic show" rather than hear the Word! So he began to heal in secret. "Tell no one," he said. My point is that miracles and revelation are inseparably related so that when God makes himself known, the man of faith is conscious of a miracle. But no one else is! God does not prove himself to nonbelievers, so they see no miracle and no God!

John, in his Gospel, tells of an incident when God spoke to Jesus, but the Pharisees said, "Oh, that was just thunder!" So without the eyeglasses of faith, they simply interpreted the same events in entirely different ways!

Say a doctor performed back surgery and feels he is responsible for helping an elderly lady patient recover. The doctor then feels resentful when the patient insists in giving all the glory to God! But the location of the miracle, for her, is not in the patient's back but rather in the patient's heart, through a renewed relationship of gratitude to God who is the source of all wisdom and all healing.

As I said before, the miracle is not between you and nature, the miracle is between you and God! For example, one of the great miracles of Jesus was the feeding of the multitudes. It is one of the few miracles recorded in all four Gospels—twice in Mark! After that miracle, some of the people followed Jesus around to the other side of the lake. They may not have seen Jesus walk on the water, but they did see that when the disciples left in the boat, Jesus was not with them, so they were a little puzzled as to how he got to the other side.

"Rabbi," they said, "when did you come here?"

And Jesus answered, "Truly, truly I say to you, you seek me not because you saw signs, but because you ate your fill of the loaves. Do not labor for the food that perishes, but for the food that endures to eternal life, which the Son of Man will give you—for on him has God the Father set his seal."

But it is clear that all of these witnesses missed the whole point of the miracle. Their bellies were full, but their souls were as emaciated as ever. Their lives were not changed, and they were no closer to God than before.

So Jesus said to them, "If you would do the work of God, then believe in me." In other words, that is the purpose of the sign: to believe in Jesus! That's what it's all about.

To that, the people replied, "But what sign will you do that we might believe in you?"

I regard this as one of the funniest stories in the entire Bible. Jesus has just fed the five thousand and walked on water, and these people were actual eyewitnesses to at least one of those events, if not both, but because they have no faith, they have witnessed no miracle.

"Yeah, so you can walk on water, let's see you swim."

"So you can feed five thousand people with a few loaves and fishes with baskets leftover—big deal—but what we want to know is what sign will you do for us that we might believe in you."

Give me a break! Isn't that funny?

The point is that miracles never prove anything. They are merely signs that point us to God, but if you refuse to follow the sign that leads to the Savior, then you will never see the miracle.

That whole incident reminds me of Moses standing before Pharaoh. Pharaoh did not believe in the Hebrew God, and he saw no signs either! I don't know if you ever noticed it or not, but God gave Moses these instructions: "And the Lord said to Moses and Aaron, 'Prove yourselves by working a miracle, then you will say to Aaron, "Take your rod and cast it down before Pharaoh, that it may become a serpent."'"

But when Moses did that, then Pharaoh summoned the wise men and the sorcerers, and they also did the very same thing with their secret arts, so it proved nothing. Pharaoh's heart was hardened, and he would not listen to them! Because he had on faith. And so it was throughout all the plagues of Egypt, none of these miracles ever impressed Pharaoh because he did not believe. So the miracles proved nothing, as almost every sign could either be explained away as a trick that Pharaoh's own magicians could pull off with their own secret devices or else it could be attributed to a natural phenomenon that still occurs to this day.

For example, in the flood season, many times the Nile has turned to blood (red tide) due to microorganisms and sediment. Also, after the flood season, there are swarms of gnats and flies from the stagnant pools. Furthermore, cattle diseases, boils, hailstones, and locust all still occur in Egypt from time to time. And the plague of darkness is so common that it has a name. It is called *khamsin*, as every March and April, hot winds from the desert darken the sky with dust storms. That is why the Bible says, "The darkness could be felt."

My point is that Pharaoh saw no miracle simply because he did not believe in the Hebrew God! So Pharaoh interpreted these same events as tricks or coincidence or natural catastrophes but not as signs from God. I tell you this because, as I mentioned earlier, my concern is that, in our modern age, miracles have sometimes become a stumbling block to belief instead of a building block and a sign from God.

Once, a little boy was telling his grandmother what he learned in Bible school. "Well," he said, "there was this mean Middle Eastern dictator named Pharaoh who took some Jewish hostages. So a secret agent named Moses infiltrated their ranks and helped the Israelis escape across a big lake in a submarine. Then when the enemy combatants came after them, Moses fired a cruise missile and blew them all to kingdom come."

"Shame on you, son," said his grandmother. "You know you didn't learn any such story as that in Bible school, now did you?"

"Well not exactly," said the boy, "but, Grandmother, if I told you what they really said, you'd never believe it!"

This brings up a very important issue about miracles. Miracles are not to be used to ridicule an unbeliever; rather, they are signs to enhance belief. Miracles are not a competency test to weed out infidels or beat them into submission. Some people think miracles are like thermometers—they can be used to measure true faith. They are a test to see how far you can stretch your belief beyond your own reason and experience.

How easy it is to forget that in ancient times, belief in magic was common. Demons supposedly caused storms and illness or even inhabited rocks. In those days, every village had its own wonder worker like Simon the Magician, so they expected *magic*, but in our scientific mentality, we do not. We find it easier to believe in Jesus than to believe in miracles, but in those days, it was just the opposite. Everyone believed in miracles. What the enemies of Jesus did not find it easy to believe in was Jesus! His enemies rarely challenged his ability to do signs and wonders, only they questioned by whose power he did them.

I once came across a story about a good man who asked God to heal his infirmity, but healing did not come. "I have served you faithfully, Lord," he said. "Why haven't you helped me?"

Fortunately, his wife was there. She tried to foresee his needs. She worried about his bitterness. But where was God? Where was the miracle he prayed for? Then one day a thought crept into his bitter heart like a revelation! He had been praying to a God who was far removed. But did he really believe that God was far removed from his everyday struggles? "No," he said, "God is not some impersonal force off in outer space somewhere. He is Emmanuel. *He is love.* God is with me here and now."

Suddenly, he looked up into the eyes of his loving wife. Then he realized that God had been reaching out to him through the only face he could see. God had spoken to him with the only voice he could hear. The miracle he had been receiving all along was the miracle of God's love and comfort through her. She helped him cope as he grew ever weaker until the day he peacefully slipped away to God!

Some scholars like to question the historical accuracy of John because it is the last Gospel to be written. But there is a similar story from the Gospel of Mark, the earliest Gospel to be written.

After Jesus has fed the five thousand with seven fish and a few small loaves, Mark says, "The Pharisees came and began to argue with Jesus," seeking from him a sign from heaven to test him. And he sighed deeply in his spirit and said, "Why does this generation seek a sign? Truly, I say to you, no sign shall be given to this generation" (Mark 8:11–12). In other words, a generation that refuses to believe is a generation that will never see a miracle. Not even Easter will be enough to persuade those who refuse to believe.

You may remember the Gospel hymn "It Took a Miracle," "It took a miracle to hang the world in space . . . but when he saved my soul, cleansed and made me whole, that took a miracle of love and grace." Faith, hope, and love are the forces that make the perception of all miracles possible! Do I believe in miracles? Of course, I do! But Jesus said, "If you would do the work of God, then believe in me." That's what it's all about! So miracles are not a test such as, "Believe whale swallowed Jonah or burn!" Making signs and wonders into barriers to push people away from God is contrary to their intent. So faith is the window, and until you believe in Jesus, miracles will explode all around you every day, but you will not see a single one! *For apart from faith, all miracles will remain unrecognized.*

YOU HAVE TO BE CAREFULLY TAUGHT

Indeed, the body does not consist of one member but of many. If the foot would say, "Because I am not a hand, I do not belong to the body," that would not make it any less a part of the body. And if the ear would say, "Because I am not an eye, I do not belong to the body," that would not make it any less a part of the body. If the whole body were an eye, where would the hearing be? If the whole body were hearing, where would the sense of smell be? But as it is, God arranged the member in the body, each one of them, as he chose. If all were a single member, where would the body be? As it is, there are many members, yet one body. The eye cannot say to the hand, "I have no need of you," nor again the head to the feet, "I have no need of you."

—1 Corinthians 12:14–21

DURING THE TIME I spent growing up in Manteo, North Carolina, there were subtle hidden customs and traditions to keep black people down. For example, all the colored people lived in only one part of town that we laughingly called California. (They all had such dark tans, ha, ha!) I am grateful that I no longer find that funny. People from "California" were not allowed to use our white restrooms, our white restaurants, our white water fountains, or our white schools. If they couldn't find a bathroom, too bad! One day the nice black man who mowed my grandmother's yard knocked on the door. It was a hot summer day, he asked for some ice water. So Grandmother gave him a mason jar to drink from.

I asked her, "Grandma, why did you give him water in a mason jar?"

Now I loved my grandmother very much, and I miss her to this day. She was a kind and wonderful woman and a very good person. But she looked at me incredulously as if she was totally taken aback by my stupid question.

"Denny," she said, "you really don't expect me to let him drink out of our good glasses, do you?"

You see, that was the way it was in those days! It was tradition, a part of the culture, I am sad to say.

My eyes were not really opened to the real tragedy of prejudice until I was nine years old and a black boy about my same age came into my grandfather's store to buy some Brazil nuts. The problem was he did not know the proper name for those nuts; the only thing he had ever heard them called was nigger toes. So instead of asking, he just pointed at the nuts and said, "I want some of dem nuts, please."

Soon, a crowd had gathered around, as people kept laughing and asking him over and over, "Tell us, boy, what kind of nuts did you say you wanted?"

Each time he was forced to repeat that humiliating N word, his head seemed to droop a little lower and his shoulders slumped all the more as he shamefully answered all of those smirking white adults standing over him.

Finally, with tears running down his black cheeks and with trembling lips, he begged, "Please, sir! My momma sent me to get some of dem nuts, so can I please have 'em now?"

A little piece of me died that day, as I lost some of my innocence, along with that young black boy's. But my eyes were opened up a lot!

No matter how you feel about Hillary Clinton, you have to agree "it does take a village to raise a child." Unfortunately, as in my case, sometimes the customs and the traditions of that a village can teach us all the wrong lessons. So it seems clear to me that a child's conscience can be seriously warped by the village as well. Mark Twain's Huckleberry Finn struggled for a while and then went against his own conscience. He decided to help the slave Jim escape, even though his conscience told him that Jim was somebody's stolen property and it was wrong not to turn a runaway slave in to the authorities. Did it ever occur to you that Jesus also grew up in a culture of prejudice? Jesus went to school where the rabbis in the synagogue taught that only the Jews were the chosen people of God and that all non-Jews were inferior infidel dogs. No wonder they had no qualms about killing every man, woman, and child when they first took the land of Israel from the pagan Canaanites. After all, these were not people; they were dogs. Even more hated were the Samaritans. Samaritans were considered half-breed traitors of inferior stock who had sold out to paganism.

My point is that just as we are often influenced by our environment, Jesus must have been influenced by his surroundings as well—some of the attitudes that shaped his childhood came not from the will of God but from group pressures, customs, and social influences of his time. Take the Samaritans for example, when his enemies tried to slander Jesus, one of the insults they hurled at him was to call him a Samaritan—"Samaritan lover!" So I can just imagine young Jesus growing up on the playgrounds of Palestine, hearing anti-Samaritan slurs and anti-Gentile jokes on his way to recess. The truth is that Jews were so intolerant of all non-Jews that the book of Ezra was written primarily to forbid marriage to foreign women and Gentiles. Ezra even made all Jewish men who had foreign wives to turn them out of the house with their children. So if this was the kind of culture in which Jesus was nurtured, it would be foolish for us to imagine that he was not in some way influenced by those same attitudes.

No wonder then that when Jesus first sent out his disciples, he commanded them, "Go nowhere among the Gentiles, and enter no town of the Samaritans, but go rather to the lost sheep of Israel!" (Matthew 10:5) Then we have the strange story that as Jesus passed through Tyre and Sidon, a Canaanite woman came out of the crowd and cried out to him, "Have mercy on me, O Lord, Son of David, my daughter is severely possessed by a demon." Now the Old Testament is filled with reproach toward the Canaanites. So when the Canaanite woman spoke, Jesus first appeared to show no compassion on her whatsoever. Instead, he turned away and ignored her pleas for help as if she wasn't even there! And the apparent reason is because she was a Gentile, a woman, a Canaanite, and a foreigner. But this woman was persistent and determined, and she continued to make a scene until, finally, the embarrassed disciples said to Jesus, "Send her away; she is crying after us!"

So Jesus replied to her, "I was sent only to the lost sheep of the house of Israel"—meaning not to a Gentile Canaanite woman.

But still, the woman would not be brushed off. She fell to her knees and cried out again, "Lord, help me!"

Personally, I believe Jesus could have been role-playing here to teach a lesson. But once again, Jesus seemed to resist her plea and gave what sounds to us like a totally uncharacteristic reply—so unlike the Jesus we know. "It isn't right to take the children's food and throw it to the dogs," he said (Matthew 15:26). But the crowds I am quite sure would have been in full agreement. "Yeah, you tell her Jesus! It isn't right to take what is reserved for us Jews, the chosen seed of Israel, and give it to a heathen, foreign Gentile woman like her." But again, the woman refused to back down. "Yes, Lord," she said humbly, still on her knees at his feet, "but even the dogs get to eat the crumbs that fall from the master's table."

By now everyone could see how, in her desperation, this brave lady's courage and quick retort had won the heart of Jesus. He had compassion for her and admiration as well for her strength of spirit and her spunk. "You are a woman of great faith," he said. "Be it done for you as you desire." Her daughter was healed. I hope the crowd learned a lesson that day.

It seems to me that this strange, even embarrassing, story, which is recorded in both Matthew and Mark, is there for a reason. To me, it represents a turning point in the life and ministry of Jesus. Apparently, up to that point, there had been some tension in his mind about the broadness of his calling—would his ministry include non-Jews or not? Just as Peter and Paul later struggled with the scope of their ministry, Jesus must have had the same struggle himself. Perhaps up to that point, our Lord's own humanity stood in the way of God's full plan. "His time had not yet come." He still had a lot to learn if he was to die for the sins of the world.

When I was in college, I had to write a paper on prejudice. My opening statement was "Prejudice is a pigment of the imagination." I thought it was cute, but my professor missed the pun and instead corrected my spelling by replacing the p with an f. So now I have a prejudice against stupid professors. Seriously, I believe that prejudice is a part of original sin. It is in the very fabric of our natures as imperfect creatures. It is so easily learned and so readily accepted because we have an innate tendency to be wary of people who are different from us. If there is one good thing I can say about prejudice, it would be that prejudice is very democratic. Everybody seems to have some in one form or another. So whether you are too tall, too blond, too short, too skinny, too fat, too pale, too dark, too gay, too straight, or even too good-looking, you can be sure that somebody will look at you in disgust just because you are the way you are.

Since 9/11, I must confess that I have personally discovered a new prejudice myself—against people who look Middle Eastern. I fight it, but I still can't help it. When I go in the dollar store and certain gas stations, motels, or convenience stores, all I can see are terrorists. My wife and I were in an airport preparing to board our flight when the airline attendants ushered a Middle Eastern man with a white cane on to the plane before other passengers boarded. That's when my wife turned to me and said, "Do you think he is really blind?"

But that is the nature of prejudice. It is being down on something that you are not up on. It is drawing conclusions on insufficient evidence. It is judging a book by its cover instead of its contents. The harshest criticism Jesus ever received in his ministry came from the "in crowd" who wanted to keep others "out." "This man receives sinners," they said, "and eats with them too." But Jesus was always crossing over forbidden barriers. He blessed the outcast, taught both women and Gentiles (against the rules). He touched "unclean" lepers. He ate with tax collectors. He healed on the Sabbath. He even plucked grain on the Sabbath. All of these things were forbidden by law at the time. In other words, he did not always follow proper regulations! To him, people mattered more than rules. "The Sabbath was made for man," he said, "not man for the Sabbath."

Jesus was very aware of the hidden caste system that kept the rich rich and the poor poor and closed doors of opportunity to the lower classes. He knew how the money changers made a killing on the poor when poor people had to buy doves to sacrifice in the temple. Also, the poor had to buy kosher foods, approved by the priests as ritually clean—after a nice kickback, of course. So Jesus made a shocking statement that made the authorities very angry. He said, "Nothing that enters a man defiles him, since it enters his stomach, not his heart, and passes on." By saying this, he declared all foods to be clean, whether they were kosher or not. No wonder the priests wanted Jesus dead. He was hitting them right where it hurt—in the pocketbook. Could this be one of the real reasons Jesus was crucified? Was this part of the hidden agenda at Calvary? "He who hates his brother is in darkness," said John. "He does not know where he is going because the darkness has blinded his eyes."

Jesus came to heal blind people like you and me. Unfortunately, most of us like our blindness. We know that in order to cure our blindness, our whole pattern of life must change. In short, "We must be born again."

Oh, I don't mean that the Holy Spirit will change you in a flash—birth always implies travail; it takes time. It comes slowly and painfully, and it hurts. Don't you see what I am trying to say? When Jesus asked us over and over to love our enemies, he knew exactly how hard a thing that was to do because, apparently, he had a hard time doing it himself. And in that struggle, with his own prejudice against women, Canaanites, Gentiles, Samaritans, and pagans, Jesus acted out the universal dilemma of all of us. He participated in our humanity. He shared in the pressures that all of us have experienced so that he could release us from our own captivity.

Let me tell you a parable about three men. I want you to try to decide which of these men best comprehends the message of Jesus. They each pass a dirty scroungy beggar sitting on the street corner, playing a guitar, singing hymns, and collecting money in a tin cup.

The first man passes by and says, "I love the human race. I just love everybody, and therefore, I'm going to put some money in this poor man's cup," and so he does.

Is he Christian? Not necessarily! Being a humanitarian with a bleeding heart doesn't necessarily make you a Christian. Linus used to say, "I love mankind. It's people I can't stand." And a lot of mushy-gushy sentimental mankind lovers are just that bad. They love everybody in general but nobody in particular.

The second man passes by and says to himself, "You know, I've ripped off a few people in my business this week, and it weighs on my conscience. Maybe if I drop some money in this poor guy's cup, I'll feel a little better. At least it will show I care, and it will help balance the books, so to speak." So he drops some money in the poor man's cup and smiles.

Is he a Christian? Not necessarily! He seems more interested in how he appears to other people, not to mention buying off a guilty conscience.

Now the third man passes by and says to himself, "Ugh, how repulsive can you get? Nothing makes me so sick to my stomach as a lazy bum like that! All of my life, I have been taught that beggars are worthless parasites on society. They are no good! But you know, Jesus loved me when I was despicable and unworthy. He said I still mattered to him. So for his sake and with his help—in spite of myself—I want to put some money in this man's cup."

Now to me, this last guy got it right. I think he best understood what I think it means to be Christian. After all, Jesus knows the power of peer pressure. He knows what it is to be afraid of people who are different. He knows how hard it is to love people that we may regard as unlovely or unworthy of our love. But he says to us, "Remember I first loved you when you were unworthy, so that is no excuse. Let me dwell in your heart, and I will love the unlovely through you." As Paul put it, "I yet not I but Christ who lives in me." Again, Paul said, "In that renewal, there is no longer Greek or Jew, circumcised and uncircumcised, barbarian, Scythian, slave and free, *but Christ is all and in all*" (Colossians 3:11).

PALM BRANCHES DRIPPING BLOOD

When I was in my last year at Duke Divinity School, I served a little student appointment way out in the country. That spring of 1968, Martin Luther King Jr. was murdered. On Saturday, I went to borrow the church's lawn mower to mow the parsonage grass when a church member yelled at me, "We finally got that damn nigger, didn't we, Preacher?"

It was bad enough that he used the N word, which I regard as profanity, but it was even worse that he made me an accomplice in the crime. I knew in my heart that I had to take a stand then and there. On Palm Sunday, I reminded the congregation that, like it or not, this man who was assassinated was a Christian minister, so now that he was already dead, perhaps they might better be able to hear what he had to say. I suppose my worst mistake was that I had brashly entitled my sermon, "Palm Branches Dripping Blood." But I was young. In hindsight, I admit that the title was harsh, but as I began to read excerpts from some of Dr. King's sermons in the *Strength to Love*—writing on nonviolence, turning the other cheek, and loving your enemies—people began to get up and leave the church until the sanctuary was virtually empty. Soon, my wife was receiving abusive anonymous phone calls. I suppose the logic was "If you like black people, you must be obscene."

The next Friday evening, a Klan rally was held in a field behind some trees across the street from the parsonage. Judy was terrified, so we crept out to our yellow Mustang and slipped off to Graham to spend the night with her parents. I thought the Klan would burn a cross in the yard and it would all be over. It was not. They did not burn a cross at all, but on Saturday night, the same group gathered once again in the center of a circle of tractor lights. It was then that I heard my wife scream, "Someone's at our bedroom window!"

I have never aimed a gun at another human being in my life, but at that moment, I went to the closet and got out my late grandfather's old Remington automatic 12-gauge shotgun and began to load it with no. 4 birdshot. I decided that if an intruder started coming through that window to threaten my wife and nephew, then God help me, I would have to shoot.

Staying with us at the time was our four-year-old nephew Tommy. He looked at me with frightened eyes and said, "Uncle Denny, I'm never going to play cowboys with you again!"

There was another Duke student serving that church named Jimmet. I called her and told her what had happened. That Sunday, she was teaching an adult Sunday school class and noticed that a number of men were nodding off.

"What's the matter fellows?" she asked. "I thought you farmers went to bed early."

"Oh no," one of them shot back." We have lights on our tractors." Everyone started laughing. They knew the score.

When the Pastor Parish Relations Committee went to complain about me to the district superintendent, he was quick to apologize, saying, "Denny is not one of my boys, and he'll be gone in June." And so I was. In June, the cabinet, in its wisdom, sent me far, far away at a low starting salary to a remote coastal fishing village fifteen miles from the nearest town. That is the way the system works.

One sweet old lady from Marshallberg said to me in her delightful Down East brogue (that reminded me so much of home), "Son, I know you think you have come to the jumping-off place, and you can almost see it from here, but the jumping-off place is really Cedar Island."

> **Those who say "I love God" and hate their brothers and sisters are liars, for those who do not love a brother or sister, whom they have seen, cannot love God whom they have not seen.**
>
> **—1 John 4:20**

SENDING SUBTLE LITTLE SIGNALS

While he was speaking, a Pharisee invited him to dine with him; so he went in and took his place at the table. The Pharisee was amazed to see that he did not first wash before dinner. Then the Lord said to him, "Now you Pharisees clean the outside of the cup and of the dish, but inside you are full of greed and wickedness. You fools! Did not the one who made the outside make the inside also? So give for alms those things that are within; and see, everything will be clean for you."

—Luke 11:37–41

ONE OF THE mysteries of the New Testament is why so many Pharisees invited Jesus to dinner when, invariably, he would end up insulting them. As you just read in Luke, a Pharisee invited Jesus to dine with him and just as you would have done, the host politely invited his guest to wash his hands before dinner. And in response, Jesus immediately went into a tirade: "Woe unto you Pharisees for you clean the outside of the cup, while the inside is full of wickedness. Woe unto you Pharisees for you choose for yourselves the best seats in the synagogue. Woe unto you, for you are like unmarked graves that men walk over. Woe to you who killed the prophets and then built them shrines!"

Now don't you think that Jesus was overreacting just a bit to the kind invitation of a gracious host to wash his hands? I can't help but wonder what Emily Post would have thought of his table manners. Heck, when I grew up, my mother always asked me to wash my hands before every meal. It was good hygiene and good manners. It was just the proper thing to do. So why on earth was Jesus so upset about it?

On another occasion, according to Matthew and Mark, some other scribes and Pharisees came up to Jesus and asked him why his disciples refused to wash their hands before they ate—breaking the tradition of the elders! Again, Jesus was miffed: "You hypocrites, Isaiah was right when he prophesied about you, 'These people honor me with their lips, but their hearts are far from me.' They worship me in vain! Their teachings are but rules taught by men."

Now the real strange thing is that Jesus probably did wash his hands quite often. In fact, every Passover, it was required that hands be washed multiple times during the meal. This hand washing even had a name. It was called the *urchatz*. It included a prayer: "Blessed art thou, O Lord, who has sanctified us and commanded us concerning the washing of hands." But you need to understand that this kind of hand washing was a ritual pouring of water over hands (hands that should probably have already been clean so as not to contaminate the sacred water). What Jesus was referring to was only a ceremonial cleansing. There was no scrubbing and no soap—it was for holiness, not hygiene. After all, germs had not even been invented yet. In every Pharisee's house, there was a large clay pot for this purpose that was used much like Catholics use holy water. Ironically, during the Dark Ages, these rituals of hand washing actually helped the Jews escape the bubonic plague. Christians who threw their waste right out into the streets and lived in very unsanitary conditions became convinced that the Jews must be poisoning their well water when, in fact, all the Jews did was wash hands!

But we still have our dilemma—what was Jesus so upset about? Isn't washing your hands the right thing to do? The answer can be found in a parallel scripture in the Gospel of Mark (7:22–24), "The Pharisees and all Jews do not eat unless they give their hands a ceremonial washing, holding to the tradition of the elders, when they come in from the marketplace." So there is our clue. They only washed hands as an act of elitism, arrogance, and superiority. Washing reminded them of their exclusiveness and separated them from the heathen in the marketplace as they symbolically washed away all contact with Gentiles, foreigners, women, and sinners. Uggah! Indeed, the very word *Pharisee* means "one who is separated."

Therefore, Jesus was not reacting against the good practice of hand washing but against the sly subtle prejudice and utter hypocrisy that was hidden behind the ceremonial act.

"Woe to you," Jesus said, "for you even tithe the spices on your spice rack, but neglect the weightier matters of the law, like justice and mercy."

The point is that Jesus was not as concerned with etiquette or even hygiene as he was with justice, righteousness, and love. He was less concerned with broken rules than with broken hearts and broken lives. The Pharisees considered themselves to be far more superior, holy, and righteous than ordinary men (and especially women). They even wore Bible verses on their hats as a symbol of their holiness. But then this upstart carpenter's son from the tiny hick town of Nazareth has the nerve to say, "Unless your righteousness exceeds that of the scribes and the Pharisees, the publicans and the harlots will enter the kingdom of God before you." The nerve!

Come on, admit it! Can't you identify with those devout and conservative Pharisees who only wanted to be pure and holy and untainted? They feared contamination from contact with lowlife people that they regarded as unclean. As they saw it, the further away they were from such unholy types, the closer they were to God. But along comes Jesus who says just the opposite. He says the closer we are, even to God's ugliest children, the closer we are to God, and whatsoever we do to the very least of them, we do to Jesus. So to separate oneself from another human being is to separate oneself from God. Thus, Jesus was willing to challenge even good customs like hand washing if they were being used to push other people away or put them down.

On another occasion, Jesus was eating dinner with a wealthy Pharisee, and once again, he insults his host. "When you give a dinner," Jesus said, "do not invite just your relatives and friends or your rich neighbors, for they will invite you back. In this way, you will be repaid for what you did. But instead, invite the poor, the crippled, the lame, and the blind (i.e., the rejects or outsiders), and then you will be truly blessed because they are not able to pay you back." Jesus is reminding us that the kingdom of God is not a stuffy boardroom for the elite and beautiful people but a banquet where everyone is welcome, no matter how marginal (by the world's standards) they may seem!

At this point, one of those rich guests tried to salvage the evening with a brilliant reply. He said, "How happy are those who will sit at the table and break bread in the kingdom of God."

Wow! Now I ask you, have you ever heard more eloquent words than these? Any poet would be happy to claim such a lovely turn of phrase as his own! But Jesus was not at all impressed because he knew exactly what the man was trying to do. He was trying to use a pious platitude to gloss over the sheer embarrassment of the guest of honor's shocking suggestion that the poor and the outcasts should have been invited to dinner! Jesus quickly saw through the sentimental façade and responded with a parable.

He described a rich man who prepared a great banquet. But all the honored guests made excuses why they could not come, from buying land to selling cattle. In order to show how silly those excuses were, let me say them upside down. I am invited to eat bread with the Master in the kingdom of God. Therefore, I do not have time to sell land or buy cows! See how stupid the excuses sound when they are reversed. At any rate, the offended host then tells his servants to go outside into the streets and bring in the poor and the outcasts and those unable to care for themselves and let them feast instead. "For I tell you," he said, "none of those men who were invited will taste my dinner." In short, the best way to thank God for your blessings is to remember those who are less blessed. "For I was hungry and you gave me food; I was thirsty and you gave me drink, I was a stranger and you welcomed me. I was naked and you clothed me, I was sick and you visited me, I was in prison and you came to me" (Matthew 25:35–39).

It amazes me how so many pious people can twist the Gospel and actually reverse its intent! A preacher was preaching on the parable of the sheep and the goats. Here was his outline:

Point no. 1:   This proves the existence of heaven and hell.
Point no. 2:   Believers (the sheep) will go to heaven.
Point no. 3:   Nonbelievers (the goats) will go to hell.
Conclusion: Believe or burn!

Sadly, that is not at all what that parable was about! It was about helping the poor, the hungry, the outcast, and the less fortunate. In short, Jesus is telling the world that rules (such as hygiene) are good but that people are worth more than rules. Our efforts at holiness should never be used to push other people away from God or to push ourselves up! So don't just wave your hands in the air and sing sweet praise songs. God does not need your flattery, he wants your service. As Saint Francis put it, "Go and preach the Gospel and, if necessary, use words!"

> I hate, and despise your festivals, and I take no delight in your solemn assemblies . . . Take away from me the noise of your songs, I will not listen to the melody of your harps. But let justice roll down like waters, and righteousness like an ever flowing stream.
> —Amos 5:21–, 23--24

THE SOFTER SIDE OF SIN

> What good is it, my brothers and sisters, if you say you
> have faith but do not have works? Can faith save you? If a
> brother or sister is naked and lacks daily food, one of you says
> to them, "Go in peace; keep warm and eat your fill," and yet
> you do not supply their bodily needs, what is the good of that?
> So faith by itself, if it has no works, is dead.
>
> —James 2:14–17

M Y SON PATRICK, before his retirement, was a chief petty officer in the Navy and a nuclear reactor operator on a submarine. As such, he was often away at sea for months at a time. So when he came home, his boys were curious observers. One day when his eldest was about three, he was watching with fascination as his dad shaved and brushed his teeth. Patrick then took a big swig of mouthwash, gargled for a few seconds, and then spit it out in the sink.

"What's the matter, Daddy?" little Cameron said. "Didn't you yike it?"

That reminds me of what God said to the church in Laodicea, "Because you are lukewarm, neither cold nor hot, I will spit you out of my mouth" (Revelation 3:16).

By sugar free, I mean a tough hardy kind of faith that is free from apathy, serious in dedication and genuine in commitment.

My wife just loves schmaltzy movies—the ones with pretty spring flowers, white picket fences, passionate romance, cute little children, bright blue skies, and happy endings. I call them chick flicks! Wouldn't it be nice if real lives were like that? But then along comes something like 9/11, mad terrorists, the Sandy Hook School tragedy, or some other horror. I call that a reality check!

I am reminded of a tale about Billy Wilder. He was trying to sell a movie plot to the late great producer Samuel Goldwyn. "But does it have a happy ending?" Mr. Goldwyn asked.

"Not exactly," said Billy Wilder. "It winds up with the poor guy in an insane asylum, thinking he is a horse."

"That won't do," said Samuel Goldwyn. "I want it to end happy!"

"Wait," said Billy Wilder. "What about if, in the end, this guy who thinks he's a horse actually goes out and wins the Kentucky Derby?"

Wouldn't it be nice if real life was like that, with happy endings every time like those sweet old black-and-white movies from days gone by, with fairy tale endings every time? But let's face it, folks, except in heaven, none of us is likely to live happily ever after. And yet there are certain religious groups that try to sell the Gospel packaged like a plastic bottle of Karo Syrup. In order to grow their congregations, these groups tell people exactly what they want to hear. They even try to sell Jesus as a way to get rich quick. They tell us to try God and increase our territory. "Just praise the Lord, and soon, you'll all be rolling in the dough without a care in the world." But where is the sacrifice? Where is the cry of the needy? Where is the call to help the helpless? Where is the cross? I am sorry to disappoint you, God is not your personal valet.

Perhaps a New Age commercial covered with a thin candy shell might sound something like this:

> Does worry and too much responsibility make your head slide off the pillow at night? Do you wake up irritable and out of sorts? Then try God-Lite! The sweet, cozy, laid-back brand for those who want all the pleasure of feeling good but without the hassle of actually having to do good! Yes, God-Lite is specially blended to please everybody with 50 percent fewer requirements. It is easy to swallow, slides down pleasingly smooth, and is far less filling. God-Lite is the home of the 1 percent tithe, the five-minute sermon, and the no-pledge-no-volunteer policy. And don't forget that spine-tingling feel-good music! God-Lite is guaranteed to be 100 percent safe with no offensive odors, no bad aftertaste, no blood, no guts, and no cross! Relax, take a load off, and chill out. You can have all the gain without the pain because, after all, you are worth it! So save time, save money, and save yourself—what a deal! Visit a soothing God-Lite center near you. God will be grateful for your visit. Your neighbors will be impressed, and you will feel especially proud of yourself.

> It's time to get lit on lite—everything you always wanted in a God and less!

Beware of "non-prophet" churches that give the people what they want to hear instead of what they need to hear. Sometimes sin can seem to be so innocent, like a warm puppy (so soft and cuddly). Such is the case for the subtle syrupy sin of sentimentality. As the apostle Paul warned long ago, "Satan disguises himself as an angel of light."

Leo Tolstoy recalled the days of the Russian czars when the aristocratic ladies would dress in warm furs to attend the opera. They would weep loudly as pain and suffering was portrayed by actors on the stage while, outside, their poor coachman, barefoot in the bitter snow, stood at attention. That is the hidden downside of sweet sentimentality— its utter selfishness. Insensitivity often hides under the warm blanket of empty emotions.

Just imagine, for example, that a poor starving boy is walking a puppy down the street. Both the boy and the dog are skin and bones. Both have dark shadows under their eyes. Both have eyes that are sunken back in their heads. A wealthy lady spies them and follows them home to a trailer park. She knocks on the rusty door of their run-down mobile home, and a thin emaciated woman with dark shadows under her sunken eyes opens the door.

"Was that your son with a little brown puppy?" the wealthy lady asks.

"Yes, it was," says the mother proudly. "Do you know him? Isn't he a nice boy?"

"Well, it's an outrage," the rich woman responds. "I have never seen anything so shameful and horrible in my whole life, and I intend to do something about it. I am going to report this travesty to the SPCA, and they are going to come and take that poor puppy away from the both of you!"

Some years ago, the citizens of San Francisco petitioned the city requesting that the words "pet owner" be dropped and replaced by "pet guardian," liking their cause to the abolition movement. Due to their efforts, the city now boasts a $7 million shelter where stray dogs and cats live in private condos furnished with wicker furniture, pillows, and framed prints. Private televisions play nature programs and cartoons. The animal shelter also has a full staff of behavioral psychologists. This facility was bought and paid for by the Society for the Prevention of Cruelty to

Animals! Did you know that in this country, more money is spent on pets, vets, pet care, and pet supplies than is collected by all churches put together?

What a pity that we do not have a society for the prevention of cruelty to people that is even half as zealous as the SPCA. Instead, we get angry at the poor for being poor. We have moved from the war on poverty to a war on poor people. That kind of callous indifference to suffering reminds me of Napoleon Bonaparte who was almost brought to tears by seeing a dog howling over his dead master in the war zone.

In his memoirs, Napoleon wrote, "The poor beast seemed to be asking for an avenger, begging for help. I was profoundly moved by the dog's suffering, and at that moment, I should have been very much in the mood to grant quarter to the enemy . . . Such is man—so little can he count on his moods! Impassively, I had sent my soldiers into battle. Dry-eyed, I had watched them marching past in an advance when thousands of them would meet their fate, and then I was shaken to the depths by the howling of a dog!"

Don't you see, sweet sentimentality has a dark, shamefully ugly, and self-centered side. It proudly turns in on itself and gloats, "Isn't it wonderful that I am sensitive enough to experience this marvelous emotion? Doesn't it speak well of my delicate sensibilities that I am able to feel so deeply this precious tender moment?"

In many of the fastest-growing churches, the question becomes not "Did we take care of the widows and the fatherless?" but "Did I have a titillating, spine-tingling religious experience today?" The emphasis shifts from doing good to feeling good, from loving my neighbor to loving myself, and from service to others to getting goose bumps under my skin. Then they can look back with nostalgia at that wonderful experience and tell people, "Oh, how spiritual it made me feel!" But listen to what Paul said about real "spiritual worship": "Present your bodies as a living sacrifice," he said. That means get off your duff and go out there and *actually* do something for others. He called that real spiritual worship (Romans 12:1–2).

In other words, as it is in tennis, so it is in life, your "service" is what really counts. By the way, the first time tennis is mentioned in the Bible is when "Moses served in Pharaoh's court." LOL. Please forgive my silly diversion, but my point is that as it is in tennis, so it is in worship. Without service, "love" only means that you have not scored one single point. That is why sweet sentimentality so rarely scores any points. Instead, it wallows in itself with empty, meaningless, feel-good delight!

Surely you have seen those TV programs and slick magazine ads asking you to adopt a pretty little girl for so much a month. But did you know that those highly expensive six-figure ads had to be purchased and the advertising executives' salaries and bureaucratic expenses come right off the top, not to mention your personal lovely eight-by-ten glossy photographs suitable for framing? And let's be honest, all people who need help are not pretty little girls, some of them are ugly, crippled, old, deformed, emaciated, and smelly. Some of them have harelips. Some are toothless old ladies and unsightly old men bent by arthritis, malnutrition, and all sorts of awful diseases. Some of them are missing ears, eyes, and limbs.

But when it comes to awful suffering like that, many pretty plastic-coated Barbie Doll, Christians are numb. They are not interested. They no longer feel responsible because they are no longer response-"able." They are no longer able to respond.

Surely, there is nothing more radiant than a young girl in love, but in spite of her joy and spontaneity, puppy love is often a shallow thing!

"I now believe in love at first sight! You are so beautiful," said the handsome young man."

"You flatter me," responded the young lady, "but I am not nearly as pretty as that girl over there."

"Where?" said the suitor as he swings around to look.

So sweet sentimentality lacks permanence. It lacks commitment and dependability! It is hollow and a whim of the moment until the next pretty attraction comes along. Puppy love is only being in love with the emotions of love. On the surface, it seems so shiny and bright, but like a new car finish, underneath, there is no depth (only hardness). Sentimentality selfishly starts with feelings and ends there. It wallows in itself, but it never accomplishes anything constructive. Real emotions set us in motion, but sweet sentimentality never seems able to translate those warm fuzzy feelings into a lasting response because sweet sentimentality substitutes the worship of feelings for the worship of God.

Now don't get me wrong, not all feelings are bad. On the contrary, feelings are truly fundamental movers. They are extremely important as long as they actually make us move. Then they can help relieve the sufferings of others through service and action. But real Christians do not sit around numbly, waiting to feel good one more time. Instead, they are dedicated to do good, whether they feel like it or not! That is why true disciples are willing to go against the in crowd and do what is unpopular, unattractive, and out of fashion. Think for a moment about some of the great men and women who have stood up to evil and injustice throughout the ages. How did they fare? Did they have time to enjoy spiritual titillation, goose bumps, and cotton-candy praise music? Hardly. To name a few:

>Socrates was poisoned.
>Jeremiah was imprisoned.
>Isaiah was sawed in half.
>John the Baptist was beheaded.
>Jesus was crucified.
>Stephen was stoned.
>Paul was tortured and beheaded.
>Peter was executed on an X-shaped (chi) cross upside down.
>The early Christians were often burned at the stake or eaten
>>by lions.

And when the news got out, thousands of people cheered with joy at the assassinations of: Abraham Lincoln, John F. Kennedy, Robert Kennedy, and Martin Luther King Jr. May God Almighty preserve us from the subtle sin of sweet sentimentality.

>**Blessed are those who are persecuted for righteousness's**
>**sake, for theirs is the kingdom of heaven.**
>>**—Matthew 5:10**

BE ANGRY BUT DO NOT SIN (EPHESIANS 4:26)

And he entered the temple and began to drive out those who were selling and those who were buying in the temple, and he overturned the tables of the money changers and the seats of those who sold doves; and he would not allow anyone to carry anything through the temple. He was teaching and saying, "Is it not written, 'My house shall be called a house of prayer for all the nations'? But you have made it a den of robbers." And when the chief priests and the scribes heard it, they kept looking for a way to kill him; for they were afraid of him, because the whole crowd was spellbound by his teachings.

—Mark 11:15–19

AT THE TURN of the century, George Crum was the chef at the Moon Lake Lodge in Saratoga Springs, New York. One day the robber baron Cornelius Vanderbilt came in and ordered the smashing new dish from Belgium called French fried potatoes. But when the waiter served them, Mr. Vanderbilt sent them back. "These are far too thick," he said. "I know, I just returned from Paris."

So Chef George sent out a second batch. These too were rejected. So Chef George became very angry and said to himself, "I'll show him."

He then cut the potato slices razor thin, dropped them into boiling oil, and sent them personally to Mr. Vanderbilt's table. Mr. Vanderbilt was truly impressed, and so was the world. In his anger, Chef George had invented the potato chip!

I share that story simply to make a point that constructive things can sometimes come out of destructive things. And even our anger, channeled in the right direction, can motivate and get our creative juices flowing into action. Therefore, I think it is a mistake to picture either God or

Jesus without some element of judgment and righteous indignation. In fact, all through the Old Testament, we have recurring images of God as an angry God who visits his wrath upon Sodom and Gomorrah and countless other sinful people. While the coming of Jesus helped us temper that understanding with forgiveness, love, mercy, and grace, even so, it would be a disservice to our Lord to deny him his rightful role as sovereign judge. Indeed, it was in that capacity that Jesus entered the temple and chased out the money changers and overturned those tables like a wild bull in a china shop! If that story of Jesus swinging a whip and turning over tables disturbs you, then you need to broaden your vision of who Jesus really was!

The famous late European theologian Karl Barth once accused us Americans of "sissifying" Jesus into Mary's pretty little lamb. After all, just because Jesus preached nonviolence and turning the other cheek did not make him an effeminate sissy. In fact, scholars tell us that according to tradition, prophets had to meet certain physical standards. The expectation of the rabbinical school was that a prophet would be a little taller and more imposing that the ordinary Joe. And not one of our Lord's critics ever accused him of being a ninety-pound weakling! So he must have had a self-assured bearing that exuded power and presence. Indeed, he was such a rough and ruddy character with skin exposed so often to the elements that people thought he was in his late forties when he was, in fact, in his early thirties.

From the time he was wrapped in coarse cloth as a baby, he had known the hard life. His father Joseph apparently died at an early age, and as the eldest son, Jesus had to support the family! In those days, there were no sawmills. Therefore, we can picture Jesus trudging the streets of Nazareth with freshly hewn beams on his shoulder. For almost twenty years, he toiled until his younger brothers could support themselves in the carpentry business. Only then did Jesus leave home to strike out on his own and began to preach. Just imagine what a powerful resonate voice he must have had to captivate thousands of people at once. And imagine the magnetic personality of a man who could inspire strangers to leave their work and follow him. He must have been quite an imposing figure, and his nerves must have been like steel. Even in the midst of a raging storm, he remained calm and serene. And in the face of his own brutal torture, he was resolute to the end. Certainly, he was no quitter. He refused to retreat or compromise his principles. His integrity remained intact even under fire.

Of course, all of us realize that, by nurture and teachings, this was a kind and gentle man—a nonviolent man. No man in history has ever been so loving and forgiving in the face of so much hatred and injustice. That is why we call him the Prince of Peace. He believed in loving his enemies, and he taught us to do the same by both precept and example. "The meek," he said, "will inherit the earth." And in Jesus, the meek did. "In the world, you will have tribulation, but be of good cheer; I have overcome the world."

Mahatma Gandhi once said that when a man slaps you in hatred, bravely turn to him the other cheek as Jesus taught. It literally does something to disarm the other man. It robs him of his power.

In Roman times, there was a law that any Roman soldier could force a non-Roman citizen to carry his armor for one mile. All Jews hated the Roman soldiers who held their land under occupation. So they constructed mileposts along the roads so that they would not have to carry that armor one inch farther than Roman law demanded. But Jesus said, "If a man asks you to go with him one mile, go with him two." Not as a sign of weakness, mind you, but as a symbol of freedom and character. The first mile you walked would be out of servitude, but the second mile you walked would be with dignity, of your own free will. And that act of quiet dignity may have a greater impact on your enemy's attitude than all the military force you could muster.

Therefore, when Jesus said the meek shall inherit the earth, he did not mean the "weak or the cowardly." Rather, he meant those who find inner strength through faith in God. Meekness originally implied the truly religious and humble gentle-minded person like Moses (Numbers 12:3) in contrast to those who are insolent and arrogant toward their fellow man. So Mahatma Gandhi used this philosophy of meekness to drive the British out of India through nonviolent defiance. He also inspired Martin Luther King Jr. and Nelson Mandela to follow the same path.

But what about the very uncharacteristic story of Jesus in the temple—violently turning over the tables of the money changers? Is this the same gentle Jesus we know and love? Surely, he must have been in quite a rage because the greedy money changers were so scared of him that they fled, leaving their money boxes behind. By the way, this story is recorded in all four Gospels. It might be added, however, that while Jesus later told the disciples to buy a couple of swords, he rebuked Peter for using one. According to John, Jesus reached out and healed the ear of the servant that Peter struck! Still, the incident in the temple reminds us that Jesus was not an absolute pacifist. Evidently, he did believe in some violence as a last resort.

Here is the background to the story: Roman law required the use of Roman coins in all business transactions. Caesar was regarded by Rome as a God; therefore, his graven image on the coins was not appropriate for the temple. So the priests set up their own relatives in the outer court to trade Roman coins for Hebrew coins at a very unfair—even crooked—rate of exchange. Now the coins were needed so that poor people could purchase overpriced doves as a sacrifice (Leviticus 5:7). Since the rich could afford to bring lambs and cattle for slaughter, the result was that the poor were being robbed and cheated in God's own house. Therefore, what angered Jesus was not the selling of the pigeons; it was the thievery—the cheating and gouging of the poor. (By the way, Jesus was not talking about church bazaars or bake sales.) Perhaps Jesus remembered how his own poor parents had to buy doves for sacrifice (Luke 2:24) at any rate, with the hawkers barking their expensive pigeons and the coins clanging in the boxes. "Step right up! Get your pigeons over here!" The temple looked more like a carnival midway than a house of worship! So not only were there mobsters making a circus of God's house, but they were also fleecing and exploiting the poor in God's name. Jesus couldn't take it anymore. He knew his time was short, and those greedy priests stood in the way of everything he stood for, so in a burst of righteous indignation, he lashed out with a whip.

How strange that when they were cruel to him, he remained calm. "When he was abused, he did not return abuse; when he suffered, he did not threaten" (1 Peter 2:23). But when he saw God defiled and the poor cheated in his Father's house, that made him angry—very angry! In the last decade or so, the common theme among action heroes in the movies seems to be to blow up the bad guy before he blows you up, the same goes for video games. Something within us wants our heroes to be tough and to be take-charge action-type guys who know how to fight and kill and who have the guts to get things done. Then we wonder why young people bring guns to school to shoot the innocent. And yet when Jesus attacked the money changers with a whip, we are shocked. It feels so wrong, so out of character. Not my meek, mild, and gentle Jesus! How can this be? We feel uncomfortable, embarrassed, and even in denial.

I think sometimes we get the impression in church that it is a sin ever to get angry for any reason. But this is not the case. Psalm 4:6 (RSV) says, "Be angry, but do not sin." The Bible speaks of the wrath of God and his fierce anger, but God does not sin! So sometimes, a little righteous indignation is the only appropriate response to evil. So where is it today? With drug abuse, child pornography, violence, pollution, and AIDS—all becoming a national epidemic—people need to get angry once in a while! In fact, I think the character of a person is partially determined by the things that make him or her angry.

One day a little girl asked her mother, "Mother, why are there so many more stupid people on the road when Daddy drives?"

I once heard a story about a little boy who hated stewed prunes. One night at supper, as the boy stuck out his lip and rolled his prunes around on his plate, his grandmother said, "Johnny, you are an ungrateful child. God made those prunes, and they are good for you. If you don't eat them, God is going to be very disappointed in you! So eat!"

"No way," the boy responded. "Never!"

"All right, young man," she said, "then you go up to your room right now!"

A short time later, a violent thunderstorm struck out of nowhere. Lightning was flashing, thunder was roaring, and the wind was whipping rain against the window panes.

"Poor boy!" the grandmother said to herself. "I'd better go upstairs and check on him to see if he is all right."

But to her surprise, she did not find the young fellow cowering in a corner. Instead, he was standing at the window with his hands on his hips shouting, "Come on, God, get a grip! It was only a few lousy prunes!"

Obviously, that boy realized that some things are worth getting angry about and some things are not!

Therefore, I believe a lot can be known about your spiritual life by the things that make you angry. Is it injustice to yourself or to others that upsets you the most? Is it petty sins like cursing or big sins like cruelty, injustice, and prejudice that invokes your anger?

Abraham Lincoln "took it" when people made fun of him: "If I were two-faced, wouldn't I wear the other face?" But he became mortally angry at the evils and oppression of slavery and dedicated his life to doing something about it.

Do you remember the old movie *Network*? It was about an angry TV news announcer who asked everybody to open their windows and scream, "I'm mad as hell, and I'm not going to take it anymore," as loud as they could. I dare say that all of us have felt that way at times in our lives, but that is pointless anger. That is rage without a target and without a constructive response. It is misdirected hostility. All that kind of anger will do is give you ulcers, high blood pressure, or a massive coronary. That kind of rage is both useless and self-destructive. But anger can also be very constructive if it get us off our duff and motivates us to spring into action and do something to make a difference in the world.

A father once said to his son, "Are you going to raise hell, or are you going to do something constructive with your life?"

To which the young man replied, "Why not do both?" and so he founded Greenpeace.

A few decades ago, a woman lost her child to a drunk driver. She was so angry that she formed an organization called MADD, Mothers against Drunk Driving. Surely, we all need to get angry about alcohol-related accidents. Indeed, there are fourteen thousand every hour of every day, and most of them involve youth or young adults who are below the drinking age.

Forty years ago, I remember driving through Smithfield, North Carolina, and seeing this huge billboard erected by the Ku Klux Klan, which depicted a hooded clansman rearing up on a white horse. It read, "Welcome to Klan Country." Then later, I learned of one relatively unknown man who fought against that sign. His name was Jonah Good. Mr. Good was the kind of man those signs were supposed to protect. He was a middle-class white Anglo-Saxon Protestant. He was also vice commander of his American Legion post and former commander of the disabled veterans in his local chapter. But Mr. Good got sick and disgusted with that hate sign in his town, and so he decided to do something about it. What he did was put up a smaller sign in his own front yard that read, "This is not Krooks, Killers, and Kowards Country. There is no hate here."

Immediately, Mr. Good was under attack, even from the mayor and his own pastor. He was branded as a troublemaker and agitator. Night riders began to blast his sign and his house with shotgun pellets. His children were harassed in school, and his wife received obscene phone calls and threats. Yet for all the anger caused by Mr. Good's six-foot homemade sign, no one seemed to be the least disturbed by the thirty-foot professional model constructed on Highway 70.

Mr. Good said, "If I had it all to do over again, I would do the very same thing."

May God bless him. "Silence isn't always golden, sometimes it is yellow."

Throughout the ages, people have stood up to evil with righteous anger. The evils of Nazi Germany drove a pastor named Dietrich Bonhoeffer to put his life on the line. He was executed for his plot to kill Hitler. Five hundred years earlier, Martin Luther grew angry at Pope Leo X for promising a pardon for dead relatives in exchange for money to build Saint Peter's Basilica in Rome. "The pope has more money than the poor people he is exploiting," Martin Luther said, "so let the pope pay for his own cathedral. Besides," he added, "if you pass by a poor beggar to send cash to the pope, you will invoke the wrath of God." So the pope had Martin Luther arrested to force him to recant. "Here I stand," Luther said, "and I can do no other."

Thus, out of anger at injustice, the Protestant Reformation was born. The more I think about it, the more I believe that when the "roll is called up yonder" on judgment day, the first question our Lord will ask is not did we curse or drink or gamble or use tobacco. On the contrary, what he will ask us is where did you take your stand, what made you angry enough to act, what causes were you willing to live and even die for, what risk did you take for the kingdom of God. *No, getting angry isn't always a sin—sometimes it's a sin not to get angry!*

THE PLACE WHERE RELIGION AND SCIENCE MERGE!

We look not at what can be seen but at what cannot be seen; for what can be seen is temporary, but what cannot be seen is eternal.

—2 Corinthians 4:18

I F YOU ARE still caught up in the old Newtonian concept of cause and effect, boy, have I got a surprise for you! If you feel frustrated because you know you are much more than what "world truth" says you are, if you feel you have a nonphysical spiritual dimension, take heart. Science may not entirely disagree. If you believe that you are more than a chance collection of chemical compounds, there is a new branch of science that sees truth, in the almost spiritual terms, of relationships. Indeed, the more that modern scientists study our universe, the more mysterious it gets, as science deals more and more with the unseen and the abstract. For example, we stand between a universe that is both infinitely large and infinitely small. On the one hand, we are part of a vast galaxy of stars called the Milky Way made up of billions of suns, and there are billions of other galaxies billions of light-years apart, in fact so far away that by the time their light reaches us, they may have already been extinct for eons. Then there is that mysterious, immeasurable, and unseen "dark matter" that fills 95 percent of the vast regions of space and quasars which, as they are being swallowed up by black holes, produce more light than a billion suns or dark energy that makes the universe expand instead of contract. Did you know that there are more stars in the universe than there are grains of sand on all the beaches of the world?

Now let's go small. Sir Isaac Newton's laws work great on the level of large planets, but not in the world of the infinitely small. Once, I had the privilege of attending a lecture by physicist Brian Greene of Columbia University. He is one of the leaders in string theory. He pointed out how subatomic particles are not really particles at all but invisible strings of energy floating around in a vast sea of empty space. In this tiny realm, there seems to be many different dimensions with multiple parallel universes. Weird, huh? Even as you read this, millions of exotic virtually massless subatomic particles with no charge called neutrinos have just passed right through you and on through planet Earth hardly slowing down. There are different kinds of neutrinos, and they can change from one kind to another as they travel. This is the strange new world of quantum mechanics.

No wonder Jesus said the kingdom of God is like "a tiny mustard seed." Truth indeed does not always lie in the very big, sometimes it lies in the very, very small where matter is merely an illusion. Why? Because on the level of subatomic particles, matter, as we know it, does not really exist. Even the word "particle" is merely a metaphor. Just suppose that you could actually enlarge a softball so big that you could hold one of its atoms in the palm of your hand. In order for that to happen, your softball would have to be enlarged to about the size of planet Earth. Then the countless atoms floating around inside that giant softball would be about the size of marbles, only they would not be hard like marbles. Inside this puff of energy that we call an atom would mainly be a few electrons on the edge of virtually nothing but emptiness. Yet even in this emptiness, there is this molasses-like non-substance that holds it all together called the Higgs boson (bit) or "God particle."

So like the planets in our solar system, the inside of our world-sized softball would be mostly empty space and inside of each atom still more empty space! At the center, just as the Earth orbits the sun, is the tiny nucleus, which is composed of still smaller non-particles like quarks. All of this tiny non-stuff drifts through this soupy void to somehow become a wonderful web of amazing interconnectedness. You see, all of these so-called particles are somehow related to one another. In other words, in the world of atomic entities, there is a wonderful inseparable web of mysterious interconnectedness to everything, which continually reaches out to make even more connections. Which is to say, that the essential nature of matter, and even of ourselves, is somehow bound to this harmonious symphony of beautiful rhythms and waves of invisible relationships that transcend time and space! . . . What I mean is that even down to the level of subatomic particles, life is engaged in a mysterious delicate dance of interrelatedness. What a beautiful concept! Einstein, however, did not like quantum theory. He said, "God did not play dice with the universe." But God knows the odds, doesn't he? So I see in the study of subatomic particles a new doorway between the physical and the spiritual realm. After all, what are these nebulous harmonious wisps of pure energy that make up all matter?

Is it possible that they may actually move from one dimension or universe to another? Could heaven be like looking at the other side of your hand? No one knows exactly what these subatomic entities actually are, but they're definitely nonmaterial. In this netherworld of the infinitely small, even the mass of the machines we use to study these so-called particles actually alters their very nature, so you can't pin them down. All you can study is tendencies. This is known as Heisenberg's principle of non-determinacy or the "uncertainty principle." What it means is there is no way on earth that we will ever be able to fully analyze these entities, except by the laws of chance.

This truth reveals to us the fallibility and limitations of our human perceptions. Even if you can figure out where these blips of energy were, you still can never know for sure where they are now or where they will be next (except by probability). In this strange invisible world, past, present, and future can become so jumbled that it is possible for one particle to be in two different places at once. In fact, two particles can actually go flying away from one to another almost at the speed of light yet doing a perfect mirror like dance across the universe just as if they were still in direct contact with each other. This is called quantum entanglement. Don't take my word for it. Google it!

I know I may sound like a nut, but it gets even more bizarre. Welcome to the Twilight Zone. It turns out that even the intention of the observer seems to have an effect to these tiny units of invisible energy. It is, to put it bluntly, as if the particle somehow has a passion of its own and is responding to the pleasure and intention of the observer.

For example, there is a famous experiment where photons are fired like bullets at two tiny slits, but when you observe them, they behave like particles, but they act like waves when you don't! Furthermore, they even seem to anticipate such observations before they actually happen in the future! How weird is that?

No wonder physicist Michael Polanyi in his classic book *Personal Knowledge* argued that science can no longer claim to act as an impartial and detached observer. We can no longer separate objectively the knower from that which he (or she) knows or the observer from that which he or she observes. So as I said in the very beginning of this chapter, the old basic Newtonian laws of cause and effect, at least in the realm of the infinitely small, have soared away into a new dimension on the gossamer wings of quantum mechanics and "God particles." So shall we all say it together, *Hello, mystery! Hello, wonder! Hello, miracle! Hello, spiritual realm!*

THE LEGACY OF ARCHIMEDES

Happy are those who find wisdom (Sophia) and those who get understanding. For her income is better than silver, and her revenue better than gold.

—Proverbs 3:13–14

WHAT IF I were to tell you that many truly new innovative discoveries and scientific breakthroughs have not come from objective empirical investigation at all but rather from what might be called revelation? Indeed, they have occurred (much like a religious experience) as inspiration in the twilight moments between wakefulness and sleep, or in what might be called the spirit realm, at the edge of our clearing in the forest of consciousness. Albert Einstein often spoke almost reverently of the strange mystical illumination that gave rise to his famous theory of relativity. "There comes a leap in consciousness, call it intuition, or what you will, the solution comes to you and you don't know why."

Sir William Hamilton said his theory on higher mathematics came from a mystical illumination he had while he was crossing a bridge. (He spent fifteen years unraveling that vision.) Friedrich August Kekule had a mystical experience in which he actually visualized the benzene ring floating before his eyes. The list of so-called objective scientists who made their greatest discoveries in the unseen realm of the spirit seems to be endless.

To me, this is not unlike the ancient prophets of Israel who received divine enlightenment from beyond. So could it be that these scientists also heard the voice of God and that "eureka" is just another word for "hallelujah"?

I still have many things to say to you but you cannot bear
them now. When the Spirit of truth comes he will guide
you into all the truth; for he will not speak on his own,
but speak whatever he hears, and he will declare to you
the things that are to come.

—John 16:12–13

HOW COULD YOU DESCRIBE A MUSTANG IN ELOQUENT DETAIL AND STILL DENY THE FORD MOTOR COMPANY?

When I look at your heavens, the work of your fingers, the moon and the stars that you have established, what are human beings that you are mindful of them, mortals that you care for them?

—Psalm 8:3–4

ONE DAY A professor of astronomy was flying in an airplane next to a minister. "Pastor, I suppose," said the astronomer, "that I could sum up your profession with one phrase: Jesus loves me, this I know."

"And I suppose," Said the minister, "that I could sum up your profession with one phrase: Twinkle, twinkle, little star!"

The story goes that when a little old lady first heard about the theory of evolution, she was so upset that she got down on her knees and prayed, "O Lord, I pray that this awful thing is not true, that we came from monkeys, but if it is true, then I pray that no one else ever hears about it. Amen." Then there was the one about the monkey who went to the library to study Darwin and figure out whether he was his brother's keeper or his keeper's brother!

Jesus never commanded us to be stupid. Instead, he commanded us to be "wise as serpents and gentle as doves" (Matthew 10:16). "There are many things I could teach you," he said, "but you are not able to bear them yet, but the Spirit will teach you 'all things.'" In other words, you will find out at the appropriate time on a need-to-know basis.

So I am not only opposed to those who would use science to undermine religion, but I am also equally opposed to those who would use religion to undermine science. I am embarrassed by those who still insist that the world was created in six earth days or that people and dinosaurs once lived together.

In my opinion, when either science or fundamentalism claims to have sole possession of the truth, truth always suffers, for example, when science says something like "Depression is *nothing but* a chemical imbalance" or "Thoughts are *nothing but* a series of physio-chemical events, and that's all there is." Scientific truth is, by definition, limited because science works within a closed system which is always dependent upon empirical verification, while religion deals with truths that can be neither proven nor dis-proven. In other words, they deal with different kinds of truth. But let's give science and technology their due.

Frankly, I am amazed at the achievements of human technology. There is no doubt that our ancestors would look in at the things we do every day in utter awe! As Psalm 8 suggests, they would almost view us as gods. At the push of a button, we can link up with someone's computer on the other side of the world and send them an encyclopedia. We can navigate in our cars with satellite guided maps. We could even fly to Mars, alter our genes, clone sheep, transplant hearts, grow new body parts, and even replicate ourselves! So in our arrogance, are we still in need of a gentle Jesus? My answer is yes, we are! In fact, it seems to me that the more God-like we become, the more we need a higher referent to guide us in using our new awesome powers wisely and ethically.

As Christians, I believe that we are merely trustees of God's creation, answerable to God as to how we manage his world. However, the danger comes when we seek to find ultimate fulfillment from creation itself. Then either the world could destroy us or else we could destroy the world. That is how technology has gotten strangely out of control and has taken on a life of its own. We no longer run our machines, they run us. No wonder we have lost our moral and spiritual moorings and have been set adrift in a sea of corporate greed without either rudder or compass.

Let me make one thing clear—this book is in no way an endorsement of so-called scientific creationism which, to me, only combines bad science with bad theology in a soup of naïve literalism which is then used to bash science on the head in the name of being scientific! That kind of silly pseudoscience only serves to cut Christians off from 90 percent of the educated people on this planet! But it does concern me that in a world where we have harnessed so many God-like powers, doesn't science still need to hear a word about judgment and values? People also need to know there is meaning and purpose in the universe and that life has a why as well as a how. So in spite of its flaws and limitations, I still have empathy with the teleological argument from design.

The question, however, is not did life on earth arise over a long gradual evolutionary process, lasting billions of years. (By all indications, it did.) The real question is could this process be possible without some kind of order, direction, and purpose. There are so many delicate variables to life, including the precise angle of the earth and its location in relation to the sun. (A few degrees off and we would either freeze or burn!) Even Stephen Hawking had to acknowledge that if the big bang events were off by just one part on one quintillion, our world, as we know it, could never have happened! So the burning question to me is, was there meaning to the process, or was it all just a lucky break? I enjoy science and almost made a career of it! I enjoy stories of dinosaur bones and black holes. But I am more concerned about the questions science cannot answer: What is our destiny? Why are we here? What is our reason for being? How do we manage this tiny fragile planet?

Even John Wesley saw creation as a gradual process over a long period, but he did not rule out God from the process. On the contrary, while regarding the strange connection between man and ape, he wrote, in 1763:

> By what degrees does nature raise herself up to man? How shall she rectify the head that is inclined toward the earth? What method did she use to transform those crooked feet into supple and skillful hands? The ape is this rough sketch of man, which bears a crude resemblance to him and is the last creature that serves to display the admirable progression of the works of God." (*The Wisdom of God in Creation: A Compendium of Natural Philosophy*)

Take note that Charles Darwin's *Origin of Species* was first published almost one hundred years later. So did Darwin read Wesley? By the way,

Darwin was not an atheist. He wrote, "In my most extreme fluctuations, I have never been an atheist, in the sense of denying the existence of God." As he concluded at the end of his book, he simply believed his theory "accords better with what we know about the laws impressed by the Creator." So he saw himself as simply uncovering the methods God used in creation. Ironically, Aristotle did a far more intricate study of animal life over two thousand years before Darwin. But the Greeks saw life as cyclic and repetitious rather than linear and progressive. The most Hellenistic book in the Bible (thanks to the influence of Alexander the Great) attests, "What has been is what will be, and what has been done is what will be done; and there is nothing new under the sun" (Ecclesiastes 1:9). So Darwin is actually indebted to the Judea-Christian culture for viewing history as moving, not in a circle but in a linear progression.

But the real questions remain: Is life an accident or a gift? Did the world bring itself into being, or was there a purposeful direction behind it? Did we emerge from a dark pool of nothingness, or was there a creative intelligence in the universe to whom we owe our deepest thanks and praise? My real concern is that if life began as an accident, then man has no spirit, no soul, and no destiny.

Auguste Comte was a nineteenth-century French philosopher who came up with a negative philosophy that he called positivism. Now don't get this confused with Norman Vincent Peale's *Power of Positive Thinking*. In fact, I think Comte's philosophy should have been called reductionism. Positivism is the secular philosophy that inspired Friedrich Nietzsche and later Adolf Hitler. The main tenant of this Godless philosophy was that the material world is the only reality there is. There is no such thing as spirituality. So if it cannot be empirically observed and quantified by scientific investigation, then it does not exist. Therefore, everything in the universe can be explained without "any reference to God" whatsoever.

By the way, positivism or secular humanism is the only religion that is sanctioned, protected, and subsidized by the United States government as the spiritual realm has been banished from the classroom in every other form (from Buddhism to Judaism). However, I argue that ultimate reality is much more than material stuff. I say life is a sacred gift, a wonder, and a mystery. The Japanese have learned how to grow bonsai trees by cutting out the taproot to force the tree to live only on the surface. As a result, what could have been a majestic oak tree grows only a foot high. It seems to me that when we materialize truth, we do the very same thing to the human spirit! Consequently, we have raised a generation that is technically full but spiritually emaciated because the taproot of the Spirit has been cut out of the curriculum and the culture! I hate to admit it, but the church is partly to blame for that. When the church attacked Kepler, Copernicus, and Galileo, we set ourselves up for payback time. Now science claims, as the church once did, to have the capstone on all truth. Both sides were wrong!

I call the former materialistic attitude justification by quantification. It regards spiritual matters as superstitious nonsense. It is as if almighty man is only answerable to himself for his behavior and religion is merely a superstitious anachronism. In other words, there is no longer any room in this "accidental universe" for the Spirit, God, mystery, or wonder because science and technology alone will save us. We are, after all, in this view, here only by a chance collection of atoms in a cold, impersonal, meaningless cosmos. So to know the truth is to become disinterested, detached, and skeptical.

For example, if someone asks you "What is a frog?" you find your answer by dissecting the frog. In other words, you kill it and dismantle it in order to understand it. The same reductionism can be seen if you ask "What is a human being?"

The biologist answers, "A human is nothing but another member of the animal kingdom, no more or no less, so biology can tell you who humans really are."

"Oh no," says the chemist. "Even our thoughts are nothing but a series of physio-chemical processes, and our DNA reveals everything about us. Therefore, chemistry can tell you who humanity really is."

"No, no," says the physicist. "Chemistry is nothing but the study of atoms, so physics can best tell you what a human really is."

"Hold on," says the mathematician. "All of physics can be reduced to higher numbers, so mathematics will tell you what human beings really are."

"Wait one minute, nothing can crunch numbers better than computers," says the computer technician. "Therefore, computer technology will tell you who you really are!"

The moral is beware of those materialistic reductionists who try to convince you that you, this world, or life is *nothing but* this or that.

Once upon a time, a baby sea turtle was dropped in a well with a tiny old freshwater turtle. "Who are you?" asked the freshwater turtle.

"I am a sea turtle," said the young turtle.

"What is the sea?" asked the old well turtle. "Is it as big as my well?"

"Oh no," said the sea turtle, "it is far bigger than your well—why, you could swim your whole life and not make your way around the edge of it."

"You are a fool," said the well turtle. "Nothing could possibly be that big. You lie!"

As Hamlet said, "There are more things in heaven and earth, Horacio, than are dreamed of in your philosophy!"

Socrates was right. As your circle of knowledge increases, so does your boundary of ignorance. The more you learn, the more you realize that there is so much more stuff you do not know.

Charles Darwin tells of primitive island natives who were awestruck by the small lifeboats that came ashore, but they were almost oblivious to the large ship offshore. They could not comprehend anything that large, and so they simply ignored it.

Happily, I can say that the world of science has begun to take on a little more humility. As I said before, from black holes to dark matter, today's science deals more and more with the invisible, the mysterious, and the unseen. The more they study the universe, the more mysterious it gets. Heck, if you can believe that one tiny little particle with the mass of the entire cosmos somehow detonated itself in order to produce the big bang and make all that there is in the entire universe over a period of 13.7 billion years, then—after that scenario, belief in God just might not seem much of a stretch.

My real concern, however, is that when science chooses to deny the spiritual side of life, it leads to a kind of fatalism that bows down to "Fat Chance" and "Lady Luck." As I see it, if there is no Creator, then there is no such thing as right or wrong—only survival of the fittest. No wonder an atheist like Ayn Rand could ridicule the very idea of altruism and strongly oppose welfare for the less fortunate. In other words, if there is no God, then we can be as greedy as we like; we can pollute the earth and waste its resources as we please. Don't you see, if human beings are no more than a chance collection of atoms, then we are set adrift in a sea of moral relativity. Morality becomes meaningless because there is no measuring stick, no higher referent, no standard, no guideline, so anything goes. Welcome to the brave new world of Friedrich Nietzsche where only the strong survive.

As a preacher's kid, we moved around a lot, so my last two years of high school were in Whiteville, North Carolina. My English teacher was Mrs. McGirt. One thing she required of all her students was to memorize and recite Macbeth's soliloquy: "Tomorrow, and tomorrow, and tomorrow," wrote William Shakespeare. (Why she wanted such negative thoughts imprinted forever on our young brains I do not know.) "Life is but a walking shadow; a poor player who struts and frets his hour upon the stage and then is heard no more. It is a tale told by an idiot, full of sound and fury, signifying nothing."

I remember a song that Peggy Lee sang back in the sixties: "Is that all there is? Because if that's all there is, then let's pass out the booze and have a ball." Who knows, perhaps Macbeth was right after all: "Life is a tale told by an idiot, full of sound and fury, signifying nothing." God help me, I refuse to believe that is true. If survival of the fittest is the goal of life, then why evolve beyond the shark. The shark is the perfect predator! It has virtually remained unchanged for millions of years. So should we emulate the shark to devour the weak and prey upon smaller fish? Should we eliminate those inferior to us that might weaken the genetic pool? God forbid! But what does happen to values like compassion and altruism in a world of cutthroat survival of the strongest? I say, morality becomes irrelevant. The greedy values of corporations (people?) replace compassion!

When I look around at creation, I see the artistic work of a gifted artist/engineer rather than happenstance and good fortune. I see a world so complex, so well designed, so beautiful, so highly organized, so intricately interconnected that it baffles my mind. How could it all be just an accident? So I affirm, with my whole heart, that I am a creature and God is my creator. I don't know how God did it. My Bible only tells me who made this universe, not how. But consider this—you have 120 trillion connections in the cortex of your brain. No other creature comes even remotely close to that. Or take your eyes, they are amazing precision instruments like no other creatures in the world. So how does life swim upstream with such resolve from lower forms to higher forms, from the very simple to the highly complex, without some outside help? Did you know that science regards the human brain as the most complicated biological structure in the known universe? Talk about leaping up the evolutionary steps. In other words, billions of complex changes would have had to occur all at once—all in a favorable direction—and then be passed on somehow by genetic code to the next generation.

We are not talking here about an elephant's trunk getting longer or a giraffe's neck reaching higher or a whale developing flippers in place of legs. That is kindergarten stuff! We are talking about highly precise and complex engineering marvels. Darwin argued that time alone, over eons, can work wonders in improving species, and that is true. We have done stuff like that ourselves by breeding horses and dogs and plants. But what guiding force can turn a collection of random mistakes into such delicate feats of workmanship that scientists study the flight of birds and bees just to learn how to build better airplanes and other such complex technical devices?

Let me give you a silly parable: Once upon a time, an electric adding machine fell in love with an IBM Selectric typewriter, and somehow they gave birth to a baby IBM computer with fifty gigabytes. Could that ever happen? Of course not, not even with a whole lot of technical encouragement, much less all by itself.

So if life is no more than a chance collection of random physical and chemical hiccups, then how do you account for the amazing complexity, the precision engineering, the delicate interdependence, the breathtaking beauty, the unique designs, the neat patterns of growth, and the astounding web of intricate interconnected relationships—even by completely different life-forms like slugs and jelly fish that are totally interdependent upon each other? (See "The Medusa and the Snail")

In the scientific community, those who find mechanisms to support the theory of order out of randomness are often rewarded with grants and articles in prestigious journals. While those who find glitches in the system are often ostracized and relegated to obscurity. But how can "random luck" work without a guiding force or a higher ordering principle in the universe? Let me put it this way: Do most of your accidents make things better for you, or do they make things worse? Think about it! How is that working for you? Here is my ultimate question to the God-doubters of this world: If we as human beings are the universe that after eons is finally able to reflect back in self-awareness upon the profound wonder of its own existence, then is that a mere fluke or an ingenious premeditated act? Consider the earth's incredible complexity, why does our planet seem to be so deliberately fine-tuned in favor of life? Is there not some unseen presence involved here? I think there is, and I call it God! Ask yourself this question: for whom do flowers bloom, and why do they smell so good? Flowers actually build runways on their petals for bees to land on, but by whose suggestion? Bees operate mostly by electromagnetic fields and in the bands of ultraviolet light. So why does a flower have to be so refined in subtle color or so beautiful in form just in order to survive? How did it know it needed to be beautiful, or even what beauty is? Why such an amazing collection of complex variations in flowers?

If you have a box of Scrabble squares and you begin to shake that box, eventually you might randomly spell the word "evolution." But without looking inside the box now and then, how would you ever know when you got it right? "OK, flower you are a beautiful pink rose. Now hold it. Stop mutating right there!" Darwin called the problem of intricate complexity the abominable question.

The Bible says that God created the world for us to enjoy as a gift. Is that true or false? Is there any other creature on earth other than man that can really appreciate the wonder of a rainbow or the beauty of a rose? "We all know that something is eternal. And it ain't houses and it ain't names, and it ain't earth, and it ain't even the stars . . . everybody knows in their bones that something is eternal, and that something has to do with human beings. All the greatest people ever lived have been telling us that for five thousand years and yet you'd be surprised how people are always losing hold of it. There's something way down deep that's eternal about every human being."—stage manager, in the play, "*Our Town*" by Thornton Wilder

O Lord, how manifold are your works!
—Psalm 104:24

THE WORLD WIDE WEB

In Caesarea there was a man named Cornelius, a centurion of the Italian Cohort, as it was called. He was a devout man who feared God with all his household, he gave alms generously to the people and prayed constantly to God. One afternoon at about three o'clock, he had a vision in which he clearly saw an angel of God coming in and saying to him, "Cornelius." He stared at him in terror and said, "What is it, Lord?" He answered. "Your prayers and your alms have ascended as a memorial before God. Now send men to Joppa for a certain Simon who is called Peter, he is lodging with Simon, a tanner, whose house is by the seaside." When the angel who spoke to him had left, he called two of his slaves and a devout soldier from the ranks of those who served him, and after telling them everything, he sent them to Joppa . . . Now while Peter was greatly puzzled about what to make of the vision that he had seen, suddenly the men sent by Cornelius appeared. They were asking for Simon's house and were standing by the gate . . . So Peter invited them in and gave them lodging.
—Acts 10:1–23

I WAS A STUDENT at Duke Divinity School, and *just by chance*, Duke Endowment sent me to First United Methodist Church in Graham to do summer fieldwork. And *just by chance*, bright and pretty Judy Bason was the junior high Sunday school teacher. *And just by chance*, after we had dated a few weeks, she got a call from her former college professor who worked as regional director for Educational Testing Service, who offered her a great new job in Durham as his private secretary, for almost twice her salary. So *just by chance*, we would both be living in Durham at the same time, and *just by chance*, since marriage had seemed a real possibility sometime in the distant future, why not now? The problem was that it was already mid-September, and housing around the

Duke campus was long gone. In fact, when I approached the lady in the Duke housing office to request an apartment, she laughed! But then a fellow right behind me in line, *just by chance,* was turning in his efficiency apartment key. "He can have mine," he said. And so, *just by chance,* we were married that September! That was one month after we had first met. Over forty years later, we are still happily married. Coincidence or providence?

Doesn't it seem strange to you how apparently unrelated events can indeed seem so interconnected beyond mere coincidence? The examples are legion. Frank Morgan, who played three different characters in the movie version of *Wizard of Oz,* needed a costume for his part as Professor Marvel, the traveling sideshow man who met Dorothy in the black-and-white opening scenes. The wardrobe staff was looking for a special kind of coat, so they went to a secondhand shop and bought fifty coats for Mr. Morgan to try on. Out of the fifty, Frank picked an old Prince Albert coat with a velvet collar that flared at the waist. It turned out that the name in the pocket of that randomly chosen coat was L. Frank Baum, the deceased author of the original story of the *Wizard of Oz.* Coincidence or what?

When Norman Mailer began his novel *Barbary Shore,* there was no Russian spy in the story line. However, he soon began to weave a Russian spy into the plot, and gradually, the spy became an even more significant character. By the end of the novel, this Russian spy was a dominant character in the book. It was not until the novel was finished that Mr. Mailer made a startling discovery! The immigration service had just arrested Col. Rudolf Abel, the top Russian spy in the United States, who had been living all that time one flight below Norman Mailer in the very same apartment building. Coincidence or what?

In the 1920s, Harvard professor William McDougall began to test the intelligence of rats by running them through a water maze. To his amazement, each generation of rats was more efficient at learning the maze than its parents, so those rats born twenty generations later were ten times as fast at running the maze as the first-generation rats.

Since a cardinal rule of biology is that learning cannot be transmitted genetically (behavior and instincts but not learning), many scientists were therefore utterly skeptical of these results and tried to debunk them. One suggestion was perhaps they smelled the old trail (ten times better?). However, even when the experiment was duplicated across the Atlantic in England, it was observed that the first generation of rats to try the maze over there was already as smart as Dr. McDougall's twentieth-generation rats. In fact, some of the rats actually went through the maze correctly the first time as if they had already been through it many times before! Coincidence or what?

Did you know that studies have found that crossword puzzles actually become easier to work as more people fill them out over time? Test subjects were actually able to raise their scores when working on puzzles that had been around for a few weeks for others to try first.

Normally, new crystalline compounds are hard to produce, that is until you produce one. After that, they become much easier to produce until they soon form easily all over the world. Since this proves to be an embarrassment to science, many excuses are offered, such as sloppy laboratory techniques that allow seeds to be carried on lab coats from place to place. But could it be that the simple truth is that reality is far more interconnected that even Hamlet dreamed. As John Muir once put it, "Whenever we touch any single object in nature, we find it hitched to everything else in the universe."

Dr. Rupert Sheldrake of Cambridge University was concerned about the way that revelations like this get swept under the proverbial rug because they are such an embarrassment to the scientific worldview. So he has come up with a name for this pervasive continuum of interconnectedness. He calls this invisible web of domino-like influence morphogenetic resonance. But whatever you want to label it, life does seem to be on a grid—touch one part and all is affected. Dr. Sheldrake compares this to radio waves or the ripple effect of a rock dropped in a pond but with one dramatic difference. These waves form clusters that actually grow stronger rather than weaker over time—like a snowball rolling down a hill. He believes, for example, if enough people know something, eventually everybody will know it.

Bolstering this argument, Ken Keyes Jr. tells the story of a particular type of Japanese monkey that was studied in the wild on a deserted island called Koshima for a period of thirty years. In 1952, due to a severe drought, zoologists broke a cardinal rule of noninterference by introducing a new food—sweet potatoes—into the monkeys' diet. The monkeys loved the tubers but hated the grit and sand that got in their mouths when they ate them. They would sputter and spit to avoid swallowing the sand. Then one day a monkey genius named Imo, an eighteen-month-old female, made a discovery. She found that by taking the raw potatoes to a nearby stream, she could wash off the grit and they were much more pleasant to eat. First, she showed her mother, and then she showed her playmates, and they in turn showed their mothers. That was equivalent in human terms to the invention of the wheel. Scientists watched with fascination as this new cultural innovation took place, so that by 1958, most of the younger monkeys had learned this new delightful technique. That was when something very strange and exciting happened according to Dr. Lyall Watson.

In the autumn of that year, an unspecified number of monkeys on Koshima were washing potatoes in the "sea" because Imo, by this time, made the further discovery that salt water not only cleaned their food but also gave it an interesting flavor. Let us imagine, for argument's sake, that the magic number was 99 and that precisely at eleven o'clock on Tuesday morning, one further convert was added to the field, but the addition of that one hundredth monkey somehow crossed over some sort of threshold because by that evening, every monkey on the entire island was washing his or her food in the ocean. (*The Hundredth Monkey* by Ken Keyes, Jr.).

Could it be that the added energy of that one hundredth monkey established a field and opened up some new dimension that transcended time and space? Because, stranger still, scientists suddenly began to observe this new food-washing behavior not only on Koshima Island but also on other surrounding islands and even on the Japanese mainland! In other words, suddenly, all the colonies, even on different islands, began to wash their food in the ocean before they ate it.

Now I must confess that when I first read that story, I did so with a great deal of skepticism because it shatters completely the materialistic worldview. It also destroys the manner in which we usually view and understand the transfer of knowledge in our universe! Think about it. Here was an awareness not transmitted by observation, books, genes, speech, sign language, or physical contact but from mind to mind, even over great distances. So consider this: If that is true for rats in a maze or monkeys on a deserted island, how much more might it be true for human beings? Yet there are some who question the value and power of corporate prayer. How sad!

Speaking of prayer, in the scripture at the beginning of this chapter, two men who lived in different towns and who had never met each other shared a common vision—each about the other—that brought them together through prayer. One was a Gentile centurion from Caesarea who heard an inner voice directing him to send two men to Joppa and seek out a Jew named Peter to be his houseguest. The vision even included the address of where Peter was to be found. Meanwhile, Peter had a dream about eating Gentile foods which the Jews considered to be unclean and a voice said, "What God has cleansed, you must not call common." Soon after that, the Gentiles from Caesarea arrived and stood at the gate. Inside the house at that precise moment, Peter had a second premonition as a voice said, "Behold three men are looking for you. Rise and go down and accompany them without hesitation, for I have sent them." So Peter returned to Caesarea with these three strangers, and there he met the pagan centurion Cornelius. So Peter preached to his Gentile family, ate their Gentile food, and then baptized the entire houschold—men, women, children, and servants—in the name of the Lord Jesus Christ. "Who was I," Peter said, "that I could withstand God?" Coincidence or providence?

Could it be that luck is simply the term God uses when God doesn't sign God's name? And could it be that another term for coincidence is providence?

One day John Wesley's carriage became mired in a mud hole. As the driver worked to pull the wheels free, a beggar approached the carriage door to beg for food. As Mr. Wesley placed some coins in the poor man's hands, he turned to his fellow passengers and remarked, "Perhaps now you can understand why it was necessary for us to become stuck in the mud."

I believe that there is indeed an unseen flow of spiritual energy out there and that prayer can tap into that energy field, especially when two or three are gathered together in his name. It is then that a field is established as oceans of rhythms flow together in clusters, guided by an unseen hand, and events begin to fall into place. Isn't that what the prophets and sages, throughout the ages, have been telling us? Life is a web, so never under estimate either the world's influence on you or your influence on the world!

William James once described life as a great cosmic battle between good and evil, in which somehow each of us are needed to turn the tide! No wonder God calls us to be children of light—to pull together and to be perfectly one! So could it be that if we all do our part at a certain point in history, as we generate together enough spiritual waves and as more and more of us tune to the same frequency guided by the Holy Spirit in our midst, eventually everybody will tune in?

Jesus said, "And the Gospel of the kingdom will be preached throughout the whole world as a testimony to all nations and then the end will come" (Matthew 24:14). Therefore, if enough people know something, eventually everybody will know it. As a field is strengthened to the point that this awareness will reach from pole to pole, I am reminded of the hymn based on Isaiah: "For the earth shall be filled with his knowledge and glory as waters that cover the sea."

"No longer," cried Jeremiah, "will each man say to his neighbor, 'Know the Lord,' for they all shall know me from the least of them to the greatest." Folks, just think. If one single monkey named Imo could influence all the monkeys in Japan, then who knows what potential we might have! Jesus was right after all. Don't you get it, "We really are the light of the world."

> Almost a century ago, the Rev. Charles Morgan was pastor of a little Methodist Church in Winnipeg, Canada. One night in a dream, he heard the sound of rushing waters and a tumult of voices calling out desperately for help! Then he saw himself posting a certain hymn number on the wall of his church. When he woke up, he still remembered that number. So for the evening service, on an impulse, he put this number on the hymn board. It was "Eternal Father, Strong to Save" (Navy Hymn)," Eternal Father strong to save, whose arm hath bound the restless wave, Who bidd'st the mighty ocean deep, its own appointed limits keep. Oh hear us when we cry to Thee, for those in peril on the sea (By William Whiting)

The date was April 14, 1912. And it just so happened that as the congregation was singing that hymn, one of the greatest sea tragedies of all time was taking place offshore in the North Atlantic. The unsinkable ship, the *Titanic*, was going down. So confident were the shipbuilders and engineers that this boat could never sink, that they did not even provide enough lifeboats on board to save all passengers. The people screamed in terror in the night. They were trapped with no chance of escape.

Now to those who believe only in objective facts and in what the eye can see, I ask you, where was hope for those poor souls who cried out in fear? Certainly, it was not to be found in the achievements of men. They found no comfort and consolation there. On the contrary, the great engineering skills that went into the building of that ship, there was only a cruel and tragic irony. Furthermore, no one was cherishing lovely thoughts about the beauty of Mother Nature. Indeed, nature and the elements seemed more like a cruel monster. And yet, somehow, out of chaos and all appearances to the contrary, something broke through the terror of that night to offer *hope*. There was an invisible something that offered peace and comfort to those troubled souls. Is it possible that this small spark of light in the darkness came from a little Methodist congregation in Winnipeg, Canada, who sang a prayer at that precise moment to a mighty God who is strong to save souls in peril on the sea? For suddenly, one woman, whose fears were strangely calmed, began to sing, "Nearer, My God, to Thee" until other hearts were touched and they too joined in on the chorus.

So I ask you, was this simply a coincidence, or was there a divine connection? Was there something more going on that night than meets the eye or that senses can perceive? Wasn't there a deeper presence, a higher truth, than what machines can calculate or instruments record? I believe there was! It was the unseen presence of God whose outstretched hand was ever present even in that God-forsaken place as prayers were offered and answered in ways too wonderful for us to comprehend in this life! I do not believe in determinism, but I do believe in the providence of God. I also believe in the power of prayer. I contend that life is a web and that all of us are somehow connected together both in this life and the next.

If one little Methodist congregation in Canada could spread the spirit of hope across the dark cold ocean, then perhaps you too can make a difference as well. So here is the question: Will the universe suffer the consequences of your indifference and your neglect, or will it reap the rewards of your deepest faith and noblest ideals? Who knows, perhaps you may be like that one hundredth monkey—you just might be the one extra light in the darkness that turns the tide.

**For where two or three are gathered together in my name,
I am there among them.**
—Matthew 18:20

BEWARE OF THE GOD EXPERTS!

For the time is coming when people will not put up with sound doctrine, but having itching ears, they will accumulate for themselves teachers to suit their own desires, and will turn away from listening to the truth and wander away to myths . . .
—2 Timothy 4:3–4

TWO LADIES WERE shopping during the Christmas rush. "I am so tired," one of them said. "In fact, I stay tired all the time. I don't guess I will ever have a chance to really lie down and rest until the day I die!"

"I know what you mean," said the second lady, "but with my luck, when I finally do lie down in my grave, it will probably be Resurrection morning, and I'll have to get right back up again!"

Before he died, Jesus knew that things were going to get very rough for his followers, so in order to give them *hope*, Jesus gave them a promise. He promised someday he would return at the end time. Not only that, but also those difficult in-between times would provide a wonderful opportunity to witness. By the way, do you know that the word "martyr" literally means "witness"? Yet over the years, we have come to associate apocalypse and the end time with disaster and doom instead of witness, with warning instead of hope, fear instead of trust.

That's the problem with words. They rarely mean what they once did. For example, when the famous British architect Sir Christopher Wren finally finished rebuilding Saint Paul's Cathedral in 1710, it had taken him thirty-five years. So he waited with baited breath to hear the queen's assessment of his work.

Queen Ann used only three terse adjectives to sum up her evaluation. She found the building to be "Awful, artificial, and amusing!"

226

How would you have felt if she said that to you? Well, Sir Christopher Wren was elated. He heaved a grateful sigh of relief, knelt humbly before his queen, and thanked her profusely. Why? Because that is the dramatic way that language has changed. You see in the early eighteenth century, the word "awful" meant "awe inspiring," the word "artificial" meant "artistic," and the word "amusing" meant "amazing." Such is the case for other religious terms like "apocalypse." Yes, in apoplectic language, there is a lot of talk about scary things and catastrophic calamities—dragons, demons, and disasters—with powerful imagery and unearthly poetry. But the message is "Don't worry, *don't give up*, endure." Apocalyptic is the language of victory and hope, not of fear, despair, and doom.

One day a mother cat and her kittens were suddenly attacked by a ferocious dog. Quickly, the mother cat hid her kittens under the porch. Then she walked right up to the dog, looked him in the eye, and said, "Ruff, ruff, grrrr!"

The dog backed up, looking surprised and confused, and then went away. The mother said to her kittens, "I hope, children, that now you can better understand what I meant when I insisted that you need to learn a second language."

Apocalyptic literature is a kind of second language found in certain books of the Bible, such as Daniel, Revelation, Ezekiel, and in a few other places. The word "apocalyptic" comes from a Greek word that means "to reveal." But contrary to popular opinion, it is not the language of prediction, prognostication, and terror. Rather, it is the language of *encouragement, hope,* and *victory!* Indeed, if you were to summarize the core message of the entire book of Revelation in one sentence, it would be Revelation 13:10 and again at Revelation 14:12, "Here is a call for the endurance and faith of the saints,"

There is in every believer a longing for the coming kingdom, where the books of injustice are balanced and God's will is finally done on earth as it is in heaven. "I have a dream!" cried the late Martin Luther King, Jr., "that one day on the red hills of Georgia the sons of former slaves and the sons of former slave owners will be able to sit down together at the table of brotherhood. I have a dream that one day even the state of Mississippi, a state sweltering with the heat of injustice, sweltering with the heat of oppression, will be transformed into an oasis of freedom and justice. I have a dream . . ."

However, as Christians, we must never confuse our "longing" for the day of the Lord with a precise prediction of the time of its arrival. In fact, numerous scriptures warn against that human folly. Jesus said it would come "like a thief in the night" or as Paul said "like labor upon a pregnant woman." In other words, that's God's business, not ours! So in my opinion, attempts to predict God's movements behind God's back are attempts to manipulate God rather than serve God.

Sneaking up from behind to look over God's shoulder or to guess what God will do next is a thinly disguised form of hubris and sinful pride. It is, in fact, an affront to the freedom of the Holy Spirit that blows where it wills! General MacArthur said, "I shall return"; Arnold Schwarzenegger said, "I'll be back"; and Jesus made the same promise to us that he would come again—but on his timetable, not ours. He is to be the judge of that, not us!

So how and when he chooses to do this is none of our business! "He said, 'It is not for you to know the times or season which the Father has fixed by his own authority'" (Acts 1:7). "But of that day and hour no one knows, not even the angels of heaven, nor the Son" (Matthew 24:36). So don't worry, be patient, and wait upon the Lord. After all, if even Jesus and the holy angels did not know when, you need to be very wary of those end-time experts who claim they know more than Jesus!

Apocalyptic language is a language of hope for the hopeless, of victory for those in the jaws of defeat. It speaks of hope to the conquered, the poor, the persecuted, and the oppressed. It is the language of "keep on keeping on" and the language of "hold fast" because someday, someway, things are going to get better. In here, God is still in charge. "In the world you will have tribulation, but be of good cheer, I have overcome the world" (John 16:33).

One more thing, when John wrote his book, it was an awful time to be a Christian. Believers were persecuted, burned at the stake, fed to lions, and banned from making a living in the marketplace. Yet you would be utterly amazed about how many times John of Patmos says in the book of Revelation that those evil Roman persecutions under 666 or Caesar (Domitian) would soon be ending—*soon* (Revelation 1:1, 2:16, 3:11, 22:6, 22:10, 22:12, 22:20). In those days, letters often stood as code for numbers, and most scholars agree that the number 666 actually stood for "Nero Caesar" or the Emperor Domitian. John even gives us a timetable of when the awful persecutions would end. He clearly says

228

three and a half years or forty-two months or one thousand two hundred sixty days (Revelation 12:6, 12:14, 13:5). And indeed, those very Roman persecutions did "soon" come to an end, thanks be to God!

Since that time, other saints throughout the ages, in times of suffering and persecution, have turned to that very same scripture to be inspired and encouraged, as they too boldly endure oppression and persecution in their own time. Revelation has helped many generations keep the faith in very difficult circumstances with renewed hope and courage to the bitter end! Why? Because they have read the last page of the book, so they already know who wins!

> **I have set before you an open door**
> **that no one is able to shut.**
> **—Revelation 3:8**

IF ONE BLIND GUIDE LEADS ANOTHER, BOTH WILL FALL INTO THE PIT (MATTHEW 15:14)

So also our beloved brother Paul wrote to you according to the wisdom given him, speaking of this as he does in all his letters. There are some things in them hard to understand, which the ignorant and unstable twist to their own destruction, as they do the other scriptures. You therefore, beloved, since you are forewarned, beware that you are not carried away with the error of the lawless and lose your own stability. But grow in the grace and knowledge of our Lord and Savior Jesus Christ. To him be the glory both now and to the day of eternity. Amen.

—2 Peter 3:15b–18

IN THE YEAR 343 BC, when Alexander, son of King Phillip II of Macedonia, turned thirteen, his mother Olympia arranged for Aristotle to be brought in as a personal tutor. Aristotle was not only a great philosopher, but he also dabbled in alchemy, the precursor of chemistry. In those days, timekeeping was by sundial, so in order to make time portable, Aristotle invented an elixir that when applied to a fabric would turn bright red in one hour and thirty minutes. By the time Alexander was sixteen, he was already commanding an army and using this new technology. His generals would dip a cloth in the solution, tie it around their wrists, hop on their horses, and make synchronized attacks on the enemy from all directions at the same time. So effective was this technique that in only a few years, Alexander the Great had conquered the known world. I am sure all of you are already familiar with this revolutionary time technology. It was known as Alexander's Rag Time-Band. Did I get you?

I tell you this silly story because everything in it was true, except the timekeeping elixir. My point is that a half-truth is far more dangerous than an outright lie because more people are seduced by it. After all, why let the truth stand in the way of a good story, right? For example, you would be amazed how easy it is to take the first chapter of Ezekiel out of context and convince people that this was really an eyewitness account of flying saucers. In fact, in 1997, Marshall Applewhite, the leader of a cult called Heaven's Gate, used that scripture to convince thirty-eight highly intelligent computer programmers to take poison and fly away with him in a spaceship behind the Hale-Bopp Comet. Of course, all they really joined was other victims of cult madness, such as the followers of Jim Jones, David Koresh, and countless others.

As I said before, once I convince you that the Bible is absolutely infallible, I already have you in my power. All I have to do is deftly cherry-pick a verse here and a verse there until I can easily twist the scriptures to my own advantage, and then you get my personal version back stamped with the divine authority of Almighty God! Jesus said, "You search sea and land for a single convert, and when you find one, you make him twice the child of hell that you yourselves are." An excellent example of this kind of malarkey can be seen in such best-selling writers as Hal Lindsey (*The Late Great Planet Earth*).

I am not sure how it happened, but somewhere along the line, the word "prophet" has been abused and confused with "fortune-teller." While it appears that some prophets like Elisha did indeed have clairvoyant capabilities, this was at best a secondary function and not his primary calling. In fact, the book of Deuteronomy clearly states, "There shall not be found among you, anyone who practices divination, a soothsayer, an augur, or a sorcerer, or a charmer, or a medium, or a wizard, or a necromancer. For whoever does these things is an abomination to the Lord" (Deuteronomy 18:10).

The word soothsayer means "one who predicts future events." So with apologies to Harry Potter and all of his ilk; wizards, diviners, fortune-tellers, and soothsayers, are *not* what a true prophet of God is called to be! In fact, according to Leviticus 20, soothsayers were to be stoned to death.

So a prophet is not primarily called to predict the future. Indeed, according Deuteronomy 13:1, "If a prophet arises among you or a dreamer of dreams and gives you a sign or a wonder and if the sign or wonder which he tells you *comes to pass*, and if he says let us go after other gods and serve them, you shall not listen to the words of that prophet." In other words, he is a still false prophet, even if he can predict the future correctly! In short, the primary call of a prophet is to "tell forth" the divine will of God rather than a "fore tell" future events.

I say this because since the Twin Towers fell in 2001, such divisive books as the *Left Behind* series by Tim LaHaye and Jerry B. Jenkins and other end-time "fiction" writers have sold like hotcakes, making these soothsayers and prognosticators into millionaires. By the way, the word "rapture" does not appear anywhere in the Bible, and the word "anti-Christ" appears only once and that is not in Revelation. It may also surprise you to know how modern all of this talk of dispensationalism and rapturing really is.

For one thousand eight hundred years, the church fathers, from Augustine to John Wesley, said virtually nothing on the subject. But in the nineteenth century, a British lawyer and former Anglican priest named John Nelson Darby (1800–1882) came up with his own strangely original interpretation of the end times. He did so by cutting and pasting together a series of obscure biblical passages into his own weirdly unique interpretation. Please note that this new creative version of the end times was distinctly different from traditional Christianity. Mr. Darby even put together his own biblical translation in order to bolster his ideas.

Later, a rather shady Kansas lawyer with no real religious training named Cyrus I Scofield gained the financial backing of a group of radical British conservatives who helped him publish a new annotated "Bible" (1909) with the crazy quilt collection of notations from Mr. Darby's own version of the eschaton included as "authoritative" commentary! The rest is history. Mr. Darby's novel opinions were quickly embraced and elevated by the American fundamentalist movement to the level of holy writ. Yes, these groups soon stamped the Schofield notes with divine authority, thus forever linking Darby's peculiar viewpoints directly to the Bible! I think the name of that dance is called the twist! No wonder Jesus said, "If one blind person guides another, both will fall into the pit" (Matthew 15:14).

I once saw a cartoon that pictured two old men with white robes and long white beards. They were both carrying signs. One read, "THE WORLD

WILL END VERY SOON!" The other man carried a sign that read, "WORLD WITHOUT END!" One observer says to the other, "I think one of those guys is an optimist and one is a pessimist, but for the life of me, I cannot figure out which one is which!"

Why is it that so many people want to use the Bible the way a gypsy uses a crystal ball? Why do they leaf through its pages like they were tea leaves looking for doom and gloom? Remember Carlie Simon's song, "You're so vain, you probably think this song is about you, don't you?" Each new generation thinks every prediction in the Bible was meant exclusively for them in their lifetime. Because of vain old human pride, they believe their age is unprecedented, so obviously, the Bible was really speaking to no one but them.

But I, for one, refuse to be a fatalist. I do not believe we are helpless puppets. I do not believe in determinism. The future is not fixed in stone. Indeed, the warnings of the prophets were never unconditional guarantees of what had to happen. They were always conditional warnings of what might happen *if.* My dad used to say that *if* is the biggest word in the English language. So the future is not immutable and predetermined, it is always subject to God's *if.* "If my people who are called by my name will humble themselves, pray, seek my face and turn from their wicked ways then . . ." (2 Chronicles 7:14 ff) With that one *if,* the option of healing and forgiveness to the whole land becomes a fresh new hope. So we are free to choose and to face the consequences of our decision either good or ill. IF.

Why do some people insist on becoming authorities on something they know absolutely nothing about as if they had the inside track on God or had Jesus in their back pocket? They do not know when the end time will be any more than you do. In fact, it is none of anyone's business. All God requires of us is to remain faithful. Jesus said, "Therefore you must also be ready, for the Son of Man is coming at an unexpected hour . . . Blessed is that slave whom his master will find at work when he arrives" (Matthew 24:44, 46). In short, *if* we want the world to be a better place, we need to do more than read tea leaves and horoscopes. We must get off our duffs to help make it better. By the way, who says God is in the demolition business? I say God is in the rebuilding business as the rainbow still reminds us! So for every forecast of doom, there is a promise of renewal and redemption: *If.*

Jesus said, "Beware that you are not led astray for many will come in my name and say 'I am He!' and the time is near, but do not go after them" (Luke 21:8).

It is ironic to me that while the message of John Nelson Darby was mostly very negative and full of fear, the message behind the powerful poetic imagery of apocalyptic literature was mostly positive. In other words, "Keep the faith. Hang in there until the end. Keep on keeping on! Last for the duration and see it through. Fear not! Don't worry, it may not be apparent yet, but if you look closely enough, you will see God's presence even in the most intolerable situations and apparent defeat" (see Revelation 14:12, 13:10). "Here is a call for the endurance of the saints, those who keep the commandments of God and the faith of Jesus."

As I have said before, that verse summarizes the message of the entire book! In other words, one day God is going to turn this world topsy-turvy and the meek *will* inherit the earth! So don't worry, have hope, and endure! That is God's word and promise in Revelation!

As I see it, one of the real dangers of the doomsday mentality is a dualistic pessimism that elevates evil up to the level of God as if Satan ruled the world. But from cover to cover, there is never any question in the Holy Scriptures that it is God—not the devil—who rules heaven and earth. "The light shines in the darkness and the darkness did not overcome it!" (John 1:5) So it is utter heresy to imply that evil has even the slightest chance of defeating God or gaining the upper hand. That is false teaching. It is heresy. It is pure BS.

For example, in the Babylonian myth of creation, the Babylonians believed that the oceans of chaos before creation were ruled by an evil dragon sea monster named Leviathan (like the monsters you see on ancient maps). But the writers of the Old Testament said, "No, God is good and created a good world. So the powerful sea monster Leviathan is not to be feared . . . For God has defeated the evil dragon and deprived it of its power." Psalm 74:13 says, "Thou didst break the heads of the dragons on the water, thou didst crush the heads of Leviathan." So Job can ask tongue in cheek, "Can you (like God) draw out Leviathan with a fishhook or press down his tongue with a cord?" (Job 41:1 ff), and Psalm 104:26 adds, "There go the ships and Leviathan that you formed to sport in it." Get the joke? The dreaded powerful demiurge of chaos is now God's little pet gold fish! LOL (see also Job 26:12–13)

So take heart. Do not fear the forces of evil or dread the future! "Little children, you are from God, and have conquered them. That is why the one who is in you is greater than the one who is in the world" (1 John 4:4). In other words, the evil dragon is no match for Almighty God— never was, never will be! Jesus said, "By your endurance you will gain your soul" (Luke 21:19). That is the message of apocalypse. So God is not looking for prognosticators, soothsayers, and fortune-tellers to outguess God's next move. Shame on those with the hubris to even dare try such a thing! Nor has God called us to make millions selling apocalyptic prediction books and made-up movies to scare people. Jesus does not seek those who choose fear and eschatological speculation about Armageddon over real action and service. Jesus doesn't call for spineless worriers but for spiritual warriors who never give up. He seeks not those who are fearful of the future but those who are fearless in the present. We don't mope about in utter despair. Instead, we serve God each day happily, faithfully, prayerfully, kindly, joyfully, peacefully, hopefully, and boldly. If we do that, I assure you we will be ready whenever Jesus comes!

Yes, there will be wars and rumors of wars, disasters, and division, even earthquakes and volcanic eruptions, but don't quit. Never give up. Don't hunker in a bunker. "Fear not, I am with you," Jesus said. So go out into the streets, the ballparks, and the fields that are ripe for harvest and live your lives in witness and service. Be engaged and get involved instead of wringing your hands and whining, "Is the end here yet?"

Be ready—not by stockpiling guns, canned goods, gas masks. Do not waste your time speculating and deliberating on what the book of Revelation tells us about politics in the Middle East! No! Instead, just faithfully serve God and keep oil in your lamps. That is all Jesus has ever asked you to do. "Blessed is the slave whom his master will find at work when he arrives" (Matthew 24:46).

In 1780, a total eclipse of the sun hit the town of Hartford, Connecticut; bats flew and chickens roosted. It was dark as night at noon. Now it happened that the Hartford legislature was in session, and when darkness fell, the lower house broke up in alarm and went home. People thought the world was about to end, and panic gripped them all. The Senate also heard a motion for adjournment so that they might also meet the Day of Judgment at home with family. But the motion was opposed by a judge named Abraham Davenport.

"I object," he said. "The Day of Judgment is either approaching or it is not. If it is not, there is no cause for adjournment. If it is, I choose to be found doing my duty."

Amen!

Satan is already defeated. Do not fear the fallen one! Let's drop all of this pessimistic paranoia about the dreadful judgment. Let's stop this silly end-of-time guessing game with God, and let's get back to work faithfully doing our duty like he told us to do!

> **He (Jesus) said to them, "I watched Satan fall from heaven like lightning. See, I have given you authority to tread on snakes and scorpions and over the power of the enemy and nothing will hurt you . . ."**
> **—Luke 10:18–19**

THE DAY THE MASTER COMES

In every age, some fools pretend,
That they know when the world will end.
Even today some claim the power
To name the year, the day, the hour!

They know a lot when God's own Son
Did not know when the end would come.
He said not even angels knew
What these impostors claim is true!

God has not called us to predict
The time that he alone can pick.
Our task is not to "fortune tell"
But seek his will and do it well.

Wise is the one who understands
Such things are best left in God's hands,
Who on his own one day will come
To seek his own and take them home.

Then heaven and earth shall be as one,
"Thy kingdom come, thy will be done!"
For why else would he have us pray
And yearn forever for that day.

Unless he knew that day upon
Which our hopes are built would come.
And what a day that day shall be
When Jesus comes to set us free.

With "Peace on earth, good will to men,"
The end of evil, crime, and sin.
No hatred, war, nor greed, nor strife
When death is swallowed up by life.

And love and joy shall have no end.
Forever we shall live with him.
Lion and lamb, the wolf and deer,
Shall play together without fear.

As people of each race and clan
Shall gather in God's Promised Land.
And sing with angels, free from pain,
The day the Master comes again.

AND TAKES HIS CHILDREN HOME!

WHY IN GOD'S NAME?

When the days drew near for him to be taken up, he set his face to go to Jerusalem. And he sent messengers ahead of him. On their way they entered a village of the Samaritans to make ready for him; but they did not receive him, because his face was set toward Jerusalem. When his disciples James and John saw it, they said, "Lord, do you want us to command fire to come down from heaven and consume them?" But he turned and rebuked them. (Other ancient authorities add, "And said, 'You do not know what spirit you are of, for the son of man has come not to destroy the lives of human beings, but to save them.'") Then they went on to another village.

—Luke 9:51–56 with footnote

FROM TOWERS ALL over the world, the minarets drone out an eerie call to prayer, and in response, the faithful people of Islam drop to their knees, bow their heads, and facing Mecca, they worship the one true God. Muslims not only recognize Abraham and all of the Old Testament prophets as their own, but they even affirm Jesus as a prophet, born of a virgin.

So Muslims, Jews, Catholics, and Protestants all worship, essentially, the very same God. How strange then that in the name of the very same Creator, they try to murder one another—from Africa to Afghanistan. "Allah be praised!" shouted the terrorists as they turned an airliner full of innocent passengers into a missile of death. Why in the name of God would anybody do a thing like that? Let me make one thing clear: there is nothing in the Koran that endorses such a barbaric act. It is just as much a distortion of Islam as the teachings of David Koresh, Jim Jones, and Applewhite were a distortion of the Bible or the FLDS, the fundamentalist Mormon cult in Texas that used the Bible to justify abusing children in the name of God. As I see it, the problem is not in religion itself but rather in the nuts and fanatics who twist and abuse the scriptures to their own unscrupulous ends.

For example the wacko from Waco, David Koresh, became convinced that it was just as important to teach his children how to use an assault weapon as it was to teach them the Holy Bible. In fact, bullets and the Bible seemed to be completely compatible to him. "Praise the Lord and pass the ammunition." I can't help but remember Peter's warning, "Beware lest you be carried away by the error of lawless men and lose your own stability" (2 Peter 3:16). But the sad truth is that killing in the name of the Lord has a long and ancient history. It is time to take both the blinders and the gloves off and face the truth!

> The Holocausts in the Old Testament (men, women, children, and animals)
> The persecutions of the early Christians
> The invasion of Spain by the Moors
> The crusades
> The Inquisition
> The conversion by conquest of Mexico and Peru
> The conflict of Protestants and Catholics in Ireland
> The extermination of six million Jews
> The suicide bombers and acts of terror
> The lynching and burning of blacks in the South

And the violent beat behind our religious history goes on!

Muslims and Christians kill one another in God's name as religion and hate walk hand in hand. I can't help but remember a tongue-in-cheek remark by Bishop Robert Blackburn, former bishop of the North Carolina Conference of the United Methodist Church. He said, "Perhaps if the people of Ireland all became atheists, they could learn how to live together like Christians." What a sad commentary that is. "May God Almighty have mercy on our souls!"

I remember how we all felt after 9/11. "Let's roll!" "Let's get them!"—we wanted them all to die! That is exactly the way the disciples felt about the Samaritans. They had been on a long journey to Jerusalem, and they were refused food and lodging because Jews and Samaritans hated each another. So the disciples got even angrier at being slighted by those infidels.

"Master," they cried, "shall we call down fire from heaven and consume them all?"—like Elijah the prophet did to the priests of Baal!

But Jesus rebuked them. Had he not taught them a new way? Shame on them! "Do you not know what spirit you are of?" he asked "For the Son of Man came to save lives, not to destroy them!"

But did you know that in saying that, Jesus stood in stark contrast to the history of Israel? For one thousand years, the Israelites of the Old Testament were a very violent and warlike people who won their land through conquest and destroyed their enemies in Holocausts—killing men, women, and children all in the name of the Lord.

Some of you have probably seen those attend-the-church-of-your-choice newspaper ads sponsored by local merchants featuring a cartoon-type drawing of some biblical scene from the Old Testament. Well, I like to doodle, and one day as I was doodling at a conference meeting, the man sitting next to me asked if I would be interested in applying for that job. The man who had done it was retiring.

I was certainly flattered, but I quickly turned it down not only because I have no training or experience as a cartoonist but, more importantly, it also seemed to me that the theme of almost every one of those ads included some sort of violence. It seemed to always be something like Sampson slaying a thousand Philistines or David cutting off the head of Goliath. In all honesty, I have often wondered why we teach our children so many of those excessively violent stories. Some of them ought to be rated R. Is it because we really expect them to learn a good lesson from Sampson's setting foxes' tails on fire or pulling down the temple on his enemies, or do they just provide easy entertainment to hold our kid's attention or even instill fear in their little hearts?

When Mohamed wrote the Koran, most of his ideas came directly out of our Bible. He even quotes Jesus. Unfortunately, the Koran, like the Bible, often sends mixed messages. For example, in the Koran, there is a strict injunction against suicide. On the other hand, there is praise for "martyrs" who die in a holy war against infidels. The Koran says, "If you kill an innocent person, it is as if you killed all humanity." But on the other hand, those who kill the enemies of Islam can expect seventy-two beautiful (perpetual virgin) maidens to wait on them hand and foot throughout eternity. No wonder some of those Islamic fundamentalists can't wait to be blown to bits! So whether it is the Bible or the Koran, the messages about war and peace sometimes become very confused, even contradictory.

For example, we often read Isaiah and Micas beautiful vision of a peaceable kingdom where swords become "plowshares" and spears would become "pruning hooks" (Isaiah 2:2–4, Micah 4:1–4). But listen to the call of the prophet Joel, "Proclaim this among the nations. Prepare for war, stir up the mighty men. Let all men of war draw near. Beat your plowshares into swords and your pruning hooks into spears. Let the weak say, 'I am a warrior; bring down thy warriors, O Lord'" (Joel 3:9–10). Isn't that exactly what many of these religious zealots want to do—Muslim, Christian, and Jew?

Ironically, did you know that about the same time that God commanded Moses, "Thou shalt not kill," Moses comes down the mountain proudly holding the Ten Commandments in his hands and promptly disobeys them? He has been so close to God that his face still glows with radiance. But when he reaches the valley, he finds an orgy of idol worshipers dancing naked before a golden calf. Moses gets so angry that he smashed the tablets of God to pieces on a rock. Then he demanded that Aaron explain himself.

And Aaron said, "I don't really know what happened. We just threw some gold in the fire, and this calf came out 'all by itself.'"

Right! Now Moses was really angry. "Who is on the Lord's side?" he asked.

The sons of Levi stepped forward, and Moses said to the sons of Levi, "God wants you to prove your loyalty by killing your neighbors and your brothers and your companions who have sinned."

And so they did, and three thousand fell that day. Oh, the horror—the inhumanity! So Moses, the very person that God had commanded "Thou shalt not kill," broke that law to pieces by murdering out of rage.

Then Moses said to his bloodstained accomplices, "Today you have ordained yourselves for the service of the Lord" (Exodus 32:25–29), blaming the slaughter on God's will! (Lord, have mercy!) Centuries later, the same house of Levi would again have blood on their hands in the bloody execution of Jesus!

Personally, I regard this account as one of the most disturbing and terrifying stories in the Bible, to think that not even a man as great as Moses could separate his own rage from the true will of God as he smashed God's commandments against the rocks. For as Paul said, "Love does no wrong to a neighbor." By the way, one thousand years later, the priestly descendants of that same violent house of Levi were at it again, still killing in the noble name of God. This time the priests of Levi were behind the arrest and bloody execution of Jesus Christ! My point is that people often blame God for the evils that they themselves do in God's name. (Christ, have mercy!)

I remember an old song by Bob Dillon, "I learned to accept it and accept it with pride. You don't count the dead when God's on your side!" But Jesus said, "Blessed are the peacemakers, for they shall be called the children of God." Let me make myself clear, I am not a pacifist. I do believe in the regretful necessity of a *just war* in self-defense and to protect the innocent. But war should always be done with sadness and as a last resort. We should never swagger in like a Texas gunslinger to shoot first and ask questions later. The sad truth is that the fanatics and the crazies have distorted the message of both the Koran and the Bible. Indeed, both holy books speak more of kindness and peace than of war and violence. We are called to be healers, not killers.

"You have heard it said of old," Jesus said, "an eye for an eye and a tooth for a tooth." He was quoting three Old Testament scriptures which actually go even further. They also say, "Life for life, hand for hand, and foot for foot" (Exodus 21:24, Leviticus 24:20, Deuteronomy 19:21). But Jesus overrides all three of those Old Testament scriptures by his own authority. In correction, Jesus says, "But I say to you, do not resist one who is evil, but if anyone strikes you on the right cheek, turn to him the other also." Yet with all of these contradictory messages, it is no wonder that people get confused.

The high priest Samuel said to Saul in 1 Samuel 15:3, "The Lord has sent me to anoint you king over Israel; now therefore, hearken to the words of the Lord. Go and smite Amalec and utterly destroy all that they have. Do not spare them but kill both man and woman, infant and suckling, ox and sheep, camel and ass" (1 Samuel 15:3 ff).

Ironically, three thousand years later, Hitler was to use that same genocide technique against the Jews themselves. But Saul had a conscience, and so he spared the life of King Agag which made Samuel angry. And in a rage, the high priest picked up a sword and hacked Agag into small pieces right before the altar of God. (Lord, have mercy! Christ, have mercy!)

In my opinion, God gets the blame for a lot of bad things that people do in his name. Surely, somebody was confused. I once saw a sixteenth-century map of North America. It looked funny. The Mississippi was way too big, the Great Lakes were missing, and Florida looked like it had swollen glands. Does that mean the shape of our continent changed that much in four to five hundred years? No! It means that well-meaning men made a mistake due to insufficient information. So the revelation of the

Old Testament was distorted and incomplete because the full truth had not yet been revealed in Jesus Christ.

Folks, God is the same today, yesterday, and tomorrow. What changed was not God's will but our perception and understanding of God's will. Listen to the words from Hebrews 1, "In many and various ways, God spoke of old to our fathers, but in these last days, he has spoken to us by a Son, through whom he created the world." That means we have a new measurement, a new guidepost, a new criterion to help us interpret the Bible correctly. The kids call it WWJD! So do not ask, "Can I find a scripture to back up what I am doing?" Of course, you can, whatever it is. Because I guarantee there is a scripture to back up almost anything you want to do, no matter how bad. No, instead ask this question, "What would Jesus do?"

Let me remind you again of the story of the disciples and Jesus taking a shortcut through Samaria on the way to the holy city of Jerusalem, but when they asked for food and hospitality, as was the custom for pilgrims, they were refused. Frankly, I don't find that very surprising, since Jews and Samaritans had hated one another for seven hundred years. It all started when the northern kingdom of Judah fell in 721 BC and the Jews began to intermarry with the Assyrian conquerors. Naturally, the Assyrians also brought their own pagan gods. So the Jews in Jerusalem considered Samaritans to be half-breeds and infidels denying them access to the temple. So the Samaritans built their own temple. No wonder they refused to offer hospitality to a group of Jewish pilgrims who were on their way to worship in a temple where Samaritans were not welcome. More than not welcome, they were despised. Many Jews thought that the only good Samaritan was a dead Samaritan. Nevertheless, when the Samaritans refused to offer them food and lodging, James and John, the sons of thunder, were ready to kill them on the spot.

"Lord," they said in anger, "let us call down fire from heaven and consume them all like Elijah did." That was Elijah the Tishbite who in 2 Kings 1, rebuked Amaziah, King of Judah for worshiping pagan gods. So the king sent an officer and fifty men to arrest him.

"If I am a man of God," the prophet said, "then may fire fall from heaven and consume you all," and it did. The king sent fifty more men, and they also were burned alive.

As cruel as that may sound, the truth of the matter is that is the typical way the ancient Israelites reacted to all Gentiles and unbelievers.

So it was not at all surprising that the angry disciples wanted to burn alive these heathen infidels who refused to offer bread to their Master.

But Jesus reacted swiftly with sharp rebuke! How awful that his disciples would even consider such a thing! "Can it be that you have been with me so long and you still do not know what manner of spirit you are of? For the Son of Man came not to destroy lives but to save them."

One of the most active and devout servant leaders I have ever pastored had a husband almost as good and kind as she was. Unfortunately, he refused to darken the doors of the church. One day as he was helping me deliver food to a needy family, I asked him, "John, you are one of the most generous men I have ever met, so why won't you ever attend church?" That is when he told me about his stern Bible-thumping father who would beat the devil out of him every night for no apparent reason, except, ostensibly, to save his "lost soul" from hell.

"Whenever I think of God," he said, "all I can picture is my angry screaming father standing over me every night, with a belt ready to beat the stuffing out of me in the name of Jesus!"

I tried my best to tell him that his image of a violent wrathful God was a false image. I told him that the Jesus he had rejected never was Jesus. But he was never able to hear me. His image of Jesus remained of an angry warrior judge with a sharp two-edged sword sticking out of his mouth, ready to strike down all evil infidels like him (see Revelation 1:16, 19:15).

But from the beginning, our Master taught a message of love, kindness, mercy, tolerance, and peace. He saw that an "eye for an eye" eventually leads to everybody going blind. So he came to cure our blindness and teach us how to forgive one another and to overcome evil with good. "You have heard it said of old, 'Hate your enemies,'" Jesus said, "but I say to you, love your enemies and pray for those who persecute you, so you may be children of your Father who is in heaven" (Matthew 5:44). It is tempting to strike out at evil in anger, but our Lord has taught us a more excellent way. "He who loves his neighbor has fulfilled the law" (Romans 13:8). Perhaps Muslims hate us because we rarely bother to practice what our Master preached.

Whoever fears has not reached perfection in love.
—1 John 4:18

THE TOWER OF BABEL IN REVERSE

Now the whole earth had one language and the same words, and as they migrated from the east, they came upon a plain in the land of Shinar and settled there. And they said to one another, "Come, let us make bricks, and burn them thoroughly." And they had brick for stone, and bitumen for mortar. Then they said, "Come, let us build ourselves a city, and a tower with its top in the heavens, and let us make a name for ourselves; otherwise we shall be scattered abroad upon the face of the whole earth." The Lord came down to see the city and the tower, which mortals had built. And the Lord said, "Look, they are one people, and they have all one language; and this is only the beginning of what they will do; nothing that they propose to do will now be impossible for them. Come, let us go down, and confuse their language there, so that they will not understand one another's speech." So the Lord scattered them abroad from there over the face of all the earth, and they left off building the city.

—Genesis 11:1–8

ONE OF THE seven wonders of the ancient world was the Ziggurat—these majestic terraced pyramids were like small mountains. So when simple nomadic sheep herders came upon these colossal structures along the Tigris and Euphrates rivers in Mesopotamia, they were awestruck.

"Who could have built such gigantic structures?" they asked. "And why can't we build things like that?"

"Is their God greater than our God?"

"And why are they so different from us?"

"They even talk differently."

In those days, the elder of the tribe was considered the repository of wisdom and faith. So his job was to pass down the traditions, memories, and knowledge of the ages in the form of stories—many of which had been passed down for a thousand years. So we can imagine the old wise elder gathering the clans around a big fire to tell them the story of Babel.

In Babylonian, the word *Bab-El* means "gate of God," but in Hebrew, there was a similar word, *babble*, which means "to mumble gibberish incoherently or to confuse." So by combining those two ideas in a marvelous play on words, a wonderful etiological parable was born.

I like to call etiological stories *how-come* stories because they are designed to explain origins. So this very ancient story of language origins has been passed down to us through the book of beginnings (Genesis).

Picture a time before there were nationalities, when all the people of the earth lived in one place, in one community, all speaking one common language. This unity gave to them great potential and power to accomplish things—amazing things! So great, in fact, that they began to regard themselves as the center of the universe—they had no need of God. "Let us make a name for ourselves," they said. In other words, let us climb into heaven by the back door behind God's back and take God's place. But God saw their arrogance and confounded their ability to communicate with one another and sent them packing over the face of the earth, babbling in different tongues.

But the sin of the Tower of Babel was not building a tower to heaven—even rocket ships cannot do that. That is silly! No, the sin of the Tower of Babel was arrogance, defiance, and selfish pride where the creature tries to usurp the place of the Creator. It is hubris that makes us dare play God and forget that we are merely God's creatures. It is hubris that destroys our ability to communicate with one another and builds walls between us. That is why we still fight and kill one another. So thousands of years later, this story is still our story. We are still prideful, arrogant, defiant, isolated, and alienated. We worship man's achievements in war, technology, computers, space travel, and genetic engineering rather than the sovereign God who made us all. But wait, that is not the end of the story.

Fast forward many eons, it is now AD 30, fifty days after Easter on the day of Pentecost when the disciples were holed up together at a prayer meeting in an upper room at the house of Mary of Bethany, the mother of John Mark. Suddenly, *like* a mighty rush, a powerful wind blew in and rushed through that room to sweep the disciples singing and laughing and babbling with joy and ecstasy down the steps and out into the streets.

At first, people thought they were drunk and no wonder with all the commotion and excitement. But this was not incoherent gibberish. These disciples had something to say, and they were saying with clarity, they were not babbling; they were communicating. They were not speaking glossolalia or "unknown tongues." Their message was understood immediately by people of different languages from all over the world. Suddenly, these small-town uneducated disciples with a Galilean accent were turning the world upside down as different people were joined together into one fellowship—that, we call the Body of Christ. And that is why we regard Pentecost the birthday of the church.

I heard a story about a bar on Franklin Street in Chapel Hill that put an ad in the University of North Carolina school paper that read, "Bring your parents here for supper Saturday night after the game, and we'll pretend we don't know you." So a local church put in an ad that read, "Bring your parents to worship with us on Sunday and we'll pretend that we do know you!"

Speaking of bars, do you remember the theme song from *Cheers*, "Where everybody knows your name and they're always glad you came"? Shouldn't that be the theme song of the church?

Someone who happened to be a recovering alcoholic once said to me, "Why can't lonely people socialize in church like they do in bars?"

You know, strangers wander alone into a bar, and soon, people are friendly and talking and laughing and singing happy songs. So why can't worship be more like a German Oktoberfest than a funeral? Actually, many hymn tunes were borrowed from bar songs, including "The Battle Hymn of the Republic" and parts of Handel's "Messiah." In the eighteenth century, when hecklers tried to drown out John Wesley in singing a ribald drinking song entitled "Nancy Dawson," Charles Wesley passed out Christian words in the same meter, and the Christians drowned out the rowdies singing in the same melody about the joy of the Holy Ghost. No wonder John Wesley exhorted us to "Sing lustily and with good courage . . . Be no more afraid of your voice now, nor more ashamed of its being heard, than when you sang the songs of Satan."

But hold on, you might say, "We can't compete with bars, can we?" They serve that social lubricant in a bottle that loosens up the crowd. To that, I say, we offer something far stronger than "spirits," we ride on the wave of the Holy Spirit. Indeed, at Pentecost, people of different tongues and nationalities were so happy together that observers thought they were plastered, hammered three sheets to the wind, zonked, stone-drunk! They were singing, laughing, dancing, and praising God. What a party, as they all joined together in mutual joy and happiness united by the power of the Holy Ghost into one body and one fellowship. No wonder three thousand souls were converted that day. I would have joined a church like that myself!

In recent years, there has been a dramatic growth in the charismatic movement, even among the high church—Episcopalians and Catholics. Certainly, an enthusiastic faith that knows how to smile is a good thing. But what concerns me is the temptation in some of these groups to become elitist and divisive as they turn in on themselves as having found the only true way to God and in so doing have built spiritual towers of Babel in order to look down on everyone else. But whenever one group of Christians begins to stick up their spiritual noses at other Christians, or even non-Christians for that matter, they have actually betrayed the whole spirit of Pentecost, which was to bring diverse people together and not to push them apart.

Take speaking in tongues for example. The apostle Paul told the Corinthians, "If a trumpet does not sound a clear call, who will get ready for battle? So it is with you, unless you speak intelligible words with your tongue, how will anyone know what you are saying? If then I do not grasp what the speaker is saying, I am a foreigner to the speaker and he is a foreigner to me. I would rather speak five intelligible words to instruct others than ten thousand words in a tongue." So if we "speak in the tongues of men and of angels," and do not love one another, we miss the point.

We may think we have the inside track on God or have captured the Spirit like a butterfly in a net, but the spirit of Pentecost blows where it wills. As Paul said, the fruits of the Spirit are things that unite us like love, peace, joy, patience, kindness, goodness, faithfulness, gentleness, and self-control. And Jesus said, "By their fruits you shall know them." Therefore, Pentecost is not a time when Christians should wrap their arms around themselves. Pentecost is a time when Christians should open their arms wide to others and reach out to those on the outside who do not feel good about themselves.

I am told that somewhere in Europe is a little reddish brown bird that sings even sweeter than a canary. The problem is that when people capture these birds and try to cage them like canaries, they stop singing, get sick, and even die! As it turns out, the loss of their voice is not just a silent protest against their captivity or deep depression over the loss of their freedom. These are very social birds who take joy in the company of each other, so much so that when they are separated, they actually forget how to sing because they learn the music from group interaction. So the people of Europe have learned to keep these birds alive and singing happily by taking them outside to the forest where the other birds sing and the little brown birds remember their song and live.

No wonder the Holy Spirit drove the disciples out of that upper room cage, down the stairs, and out into the streets so that they could sing their happy spirit songs among the people. As Psalm 4:7 says, "Thou hast put more joy in my heart than others have for their corn and wine." Amen to that! Don't you see, real Pentecostal power opens doors, breaks down barriers, and brings people together in love, peace, and joy. It does not divide, it unites. So while the end of the Tower of Babel was confusion, division, estrangement, distrust, and even war, the day of Pentecost led to unity, fellowship, love, and joy as barriers were broken down between people of different nations, languages, races. Frozen souls were forever thawed by the warmth of God's amazing love.

"In that renewal there is no longer Greek and Jew, circumcised or uncircumcised, barbarian, Scythian, slave or free, but Christ is all and in all" (Colossians 3:11). In short, nobody has a monopoly on the Holy Spirit. So beware of those who claim that they do! Does a fish have a monopoly on the ocean?

I want you to imagine that there has been an earthquake. A large building has collapsed, and men, women, and children have been trapped in an airtight chamber. It will take days to dig them out, but right now, the first concern is to get them enough oxygen so that they can breathe. A crew is working desperately to drill a small hole into the chamber before the oxygen runs out and they suffocate. Suddenly, there is a popping sound, the wall is breached, and air can get in. Folks, it is no accident that the word for spirit, breath, wind, and air is all the same in both Hebrew and Greek. Nature does not like a vacuum, and even if you only open a small hole, the air will literally rush in to fill every corner of that empty void in a matter of seconds. The same thing goes for your heart. Some people are Spirit-tight, and some churches are Spirit-uptight. So open up and do a little spiritual house cleaning. Push out everything that keeps the Holy Spirit out of your life, unplug the hole in your heart, and let the Spirit—like fresh air—come rushing in to fill the void.

Remember, the Holy Spirit is not a self-service pump. It is God that does the filling. Therefore, it takes no special skill on your part. All you have to do is offer God room in your heart. God does the rest. Furthermore, to be "Spirit-filled" "or filled with the Spirit" does not mean that you get more of God than your neighbor. Rather, it means that God gets more of you! It does not mean that you can proudly wrap spiritual arms around yourself as one of God's frozen chosen. God gets the glory, not you! All you did was remove the padlock from your own freezer door to open up your ice-cold heart. The Holy Spirit did the rest. Now the fresh warm air of the winds of God can swoop quickly in to replace that stale chilly void in your soul.

WARM SPIRIT WIND

Warm spirit wind of power and might,
Sweep through our world and bring us light.
O breath of life from heaven above,
The source of everlasting love,
Wake us from slumber, rain down fire,
Let your will be our one desire,
And as affections overflow
And we are captured by the glow,
Let Pentecostal power grow
Around the world so each will know
Intoxicating joy and fun
That comes when all of us are one.

CATCH THE SPIRIT!

A ROSE BY ANY OTHER NAME

While Paul was waiting for them in Athens, he was deeply distressed to see that the city was full of idols. So he argued in the synagogue with the Jews and the devout persons, and also in the marketplace every day with those who happened to be there. Also some Epicurean and Stoic philosophers debated with him. Some said, "What does this babbler want to say?" Others said, "He seems to be a proclaimer of foreign divinities." (This was because he was telling the good news about Jesus and the resurrection.) So they took him and brought him to the Areopagus and asked him, "May we know what this new teaching is that you are presenting? It sounds rather strange to us, so we would like to know what it means." Now all the Athenians and the foreigners living there would spend their time in nothing but telling or hearing something new. Then Paul stood in front of the Areopagus and said, "Athenians, I see how extremely religious you are in every way. For as I went through the city and looked carefully at the objects of your worship, I found among them an altar with the inscription 'To an unknown God.' What therefore you worship as unknown, this I proclaim to you. The God who made the world and everything in it, he who is Lord of heaven and earth, does not live in shrines made by human hands, nor is he served by human hands, as though he needed anything, since he himself gives to all mortals life and breath and all things. From one ancestor, he made all nations to inhabit the whole earth, and he allotted the times of their existence and the boundaries of the places where they would live, so that they would search for God and perhaps grope for him and find him—though indeed he is not far from each one of us. For 'In him we live and move and have our being'; as even some of your own poets have said, 'For we too are his offspring.'"

—Acts 17:16–28

A HIGH SCHOOL HISTORY teacher was trying to tell her senior class about Mahatma Gandhi. She said, "He came from the very poor nation of India where many people didn't even own a pair of shoes and even fewer could afford transportation, so this holy man preferred to walk barefoot as much as possible. So his feet were often blistered. And being a man of devout faith and prayer, he would often meditate for hours and fast for long periods in protest to the injustice and oppression of the British government. It is said that this fasting not only left him emaciated but also with a terrible acetone breath." After a pause, one student raised his hand. "Mrs. Jones," he said, "does that mean that he had become a super calloused fragile mystic hexed by halitosis?" Shame on me for such a shallow pun about a truly great man.

Once, while Gandhi was a college student in apartheid South Africa, he visited a Methodist Church to worship, but because of his dark skin, he received a very cool reception. The minister kindly referred him to another church for his kind down the street. He found the worship dull and the preaching uninspiring, anyway, so he never returned. Therefore, one of the most influential men in history went to worship in a church with a tradition of inclusiveness and a heritage of warm heat, only to find such coldness, spiritual deprivation, and blatant discrimination that upward of four hundred million Indian souls were affected in one generation alone.

Here was a man who seriously considered becoming a Christian. Yet not only was he able to extrapolate the teachings of Jesus from the racist attitudes of so-called Christians, but he also took the teachings of Jesus far more seriously than they did. Indeed, through peaceful, nonviolent protest, he was able to bring the powerful British Empire to its knees. Nevertheless, Gandhi had a problem. He came from a nation of non-Christians, and though he was strongly drawn to Jesus, he felt that to profess him openly would only serve to alienate himself from his own people and limit his ability to lead them.

So while I have always admired Gandhi as a truly great man of faith, it still frustrates me that he never openly professed Jesus as his Lord and

Savior. Yet by every action and every word, he seemed to live out the Gospel which, by the way, he quoted with authority.

On one occasion, Gandhi talked about going to a Hindu temple as a boy and was surprised to hear the Hindu priest read from the Muslim Koran. "But today," he said sadly, "Hindu Muslims only wish to kill one another." So his prayer was that one day all people would live in peace and be perfectly one. Therefore, when someone would ask him what religion did he profess, he would reply, "I am a Hindu, a Christian, a Buddhist, a Muslim, and a Jew." In other words, he went to the heart of the great world religions and at the center, beneath the fanaticism and weird doctrines, behind the pagan rites and strange creeds, beyond the rituals and ceremonies and various forms of worship, and way past the radical extremists and hate mongers. He found a common core of truth, a common thread interwoven throughout. He found the way of the Spirit a reverence for life, compassion, and peace. He found that we are all pilgrims of the soul, searching for a sense of the sacred, for harmony, and for meaning. He observed a common quest for hope, faith, righteousness, good will, and a universal need for "spirit-crafting."

Of course, as Christians, we believe that the ultimate revelation of God came to us through our Lord and Savior Jesus Christ. "No man has ever seen God," said John in his Gospel, "but the only Son, who is in the bosom of the Father. He has made him known."

"In many and various ways, God spoke of old to our fathers," says Hebrews, "but in these last days, he has spoken to us by a Son, whom he appointed heir of all things and through whom he created the world."

So without apology, it is our affirmation as Christians that the Word that was with God and was God and the Word became flesh and dwelt among us. "He was in the world, and the world was made through him, and the world knew him not."

But what about the fate of nonbelievers and those of other religions? If Jesus is the way, the truth, and the life, and if no one comes to the Father except through him, then what is God going to do with three billion pagans out there? Are they all doomed to hell? Could it be that the doctrine of the Holy Trinity, which reminds us of the multifaceted nature of the one true God, is our bridge to the world religions?

After all, the Native Americans knew of the Great Spirit long before the white man arrived, and in many ways, they acted more like Christians toward the white man than the white man acted toward the Indians.

No wonder then that the apostle Paul, sensing the cosmic scope of the Gospel, boldly stood before the pagan people of Athens and proclaimed, "What therefore you worship as unknown' that I now proclaim to you—the God who made the world and everything in it, who gives life and breath and everything else to all men. From one man, he created all races and made them to live over the whole earth. He did this so that they would perhaps find him as they felt around after him."

Felt around—isn't that a powerful and graphic image? I can almost see a blind man groping in the darkness, seeking the light. Isn't that a wonderful paradigm for what all religions are about—a groping around in the darkness in search of God and ultimate enlightenment?

So what about people of other faiths and other religions? Are they denied access to God simply because God is the exclusive possession of Christians? Dare we be that presumptuous, and is God that narrow-minded? "Yet he is not far from any of us . . . For in him we live and move and have our being." So in that case, what does it mean to believe in the name of Jesus—is he particular, or is he universal? I believe he is universal. He is not just world-class but cosmic-class! We are the fish, and he is the ocean!

In Hebrew, the word "name" refers to the essential essence and real meaning and nature of a thing. So when people changed their character, they would often change their name as well. That is why Abram became Abraham, Jacob became Israel, Cepheus became Peter, and Saul became Paul. So to believe in Jesus's name is to believe in his nature. It is to believe in goodness, grace, holiness, compassion, truth, kindness, forgiveness, and love.

But wasn't Shakespeare right? Doesn't a rose by any other name smell as sweet? So why can't people experience the spirit of Jesus, our Rose of Sharon, in their hearts without placing that particular label on that particular experience? Furthermore, the name of Jesus is not a certain sound, as each language and culture often spells and pronounces his name differently. For example, Jesus is really Greek for the Hebrew name Joshua. But no one goes around saying, "By no other name than Joshua will you be saved!" Besides, Jesus has countless other names all throughout the New Testament. I do not have the space to name them all, but here are a few: the I Am, the Way, the Alpha and Omega, the Good Shepherd, the Light of the World, the Son of God, the Son of Man, Savior, Redeemer, the Door, the Bread that came down from heaven, the

Prince of Peace. So who are we to say that the spirit of Jesus cannot speak to the heart of a Hindu, a Muslim, or a Jew?

I like the way one little boy put it, "I think all religions are just different ways of voting for God!" If, in Jesus, there is neither Jew nor Greek, male nor female, then Christ is already present. If Christ is all and in all and if his spirit is "poured out on all flesh" and "all flesh shall see it together," then he is already here. If "in him we live and move and have our being" and "all things are held together by him," then all of us are a part of Christ and he is a part of all of us, whether we acknowledge it or not.

There is an interesting story that when Britain first conquered China, Christian priests baptized thousands of Chinese people with fire hoses. So the message was "Jesus died for you, whether you know it or not! For he is not far from any of us." Therefore, Jesus is already in us and through us, even if we do not know he exists and even if we deny him altogether. So isn't it possible to encounter Jesus and know the warmth of his spirit before we put any particular label on that experience? After all, does a fish really know that the vast ocean it swims in exists?

Helen Keller's teacher had been able to communicate to this young girl who was deaf, blind, and unable to speak. She told her all about God's world but not about God. Finally, she decided it was time to try to talk to her about the abstract concept of God. But how do you communicate such a nebulous concept to a fourteen-year-old child who cannot speak, see, or hear. But with great patience, her teacher began to tap out the sacred message of the divine creative force in the universe. As Helen held her sensitive fingers to her teacher's lips, all of a sudden, Helen's face lit up. Her expression was one of both relief and joy. "Oh," she said, "I am so glad he has a name. He has spoken to me so often, but this is the first time anyone told me who he was."

Whenever people tell me that they are unable to experience Christ, I usually ask them, are you so sure you haven't experienced Christ already, only you didn't put that particular label on that experience? Could it be that God simply spoke to you in ways you did not expect or imagine? After all, what is it to experience Jesus in your heart anyway! Is it to see fantastic visions from above or to hear booming voices from the great beyond? Or is it to know deep warmth, happiness, tenderness, and love to feel the power of faith, to experience beauty and the sacredness of soul through an act of healing or of courage? Or is it in a gesture of kindness or mercy or perhaps the glory of a sunrise or the fragrance of a rose or the innocence of a child? Or is it an act of bold integrity, honesty, or justice? Could it be in the care of an old friend? Or is it the compassion and warmth of a pure heart or the sensitivity of a touch? Or is it a serenity of spirit or the grace of forgiveness? Could these things not be an experience of the very presence of Jesus in our midst, with us in spirit and in truth yet unnamed and unrecognized?

Jesus is God touching us at the very center of our being! In *The Quest for the Historical Jesus*, as Albert Schweitzer put it, "He comes to us as one unknown, without a name, as of old by the lakeside, he came to those men who knew him not. He speaks to us the same words: 'Follow thou me!' and sets us to tasks which he has to fulfill for our time. He commands. And to those who obey him, whether they be wise or simple, he will reveal himself in the toils, the conflicts, the sufferings which they shall pass through in his fellowship, and as an ineffable mystery, they will learn out of their own experiences who he is."

Don't you see, our Lord is not confined to dusty old books. He is alive and active in this world. So seek him there where children play, friends chat and laugh, when the sick are cared for, the hungry fed, and people touch souls deep down inside. Seek him when the lonely find companionship, the hurt are comforted, and the homeless find refuge. For he is in the midst of every sorrow, every tear, every act of kindness, and every celebration of joy. He stands where the oppressed are treated unjustly or the poor are trodden under foot. He is in us all. He has been there all along. Jesus said, "The kingdom of God is within you."

I think part of our problem is we limit the ways that Jesus can speak to us. As the prophet Isaiah put it, "By men of strange lips and with an alien tongue, the Lord will speak to his people." So the same God that spoke to Balaam by his ass can speak to us in countless ways that we might never imagine or expect. So woe unto us if we try to limit the ways that God speaks to only churches, preachers, and the Bible. Just remember what Peter said to the people of Pentecost who, by the way, were a rainbow of different languages, different cultures, and different nationalities, "The Spirit has been poured out on all flesh!"

Folks, I am going to let you in on a little secret: Jesus has been let loose on the world, and now he permeates every part of it. Church walls cannot hold him. Therefore, I say to all you gropers in the dark out there who are feeling around after him, seeking the light, stop and do a double take. He is already here. I offer you Christ Jesus in your midst, not as a know-it-all but as a hungry humble beggar sharing with others where he has found some wonderful life-giving bread.

> KNOCK, KNOCK!
> **Who's there?**
> JESUS.
> **Jesus who?**
> **Jesus who died for you, whosoever you are!**
>
> **Just knock and it shall be opened!**

ONE WHALE OF A MESSAGE

When God saw what they did, how they turned from their evil ways, God changed his mind about the calamity that he had said he would bring upon them; and he did not do it. But this was very displeasing to Jonah, and he became angry. He prayed to the Lord and said, "O Lord! Is not this what I said while I was still in my own country? That is why I fled to Tarshish at the beginning; for I knew that you are a gracious God and merciful, slow to anger, and abounding in steadfast love, and ready to relent from punishing. And now, O Lord, please take my life from me, for it is better for me to die than to live." And the Lord said, "Is it right for you to be angry?" Then Jonah went out of the city and sat down east of the city, and made a booth for himself there. He sat under it in the shade, waiting to see what would become of the city. The Lord God appointed a bush and made it come up over Jonah, to give shade over his head, to save him from his discomfort; so Jonah was very happy about the bush. But when dawn came up the next day, God appointed a worm that attacked the bush, so that it withered. When the sun rose, God prepared a sultry east wind, and the sun beat down on the head of Jonah so that he was faint and asked that he might die. He said, "Is it right for you to be angry about the bush?" And he said, "Yes, angry enough to die." Then the Lord said, "You are concerned about the bush, for which you did not labor and which you did not grow; it came into being in a night and perished in a night. And should I not be concerned about Nineveh, that great city, in which there are more than a hundred and twenty thousand persons who do not know their right hand from their left, and also many animals?"

—Jonah 3:10–4:11

LITTLE JOHNNY WAS talking to his teacher about whales. "A big whale swallowed Jonah," he said.

The teacher disagreed. "It is physically impossible for a whale to swallow a human because even though it was a very large mammal, its throat is made of filters to catch very small creatures."

Little Johnny responded by saying, "Jonah was too swallowed by a whale!"

Irritated, the teacher reiterated that a whale could not swallow a human; it was physically impossible.

Little Johnny said, "When I get to heaven, I will ask Jonah."

The teacher asked, "What if Jonah isn't in heaven? What if he went to hell!?"

"Then you ask him," replied Johnny.

I love a good story, and so did Jesus. Parables are short pithy tales that usually have a surprise twist at the end and hammer home a single message or moral. The question you need to ask about Bible stories is not is it factual but is it true, what does it say about my life, my relationship to my neighbor, and my relationship to God.

Often parables were humorous, or should I say, they were meant to be humorous. Some people take them so down-in-the-mouth serious that they lose their spark and joy altogether. When you read a parable with too much seriousness, you not only lose the lighthearted nature of the story, but sometimes you lose the real message behind the story as well. The Bible does not say the people heard Jesus sadly; it says the people heard him gladly! In other words, he made them laugh!

Of all the Old Testament books, I believe the one that stands out best in reflecting the attitude, style, and teachings of Jesus is the story of Jonah. Unfortunately, very few people realize this because the powerful message of the book of Jonah has sadly been reduced to a big-fish story. That is all most folks remember! Now don't get me wrong, I was raised on an island, and I love a good fish story as well as the next fellow. Do you remember the one about the poor guy who fished all morning without as much as a nibble? So on the way home, he stopped at the local fish market and said to the proprietor, "How about tossing me a half dozen of those nice blues over the counter so that I can catch them. I may be a lousy fisherman, but I ain't no liar!"

Yes, we have all heard stories about the big fish that got away. We find these stories quite amusing. They make us laugh. So why is it then that we fail to see the wonderful hilarity in the story of a big fish that caught a man who got away? Was he so small that the fish threw him back? Or did he taste so bad that the fish barfed him up? Who says God doesn't have a sense of humor? How sad then that so many well-meaning Christians, instead of laughing together and enjoying this delightful story, choose instead to close ranks and get into arguments over who swallowed what. Some people even want to use the whale story as just one more litmus test for true believers when even the Bible itself is not clear on the facts. For example, the New Testament says Jonah was swallowed by a whale, but the Old Testament says it was a fish. Yet in either case, whale or fish, to argue and to fight over whether or not you can swallow this fish story whole is to negate the purpose of the book which was written to promote peace, tolerance, and understanding.

As that teacher said to the little boy, most whales could not swallow a man because they filter plankton from the sea through gill-like mouths. But take heart, I have read that according to the official records of the British Admiralty, one sailor did survive for fifteen hours in the belly of a sperm whale—the largest creature on earth. He didn't, however, compose any songs and sing them during his brief stay in the whale's belly. But seaman James Bartley was swallowed by a sperm whale in February of 1891 and lived to tell the tale. He was a crewman with the British whaling ship *Star of the East* in the South Atlantic. When the men in his longboat harpooned the giant monster, it slammed into the small craft and threw the crew up in the air. When James fell back into the sea, he was engulfed by a gigantic mouth. There were sharp stabbing pains as he swept across the rows of knifelike teeth. He kicked and fought for breath and then passed out. Ten hours later, the ship's crew saw the dying whale float to the surface. They pulled alongside and began to peel off the thick blubber. Shortly after eleven o'clock, working round the clock, by lantern light, the tired crewmen suddenly discovered James Bartley's foot and pulled him out. He was unconscious but alive. For almost four weeks, he lingered between life and death, strapped in a bunk in the captain's quarters. As a result of his fifteen-hour ordeal inside the whale, he lost all the hair on his body, his skin was bleached to an unnatural white, and he was almost blind for the rest of his life, which he spent as a cobbler in his native Gloucester.

So it is silly to ask the obvious—could God arrange for a whale to swallow a man and spew him out alive up on the beach? Of course, God could do that. After all, God is God! But let me tell you something: If you are one of those folks who likes to impress God by believing things that are very hard to believe, have I got some good news for you. There are other weird things in the book of Jonah that are much harder to swallow than the story of the big fish. Take for example the desert plant that grew into a large shade tree overnight, only to be eaten up by a single worm the next day. Or more importantly, consider this, a reluctant prophet makes his way to the capitol of his mortal enemies, where he denounces them in their own language and threatens them with annihilation in forty days! But get this, rather than laughing him off as a nut or forming a lynch mob, they actually listen. So Jonah converts the whole pagan nation into believing in the God of the Jews—the God of their enemies! How about that for a miracle? No wonder that even Jesus envied Jonah. "This generation is an evil generation," Jesus said. "It asks for some sign, but no sign shall be given it, except the sign of Jonah—for the people of Nineveh will rise up and condemn you in the judgment, for they repented at the preaching of Jonah and behold something greater than Jonah is here" (namely the Son of God) (Luke 11:32). So the real sign of Jonah was repentance and conversion. Don't you see the irony? While no other prophet could convert Nineveh—not Moses, not Jeremiah, not Isaiah, not Amos, not Hosea, not even Jesus Christ himself—Jonah manages to convert Israel's mortal enemies in no time flat. So if you want to point to something truly miraculous and supernatural about the book of Jonah, then point to the dramatic repentance and conversion of the Ninevites— that is the real sign of Jonah. But for goodness's sake, let's call a truce on the whale.

You see, I think the book of Jonah is one of the most significant books in the Old Testament. It has a whale of a message to tell. But get this, if the whale or the big fish were completely eliminated from the story, this would have absolutely no effect on the central message of the book. Now think about it, when you read God's word, isn't the most important question "What is God saying to me in this book?" After all, if you ignore God's message for you in the book of Jonah, do you think God will be impressed because you remember the whale? Unfortunately, the real message rarely gets told.

I have heard innumerable sermons on Jonah's fleeing from God's call to preach. What a cop-out! Jonah loved preaching, and he loved being a prophet. His problem was the audience to whom he was called to preach—not preaching. He just did not want to preach to those nasty Ninevites—the mortal enemies of all Jewish people. They were his problem, not preaching. Nineveh was the wickedest city in the world. It was the capital of the Assyrian Empire. So perhaps now you can begin to understand poor Jonah's shock when God told him to go there and preach. It would be like God calling me to go to preach in Iran. No wonder Jonah did not want to go. By the way, ironically, Nineveh just happens to have been about twenty-five miles from today's Baghdad. So if you think some of the people of Baghdad hate Americans who occupied their country, that is not even close to the level of hatred the Jews felt against the Assyrians for taking their best people off into captivity, raping their women and children, and even salting their land so it would not grow crops. They hated Nineveh!

Remember our anger at the fall of the Twin Towers on September 11? Well, listen to the prophet Nahum's rebuke against the city of Nineveh and you can almost hear our rage against the terrorists: "Ah! City of bloodshed, utterly deceitful, full of booty—no end to the plunder . . . piles of dead, heaps of corpses, dead bodies without end—they stumble over the bodies!" (Nahum 3:1 ff) No wonder Jonah tried to flee to Joppa in Southern Spain—as far from Nineveh as he could get. Who could blame him for his anger? Jonah did not want mercy on these nasty Ninevites; he wanted vengeance. He did not want forgiveness; he wanted retribution. He did not want peace; he wanted war. Indeed, he could cry out with the psalmist of old, "Let burning coals fall upon them. Let them be cast into the pits, no more to rise! O daughter of Babylon, you 'devastator'! Happy shall be he who requites you for what you have done to us. Happy shall he be who takes your little ones and dashes them against a rock!" (Psalm 137) That's how Jonah felt, but God had a different plan for Nineveh—mercy and reconciliation. But Jonah did not want to deliver it.

So back to the story—Jonah flees from God, and a storm comes up, and Jonah volunteers to be thrown overboard, and then the storm abates. So God sends a great fish which gulps up Jonah and, three days later, spews him up on the beach. But I ask you, did Jonah have a conversion experience inside the whale? Did Jonah change? Did his attitude toward Nineveh improve? *No!* Absolutely not. He hated the Ninevites after the whale just as much as he hated them before the whale. Only this time what choice does he have? But as he begins to give them hellfire and brimstone sermons and sees that look of fear in the eyes of these infidels, he actually starts to enjoy himself. This was fun! "In forty days, God will lay waste to this city!" he bellows. But lo and behold, they did repent. Ooops!

In fact, the king arose from his throne, removed his robe, and covered himself with sackcloth and ashes. Then he made a proclamation, "By the decree of the king and his nobles, no human being or animal, no herd or flock, shall taste anything. They shall not feed nor shall they drink water. Human beings and animals shall be covered with sackcloth, and they shall cry mightily to God. All shall turn from their evil ways and from the violence that is in their lands. Who knows, God may relent of his anger and change his mind so that we do not perish." Lo and behold, that is exactly what happened. God saw what they did, and God had mercy upon them and changed his mind about the calamity he almost called down upon them! So much for immutable predetermined prophesy!

Remember, the predictions of the prophets were never set in stone. That is determinism, not free choice! All prophetic predictions were subject to change based on the response of the people. That is the *"if"* factor. Furthermore, most of the prophets of doom in the Old Testament did not want their predictions of disaster to come true. No way! They hoped the people would repent and God would heal their land. They hoped they were wrong about doom. But not Jonah. Jonah did not want the Ninevites to be saved. He wanted them all to be destroyed in forty days—just as he predicted. He wanted doom to come! He wanted them all to burn in hell for what they had done to his people!

"I pray thee, Lord," said Jonah. "Is not this what I said would happen when I was in my country? That is why I made haste to flee to Tarshish for I know that you are a gracious God—merciful, slow to anger, and abounding in steadfast love and ready to relent from punishing." The very thought of God forgiving those evil Ninevites was just too much for Jonah to bear. "It is better for me to die than to live." In other words, Jonah would rather die than see those wicked Ninevites forgiven!

Do you get the amazing irony here? According to the story, Jonah has just become the most successful prophet in history. But instead of celebrating his victory, he pouts as he sits outside the city where he had waited forty days in anticipation to watch the devastating fireworks as God was supposed to fry them all to a crisp! So God sends a miraculous plant overnight to spring up and shade Jonah from the hot desert sun, and then God sends one (giant?) worm to devour that bush. Now Jonah is even angrier.

"Are you angry over the bush?" God asked asks.

"Yes," said Jonah, "angry enough to die."

"So you miss that plant that you did not create and yet you fail to see why I have compassion on 120,000 souls that I did create?"

So the message of the book of Jonah is simple: All of us are God's children, and so God is not only on our side, but God is also on everybody's side. He wants our fragmented Humpty Dumpty world glued back together again! In other words, God wants us all to live in harmony! For God so loved the world—ugly as it is, warts and all—that he sent his own Son to save it. He said, "Love your enemies and pray for those who persecute you!" *Repay no one evil for evil.*

But, Lord, what about the terrorists? These evil people are crazy, they are not even human; they drape themselves in bombs to blow up the innocent. We hate them with a passion!

"Vengeance is mine, I will repay," saith the Lord.

How frustrating! Now don't get me wrong, God is not telling us to lay down our arms and become pacifists. He is warning us not to let hatred warp our souls and destroy our spirits—defense, yes, but glee in sweet revenge, no! It is our bounden duty to defend the weak and to protect the innocent with all of our might but not to hate.

I am not so naïve that I do not understand that there are wicked and ruthless people who are bent on our destruction at any cost. And yes, they make me unspeakably angry, but on the other hand, I still believe in the sovereignty and providence of God and, therefore, in what God told us to do. Besides, I cannot see any way, by ourselves, that we can ever force people to like us or police the whole world or make all people into our Western image or force all people of different cultures to be free, whether they want to or not. After all, we are a minority in this world! Someone has calculated that roughly 70 percent of the world's population is nonwhite, non-Christian, illiterate, and underfed. No wonder so much of the world looks at us in envy and even hate.

Do you remember Aesop's story about the contest between the North Wind and the Sun—over who could make a man remove his coat? The harder the North Wind blew, the tighter the man held his coat, but the warmer the Sun got, the quicker he removed it. By the same principle, the more we throw our weight around like tough guys to intimidate other countries, the more they will hate us and the tighter will be their resistance against us. So I think we need to approach them as friends and not bullies!

People of God, our world is in a mess. The name of our world is Humpty Dumpty, and all the king's missiles and all the king's planes cannot put our Humpty Dumpty world back together again—that is, without God's help. So we have to fix it God's way and not our way. Even though our enemies may be evil, it does not give us an excuse to forget our Lord's teachings—like the golden rule—or trash the Sermon on the Mount as too sensitive or the constitution as too idealistic. "Do not be overcome by evil," said Paul, "but overcome evil with good!" In other words, we must never become so angry at evil that we become evil ourselves—God forbid!

My friends, the end does not justify the means. Two wrongs never make a right. Evil men should never make us forget our Lord's commandments or flee like Jonah from God's call for reconciliation. So hear me on this: if our enemies make us forget our faith until we no longer believe in the teachings of the Prince of Peace and take on the nature and tactics of our enemies, then we have already lost the war on terror and our enemies have already won! That is why the real message of Jonah is so much greater than a big-fish Story. No wonder it is so hard for some people to swallow. *That is why true religion should always be sugar free.*

Printed in the United States
By Bookmasters